MOTORING WEST

VOLUME 1

MOTORING WEST

VOLUME 1
AUTOMOBILE PIONEERS, 1900–1909

Edited by
PETER J. BLODGETT

UNIVERSITY OF OKLAHOMA PRESS
Norman

Also by Peter J. Blodgett
Land of Golden Dreams: California in the Gold Rush Decade, 1848–1858 (San Marino, Calif., 1999)

The reprinting of chapters 1 through 5, pages 5 through 45, from Floyd Clymer's edition of "Coast to Coast in Brush Roundabout" (1952 pamphlet) is reprinted with permission of VelocePress.

Library of Congress Cataloging-in-Publication Data
Motoring West : automobile pioneers, 1900–1909 / edited by Peter J. Blodgett.
volumes cm
Contents: volume 1. 1900–1909
ISBN 978-0-87062-383-7 (cloth)
ISBN 978-0-8061-5595-1 (paper)
1. Automobile travel—West (U.S.)—History. 2. Automobile travel—United States—History. 3. Automobile driving—West (U.S.). 4. Automobile driving—United States—History. 5. West (U.S.)—Description and travel. I. Blodgett, Peter J. (Peter John), 1954–
GV1024.M9125 2015
917.8—dc23
2014032094

The paper in this book meets the guidelines for permanence and durability of the Committee on Production Guidelines for Book Longevity of the Council on Library Resources, Inc. ∞

to

Sue,

as ever

Contents

Illustrations

MAP

FIGURES

Acknowledgments

No matter how solitary the process of researching and writing may feel while it is underway, no historian fails eventually to realize the innumerable kindnesses and courtesies that have made the successful conclusion of any project possible. Those who undertake the editing and publication of documents from the past are perhaps especially aware of how much they depend upon the assistance of others, including those individuals whose labors ensured the survival of the original sources. In my case, although I never met him, I am particularly grateful to the late Carey S. Bliss, former Curator of Rare Books at the Huntington Library, whose personal passion for acquiring the published accounts of twentieth-century automobile travelers in the American West built a notable collection that, in turn, inspired my desire to bring many of those stories back into the light.

Once launched upon this endeavor, I had the great good fortune of finding a host of willing confederates. At the Huntington, Carey Bliss's splendid successor, Alan Jutzi, Avery Chief Curator of Rare Books, has not only been an exceptional steward of the Bliss materials, expanding judiciously upon them through the years, but has cheerfully shared his unparalleled understanding of them with me. Such warm generosity extended all across the Huntington (rightly renowned as one of the premier research libraries in the world), as I benefited from the assistance of colleagues such as Kevin Miller, Mark Fleming, and Mario Corral in the Rare Book stacks; Manuel Flores, Brian Moeller, and Devonne Tice in Imaging Services; Catherine Wehrey in Reader Services; and particularly Sara S. (Sue) Hodson, Dixie (Dillon) Lane, Dan Lewis, Julia (Jill) Palmer, and

Mary Robertson in my intellectual and professional home, the Huntington's Manuscripts Department.

Other archivists and librarians at other institutions—including Gary Kurutz, former Director of the Special Collections Branch of the California State Library; Morgan Yates, corporate archivist at the Automobile Club of Southern California; and Claude Zachary, Associate University Librarian and Archivist at the University of Southern California—have generously made available their knowledge, their enthusiasm, and their time to assist in the development of this series and in the location of various sources. Meanwhile, research assistants at both the Huntington and elsewhere have rummaged through card catalogs and online databases, chased down fugitive titles, and staggered out of library stacks under the weight of armloads of vintage periodicals in search of the nearest Xerox machine. My particular gratitude goes to Dixie Dillon and Jill Palmer at the Huntington, Sarah Fearon at Dartmouth College, and Emma Dodds and Jessica Mitzner of the University of Oklahoma.

Although scholarship is typically portrayed as a loner's enterprise, it is actually the friendships that we form in the process of research that enable us to emerge from the endeavor with both sanity and good humor still intact. In my case, I have had the particular good luck to be toiling in the vineyards of tourism and recreation at the same time as Catherine Cocks, Lary Dilsaver, Marguerite Shaffer, Terry Young, Yolonda Youngs, and David Wrobel. Unfailingly generous with their time, their expertise, and their congeniality, they have helped to make straight this highway through many a wilderness while demonstrating the restorative powers of beer, burgers, and pie à la mode.

Even in the rapidly changing world of e-books and digital production, an author without someone to publish her book is merely a scribbler in the darkness. I therefore consider myself incredibly lucky to have had the opportunity to join the family of Arthur H.

Clark Company authors. Bob Clark, third-generation scion of this distinguished publishing enterprise, played an indispensable role in shaping this project at its earliest stages, transforming an inchoate jumble of ideas into a full-fledged documentary editing project. Bob's lively interest, unstinting enthusiasm, and sharp insights helped me to sustain this enterprise when the press of other tasks threatened to completely overwhelm it. And when Bob shepherded the acquisition of the Arthur H. Clark Company by the University of Oklahoma Press, he ensured that the legacy of the Arthur H. Clark Company would be entrusted to another press of exceptional quality in the field of western American history.

The presence at Oklahoma of a cherished friend and fellow historian, Charles E. Rankin, editor-in-chief of the University of Oklahoma Press, has proved a distinct godsend. Chuck's astute editorial eye, persistent good cheer, and imaginative grasp of publishing's possibilities have been invaluable resources upon which I have come to depend. Through Chuck, I've also been introduced to the exceptional team at Oklahoma, all of whom dedicate their considerable talents to maintaining the Press's well-deserved reputation for excellence. Amy Hernandez, Emily Jerman Schuster, Kathleen Kelly, Jessica Mitzner, Ariane Smith, and Rowan Steineker have each contributed notably to propelling this project off the launching pad with their energy, their enthusiasm, and their professionalism.

Finally, there are two individuals without whom this journey might never have been begun and certainly would never have been finished. Howard Roberts Lamar, now Sterling Professor Emeritus of History at Yale University, not only mentored me through an unusually lengthy voyage in pursuit of a Ph.D. with his customary grace and wisdom, but throughout my career has offered steadfast and generous encouragement. As has been true for generations of other Yale graduate students, I have treasured Howard's friendship and aspired, as far as it has been within my power, to follow the example he has set.

No one, however, has had a more personal and immediate sense of what this project has meant than Sara S. (Sue) Hodson, cherished colleague and companion. No matter how immersed in the demands of her own distinguished career as the Huntington Library's Curator of Literary Manuscripts, she has spared neither time nor effort to contribute to my progress. No one has been more sublimely confident of *Motoring West*'s potential or of its ultimate value; no one has been more ready to lend a hand to bring it to fruition or more excited about the prospect of its completion. It seems only fitting, therefore, that I offer her, yet again, my undying gratitude and love for all she does as we travel this road together.

PETER J. BLODGETT
San Marino, California
April 2014

Editor's Note

The editor has chosen to arrange the contents of this volume in order of publication date *except* in the case of those texts published long after the date when the events they described had occurred (such as the 1905 journey of the two Oldsmobiles documented in *From Hell Gate to Portland*, published in 1931, and Florence Trinkle's account of the trip in the Brush Runabout, which appeared in 1952). In such instances, I have relied upon the dates of the actual events as the rationale for selecting their placement.

In dealing with the original texts, on the whole I endeavored to keep the original modes of expression completely intact, even to the point of accepting some idiosyncrasies such as the reliance upon numerals rather than spelling out numbers (whether weights or distances or speeds) and retaining such now obsolete choices as leaving "State of Nevada" capitalized while "Mississippi river" appears with "river" lowercased in an effort to retain as fully as possible the full flavor of these texts as artifacts from another time. Occasionally, various abbreviations have been fully spelled out, the first names of various individuals have been inserted, and some usages of punctuation have been modernized for the sake of clarity, but otherwise the texts are presented as close to original form as feasible. Similarly, I have relied upon the introductions for the volume as a whole and for the individual entries to establish the basic context for the authors and their essays rather than engaging in extensive annotation of the texts.

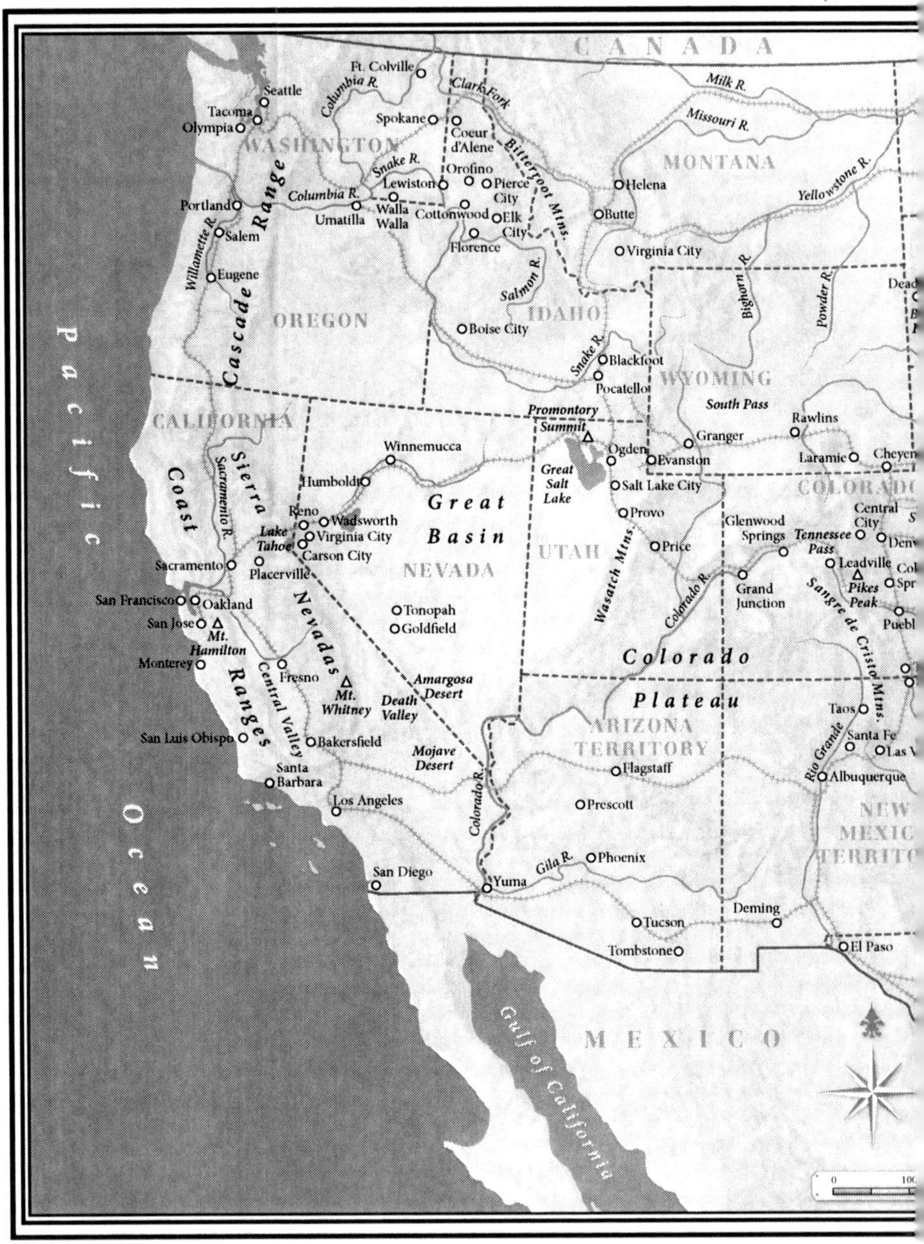
CANADA
MONTANA
WASHINGTON
OREGON
IDAHO
WYOMING
CALIFORNIA
NEVADA
UTAH
COLORADO
ARIZONA TERRITORY
NEW MEXICO TERRITORY
MEXICO
Pacific Ocean
Gulf of California
Great Basin
Colorado Plateau
Cascade Range
Coast Ranges
Sierra Nevadas
Bitterroot Mtns.
Wasatch Mtns.
Sangre de Cristo Mtns.
Seattle
Tacoma
Olympia
Portland
Salem
Eugene
Spokane
Ft. Colville
Coeur d'Alene
Lewiston
Orofino
Pierce City
Walla Walla
Umatilla
Cottonwood
Elk City
Florence
Boise City
Helena
Butte
Virginia City
Blackfoot
Pocatello
Promontory Summit
Ogden
Evanston
Granger
Rawlins
Laramie
South Pass
Great Salt Lake
Salt Lake City
Provo
Price
Winnemucca
Humboldt
Reno
Wadsworth
Lake Tahoe
Carson City
Sacramento
Placerville
San Francisco
Oakland
San Jose
Mt. Hamilton
Monterey
Fresno
Mt. Whitney
Death Valley
Amargosa Desert
Mojave Desert
Tonopah
Goldfield
San Luis Obispo
Bakersfield
Santa Barbara
Los Angeles
San Diego
Yuma
Phoenix
Prescott
Flagstaff
Tucson
Tombstone
Deming
El Paso
Albuquerque
Santa Fe
Taos
Glenwood Springs
Grand Junction
Tennessee Pass
Leadville
Pikes Peak
Central City
Columbia R.
Snake R.
Clark Fork
Milk R.
Missouri R.
Yellowstone R.
Bighorn R.
Powder R.
Salmon R.
Willamette R.
Sacramento R.
Central Valley
Colorado R.
Gila R.
Rio Grande

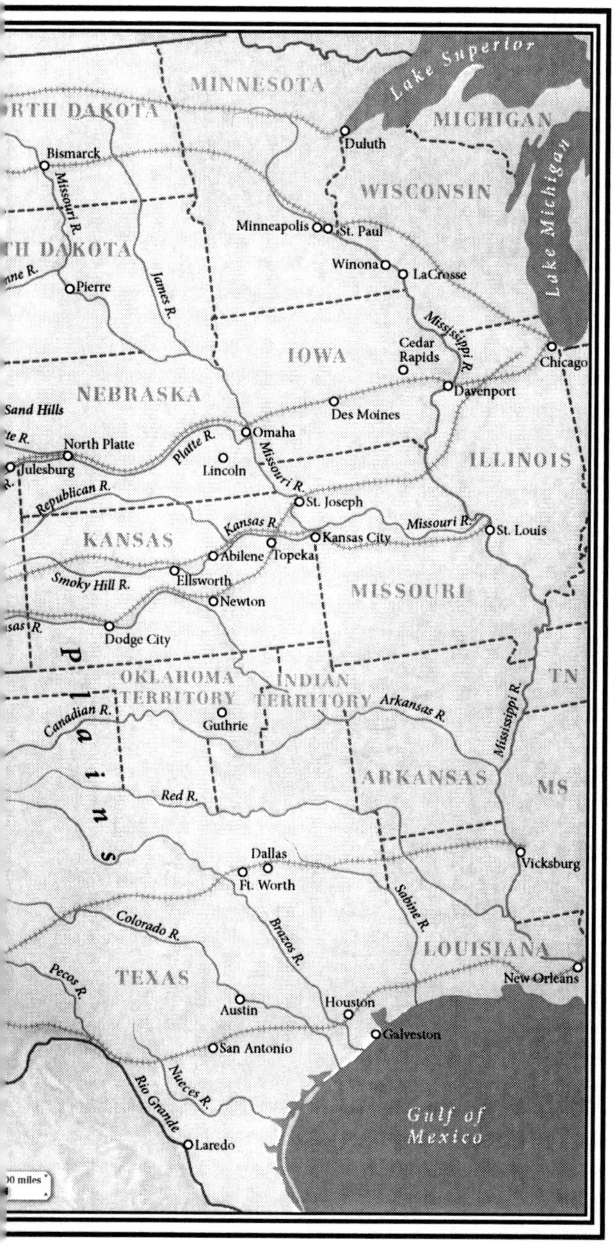

MOTORING WEST IN 1905
This map of the trans-Mississippi West in the early twentieth century places the trips made by these pioneering automobile travelers in the geographical context of the region as a whole. The profusion of mountains and rivers—as well as the total absence of highways—depict the many obstacles confronted by motorists while the presence of railroad lines reminds us that the iron horse represented the predominant means of moving people throughout the West at the dawn of a new century.

Series Introduction

Motor touring across the great spaces of the trans-Mississippi West grew after 1900 from an audacious stunt to a curiosity to a commonplace occurrence over only a few decades. For aspiring western travelers, automobiles became an integral part of their continuing search for new experiences and new destinations. At the very same time, the unrelenting expansion of mobility that automobiles guaranteed for growing numbers of travelers gave rise to a wide array of western businesses that cared for the needs of both car and driver. By mid-century, the resulting infrastructure of automotively oriented attractions and services had helped establish tourism as a crucial underpinning of the entire region's economy while motorized excursionists explored western landscapes, communities, scenery, and history.

As one historian has observed, "from its introduction in the United States, the motor vehicle appeared to offer substantial utilitarian advantages over the horse-drawn vehicle," ranging from perceptions of greater economy to enhanced efficiency in areas ranging from maintenance to performance. In addition to such "utilitarian" notions, "nonutilitarian" conceptions "greatly enhanced the attractiveness of the innovation to Americans," including the lure of geographical mobility and the love of individual autonomy.[1] That conjunction of the automobile's practical and symbolic appeals, as well as its rapid evolution into an ever-more dependable means of long-distance transportation, made automotive technology increasingly indispensable all over the United States, including the trans-Mississippi West, within very few years. Americans integrated this new machine into many of their customary endeavors, transforming everything from business practices to leisure habits.

Many of the motoring tourists who rode their horseless carriage across the West at the turn of the last century left written accounts. These are an invaluable resource for understanding the early-twentieth-century West and the roots of recreational motoring. There are scores of articles, pamphlets, and books published by travelers who motored across and around the region between 1900 and 1940, varying wildly in length, depth of detail, literary quality, and perspicacity of observation. They illuminate the motives that propelled these travelers to venture into the West and their diverse perceptions of western landscapes, western communities, and westerners themselves. They also reveal the enduring cultural significance of the region's history, natural beauty, and recreational opportunities and the insatiably magnetic attraction of western national parks and other tourist attractions, as well as the evolving infrastructure of western tourism and the sometimes elusive visions of the West embedded in the minds of its auto-borne visitors.[2] From these same sources, we can also capture many insights about the amazing advances of automotive technology during the era, the influence that the steadily expanding presence of the automobile exerted upon the development of the West, and the similarities and differences in the ways that men and women engaged both the automobile and the many Wests that they encountered in their travels.

The vast majority of these accounts have been lost to readers' eyes in the decades since they were first published. Although a handful of individual accounts such as those written by Alice Ramsey or Emily Post[3] have come in and out of print through the years, almost all others have been consigned to near-absolute oblivion, especially those articles that originally appeared in periodicals that once graced the homes of thousands of middle- and upper-class Americans. Even lengthy volumes written by such once-prominent authors as James Montgomery Flagg, Lewis Gannett, Dallas Sharp, and Frederic F. Van de Water to describe their continent-spanning adventures eventually disappeared beneath the waves of changing literary tastes, leaving few if any traces behind them.[4] The volumes that will comprise *Motoring West* shall resurrect a generous selection of these accounts, making them available for a new generation of readers who are eager to explore America's protracted affair with the automobile and the changing character of western landscapes during the twentieth century, as well as the enduring impact of tourism upon the trans-Mississippi West during those years and the allure of the automobile as a talisman of the American affection for constant mobility.

Building the Roads

The pioneering auto traveler confronted numerous challenges beginning with the wretched state of the average American highway in the pre–World War I era. Indeed, based upon the figures assembled by advocates of better roads at the turn of the twentieth century, it would be hard to argue that America possessed anything even vaguely reminiscent of modern highways. As one contemporary student of transportation history has concluded, "it was more difficult to travel west by road in 1900 than it had been in 1858." A 1904 census of American roadways, conducted by the U.S. Department of Agriculture's Office of Public Roads, revealed that of the national total of 2,152,000 miles of rural roads, only 154,000 miles (or slightly more than 7 percent) were surfaced at all—the vast majority only gravel mixed with a binder to hold it in place. Agitation for a significant improvement and expansion of routes outside the boundaries of cities had been building for nearly two decades. During the 1880s and especially the 1890s, segments of the farm populace grew increasingly vocal in their calls for better roads, in hopes of reducing both the costs of transporting their crops to market and the isolation in which so many farm families lived. Over time, their appeals were bolstered by the promotional efforts of the rapidly growing ranks of bicycling enthusiasts. Those individuals, in turn, through their national association, the League of American Wheelmen, exerted all the pressure they could in favor of better roads that would carry bicyclists farther and faster through new landscapes. As these groups and others began to coalesce around the issue of highway improvement, the Good Roads movement took shape.[5]

Good roads, as a cause, enlisted many different interests to march behind its banner. Bicycle manufacturers, road builders, and the nascent automobile industry lent what weight they could to the work. Despite their disparate identities, these champions of highway betterment pressured governments on various levels through public information programs and direct lobbying. With the creation of the Office of Road Inquiry in the Department of Agriculture in 1893, the Good Roads movement had even established a beachhead within the federal government. Before many more years had passed, various advocates within the movement focused more of their efforts on enlisting more expansive federal support.[6]

Even as the cause began to take hold more deeply, making inroads into the wider public's consciousness, the relationships among its constituent elements altered in response to changing national circumstances. Thus by 1903, one scholar has argued, "automobile interests rapidly displaced bicycle organizations as the dominant force [in support of good roads]," as the horseless carriage's popularity expanded. With the upsurge in automobile ownership during the first two decades of the twentieth century (spurting from less than 10,000 in 1900 to nearly half a million ten years later and then rocketing upward to a total of 2,446,000 cars and trucks by 1915 and 9,232,000 by 1920), the influence of the motor-vehicle community upon public affairs increased. National good-roads conferences drew more attention and wider political support. Even so, the automobile's friends and sponsors struggled for years to push road building into new directions. Laws providing for tax-supported construction and maintenance of local roads by counties and states worked their way through more than half the state legislatures by 1913; three years later came the capstone of all these efforts with the passage of the first Federal Aid Road Act.[7]

Enactment of the federal legislation made available seventy-five million dollars over five years for the cause of improving rural roads, though only if the states could match allocated funds, dollar for dollar, and agreed to establish highway departments at the state level. Although hardly establishing a dominant role for the federal government in the process, such stipulations clearly inserted the government into activities once left almost entirely to the locality. Just as the federal government made its first tentative foray into the road-building enterprise, the first of a number of private organizations also took on the task of encouraging highway improvements. The Lincoln Highway Association, under the flamboyant leadership of Carl Fisher, represented the kind of application of private means to achieving public purposes that often characterized the development of American highways at the beginning of the twentieth century.[8] They envisioned a "Coast-to-Coast Rock Highway" built through endorsements and donations from auto makers such as Packard and Willys-Overland, manufacturers such as the Goodyear Tire and Rubber Company, and automobile clubs and enthusiasts.[9]

Far beyond the reach of the Lincoln Highway, in every section of the country, the alluring prospect of tourist dollars intrigued other civic boosters as well, inspiring the creation of dozens of other private highway associations between 1913 and American entry into World War I in 1917. Ranging in their scope from the grandest transcontinental vision, often in conscious competition with the Lincoln Highway (as in the case of the National Old Trails Road, Pikes Peak Ocean to Ocean Highway, Theodore Roosevelt International Highway, and Victory Highway), to the thoroughly parochial (such as the Big Four Trail from Terre Haute, Indiana, to St. Louis, Missouri; or the Corn Belt Route from Effner, Indiana, to Burlington, Iowa), these organizations promoted the advantages of their particular routes and the attractions of the communities adjacent to them with the clear intention of profiting from the tourists who would travel these roads. In doing so, they also began, usually without a conscious intent, to redefine many large swathes of the American countryside. Towns, cities, or counties that might once have never imagined they shared any common ground with each other now might discover themselves linked by the Arrowhead Trail, the Dixie Highway, or the Old Spanish Trail. Not only might one of these paths to potential profit unite their various aspirations to economic growth and development, but in a number of instances, the organizing theme might create a new identity for the realms through which a highway passed. Whether commemorating national heroes (Thomas Jefferson, Abraham Lincoln, or Theodore Roosevelt), historic events or places (Custer Battlefield, the Oregon Trail, or the Old Spanish Trail) or prominent sites on the map (Geyser to Glacier, Pikes Peak or Ozark), the names of many highways conveyed a certain sort of grandeur to any localities associated with them.

In the West, various highways cropped up throughout the nineteen-teens, either spanning the region as part of a larger transcontinental enterprise (the Lincoln Highway, the National Old Trails Road, the Yellowstone Trail) or knitting together western landmarks (the Denver-Yellowstone Highway, the Geyser-to-Glacier Highway, or the National Park to Park Highway). While some tried to capitalize on the aura of the region's history (the Lewis and Clark Highway or the Oregon Trail) and some were relentlessly pragmatic (the Chicago-Buffalo Highway or the Texas–New Mexico Mountain Highway), still others (as noted above) focused upon one particularly distinctive feature of the region, its national parks. Given the prominent role that national parks had already come to play in all forms of tourist advertising for the Far West and especially for the Rocky Mountain states, the frequency with which "Yellowstone" in particular or the general term "National Parks" appeared in the titles of western highway associations is not surprising. The images provoked by references to the nation's scenic crown jewels remained sufficiently compelling that many highway promoters sought the same sort of identification with national parks that other advertisers already had been employing.[10]

The escalating numbers of highway projects, unfortunately, brought no commensurate improvement in highway quality during this period. The Lincoln Highway, after all, had been forced by the realities of fundraising to abandon its most ambitious road-building schemes, resorting instead to the construction of demonstration projects (the so-called "seedling miles") along its route in hopes of establishing a standard to which, its organizers hoped, county and state governments might aspire. Other "highways" or "trails," living on far more restricted financial means than the Lincoln Highway, could do little more than promote the notion of good roads through their advertising and try to plot out a route that could attract more backers by accommodating as many local interests as possible. Projects such as the Arrowhead Trails Highway, envisioning a southwesterly path from Salt Lake City across Utah and Nevada to Los Angeles, had to rely upon nothing more tangible than aggressive salesmanship through the distribution of literature filled with "photographs, strip maps, information on tourist accommodations [and] verbal descriptions of all that was to be experienced [by motoring tourists]." Moreover, despite the best intentions of their founders, the increase in proposed highways generated considerable confusion. Forced in many parts of the country to rely upon a relatively small number of through roads, various associations mapped out the same routes, festooning them with their different signage until, in the words of the Lincoln Highway's history, "it was not uncommon for a single pole to carry the insignia of as many as a dozen routes." As a later student of the movement has argued, "These roads were usually the product of local boosterism; civic pride on the part of townspeople and businessmen promoted them to climb on the good-roads bandwagon." With operating funds often in short supply and the responsibility for road construction and maintenance still laid in large measure at the doorstep of local governments, the private-highway movement faced great challenges in trying to bring about a new era of highway improvement. Right up through the World War I years, American highways in general ranged from mediocre to disastrous.[11]

Even after the passage of the first Federal-Aid Highway Act in 1916, little immediate progress in road building occurred. Only after the passage of a second Federal Highway Act in 1921 that clarified jurisdictions and established the priority of state agencies as road builders did federal funds exert a significant role in bringing about better roads. Those funds proved particularly crucial to many states all over the West, whose ability otherwise to pursue such programs would have been severely hampered by the great distances and the lack of state funds found in these sparsely populated states. One historian of federal highway programs has estimated that the 1921 act funded as much as three-fourths of state highway construction in some western states within five years of its passage.[12]

As difficult as the first thirty years of the century had been for good-roads advocates, the decade of the 1920s brought highway construction and development into a more prominent role than ever before, driven in large measure by public funding.

The downward spiral of the national economy during the Great Depression affected road construction and the funds necessary to pay for it. As the leading scholar of American highway policy has put it, "[T]he highway boom of the 1920s continued . . . as road builders faced a sharp drop in funds only during 1932 and 1933." The leading indicator of growth, the total mileage of surfaced highways, rose from 694,000 miles in 1930 to 1,367,000 miles in 1940. Expansive new sources of federal funds soon opened up, particularly during the New Deal years, as highway building became a magnet for public-works spending to help alleviate unemployment. For our immediate purposes, however, it is sufficient to observe that the decade that ended with American entry into World War II carried forward in handsome fashion the development of the highway infrastructure essential to the ongoing influx of tourists to the Rocky Mountain West.

The states of that region, having relied upon federal aid through the 1920s for critical support in the road-building business, continued to do so through the following decade when the rising tide of out-of-state visitors made highway expansion critical. A 1929–30 traffic survey conducted by the Bureau of Public Roads on federal-aid roads in the Far West demonstrated that in Colorado 20 percent of all out-of-state automobiles had come from east of the Mississippi with the same percentage observed in Wyoming, almost 14 percent in Utah, and nearly 10 percent even in Idaho. For the region as a whole, it concluded, 22 percent of such traffic originated in the Central Plains states, with another 12 percent traveling from the Northeast and Californians supplying nearly one out of every four out-of-state cars observed in the study. As it mapped out the routes carrying the heaviest concentrations of this traffic, the study laid out a configuration of roads that paralleled the Front Range of the Colorado Rockies through Colorado Springs and Denver north to Cheyenne, Wyoming, and then swung west through the southern part of the state as it angled down toward Salt Lake City, from which another corridor appeared leading north to Pocatello, Idaho, and then curved to the northwest across the state. Mirroring in part the broadest outlines of the original emigrant trails of the mid-nineteenth century and reflecting a pattern eventually adopted by the interstate highway system, the layouts of this traffic also illustrated that other networks of automobile travel had spread away from the main arteries, weaving their way across all of these states in response to the requirements of the automobile age.[13]

State highway departments celebrated their successes as road builders and advertised the virtues of their labors through a variety of publications such as one 1935 pamphlet from the Montana State Highway Commission, which boasted of its "modern graded . . .

smooth, fast highways rolling across the prairies and over the Rockies," or a 1937 brochure from the same agency that touted the "oiled or asphalt surfacing" and its "safe, dustless all-weather highways," ensuring that Montana had a "black top" heaven for tourists. This literature, making the argument of convenience and ease of travel, routinely broadcast the notion that the tourist could find no better circumstances in which to travel than the completely up-to-date highways of a state like Montana, "free of detours, bumps, stiff grades and sharp curves," as built up by the people of the western states.[14]

The state guidebooks produced by the New Deal's Federal Writers' Project chimed in with their own observations about the progress of the automobile age as seen in highway construction. By 1939, for example, the Montana guide could note that the total coverage of the federal aid system extended to just over five thousand miles at that point, linking tourists to even more thousands of miles of state highways. The 1940 guide to Utah boasted that tourists could cross the state on any of six federal highways or strike off onto "a network of graded roads [connecting to] small towns and recreation areas." Travel advertising through the 1930s urging tourists to visit the Rocky Mountain states by car could presume with ever increasing certainty the presence of good roads. The Denver Convention & Visitors Bureau, one of the region's principal promoters, thus could encourage potential visitors in 1940 to "Drive Covered Wagon Trails Now Broad, Smooth Highways," celebrating the "wide, surfaced roads paralleling pioneer trails of the [1860s] where the Spirit of the Old West still lives . . . a few hours comfortable driving over easy grades!" and the Standard Oil Company in the same year could distribute colorful folders based on the same general premise. "How to See the Best in the West" assured motorists that a staggering assortment of "natural and man-made wonders" could be reached on "main highways" or by other "good roads" (along which could also be found, not coincidentally, Standard's system of service stations under the "Chevron" insignia).[15]

Finding the Roads

Before American tourists could benefit from these new possibilities, however, they had to overcome the other great challenge to auto-touring bliss in the early part of the twentieth century: they had to obtain more and better information about the road ahead. In a sense, of course, that challenge had no novelty about it, for generations of Euro-American travelers who had journeyed across or around the trans-Mississippi West had faced the same challenge, reaching back to the great age of exploration personified by Meriwether Lewis and William Clark. As the westward movement of immigrants from the fledgling United States to regions such as Oregon Territory or Alta California grew in the 1830s and 1840s from a trickle to a torrent, an array of authors and publishers had stepped into the breach with offerings of wildly varying quality. Though often intended for the potential settler or investor as much as for the traveler, many of these volumes were celebrated or excoriated for the help or hindrance they furnished to westward-bound Americans. In the words of one historian of the nineteenth-century overland migration, "Guidebooks published prior to the gold rush contained a wide variety of 'useful reading' for emigrants, but nearly all attempted to supply the two kinds of practical instruction expected by the prospective traveler: a description of the route to be followed and advice on preparation and method of travel." Driven by the enormous demand for such information at the height of the California gold rush, the publication of guides conforming to that model continued to flourish into the last quarter of the century, even as they were being supplanted in turn by the "tourist guides." Like their literary forebears, these guides sought to distill a wide array of information and experiences into a comprehensible (if not comprehensive) package, in this instance offering "detailed information on train schedules, accommodations, noteworthy sites and cities all along the [railroad] routes [which] made planning a long trip westward entertaining and helped make the journey itself enjoyable and worthwhile." Incorporating what one scholar has characterized as "a strong element of regional pride" into the fabric of their presentations, these guides consciously sought to respond to the interests of a significant new population of west-bound travelers who desired adventure or excitement or recreation rather than profit or permanent residence. In doing so, their creators accelerated the transformation of this genre into a tool for leisure and pleasure, prefiguring the rise of a utilitarian literature that would be of great importance for the motorist who headed west in the twentieth century.[16]

By 1901, the automobile had made sufficient inroads into the character of everyday life that its use for a variety of purposes, including the recreational, demanded not only more and better roads but more and better information about how to navigate them. In the words of one advocate of auto touring, "There is one essential for the motorist who sets out to travel . . . and that is accurate information covering every important detail."[17] As a result, a variety of channels intended to accumulate and then disseminate useful details developed in the first two decades of this century. Unhappily for the aspiring motorist in those years, the documentation of roads then in existence generally proved at least as wretched as the quality of the roads themselves. Thus, every excursion by motor car could prove an unintended voyage of discovery, especially for the aspiring long-distance traveler. With the numbers of motor tourists increasing through the 1900s and 1910s, drivers seeking directions and particulars about what lay ahead interrogated each other and, wherever possible, the local citizenry. The question uppermost in every mind—"How's the road?" (a question so ubiquitous that it served as the title for one of the better published accounts of American auto touring)—rapidly evolved into the essence of most conversations at rest or along the wayside. Such conversations, representing what one historian has called the "casual shop talk" of the auto tourist, served to fill in the huge gaps in highway knowledge reflected in the early years by the dearth of published sources. Indeed, as part of the developing camaraderie of the road, "it was a cardinal rule of motoring to 'pass it on.' Just as tramps informed each other of hospitable farm houses and hostile police, tourists talked of bad roads, bad hotels and dishonest garages." Similarly, motorists reporting on their trips acknowledged the assistance of the people they met by the side of the road. One traveler, recounting the course of his voyage, reported that "Residents along the way were always obliging and willing to give information in regard to roads, etc."[18]

To many tourists, gleaning the facts through frequent conversation proved a gratifying method of getting to know their fellow Americans. As the motoring public grew substantially, however, demand for other, more formal means of circulating travel intelligence escalated as well. Drivers in need of directions, for example, could not always count upon encountering a fellow motorist or an obliging and well-informed local just at the moment of losing their path across the unmarked prairie or on a mountain road. Furthermore, even the best-intentioned residents of a specific community might have no more familiarity with the landscape beyond the county line than did the out-of-state tourist. Others proved susceptible to bursts of local pride and excessive optimism about the progress of local road construction, leading one observer to remark wryly that "when [a southerner] tells you a road is good, he means that it once was good. When a Westerner tells you the same thing, he means that it is going to be good at some happy future date." And, of course, the "facts" about any individual road might vary considerably, depending on who reported them; as one historian observed, "tourists learned quickly that not everyone knew the right directions and that fellow motorists tended to exaggerate hardships."[19]

Fortunately for the purposes of the motor tourist, the traditional American enthusiasm for collective fellowship in pursuit of a common goal had taken root early on amongst the first automobile owners. Organizations such as the Automobile Club of America (ACA) and the American Automobile Association (AAA) (AAA characterized by its evolving network of local and statewide affiliates) provided channels through which demand for and eventually the creation of reliable maps and guidebooks could be directed. By 1901, various entrepreneurs had begun publishing bound volumes of itemized directions, narrating the course to be navigated by a motorist going from point A to point B. Characterized by one student as "verbal guides," these sturdy tomes would include "lengthy descriptions of specified routes including indications of road conditions, points of interest along the routes and highly detailed descriptions of intersections where changes of direction were necessary. Each change of direction or point of interest was indicated as being at a specific distance from a pre-determined starting point. Thus, even the shortest and most simple route had to be accompanied by hundreds of words of description."[20]

Made both cumbersome and expensive by such bulk, this variety of guidebook remained popular though not unchallenged for nearly two decades. As the technological possibilities of the automobile and the camera continued to evolve, photographic guides and slimmer narrative guides relying upon odometer readings rather than ephemeral landmarks of the natural or the built environment provided new competition, enhancing the struggle for the motorist's patronage and thus for economic survival among their many publishers.[21] At the same time, the swelling reach of the automobile, a function of its increasing power and reliability, heightened the need for even more complete guides covering even wider swathes of the landscape.

No matter their form, however, road guides in any incarnation were absolutely dependent on accurate information gathered through first-hand investigation. To conduct such investigations, organizations such as AAA sponsored a new kind of frontier scout, the highway "pathfinder." Just as the pathfinders laid out the actual routes for many early-twentieth-century highways, so they also plotted out the directions to those routes that became the foundation for travel guides of all types, including the increasingly popular cartographic guides that relied upon information assembled in the form of maps. In their pathfinding capacity, these pioneers not only rattled all over the landscape, identifying the best routes for motorists to follow, but they compiled the data and promoted the chosen paths to motorists all over the region and eventually the country through a variety of means. Sometimes, as in the case of W. D. ("Bill") Rishel of Utah, they even drew the maps. At the very least, like A. L. Westgard of the American Automobile Association, they glad-handed politicians and civic leaders of every stripe as well as chambers of commerce and local automobile clubs to raise popular consciousness about the virtues of automobility, especially in areas where good-roads campaigns were under way. Sponsored by a variety of organizations—including advocates of the automobile such as AAA or the National Highways Association, metropolitan newspapers such as the *Salt Lake Tribune* or the increasingly ubiquitous private highway associations—pathfinders such as Rishel or Westgard or Maj. Charles E. Percival threw their energies into championing what Percival called "a motorized age in which the only use for legs would be to walk out to the garage." Although the resulting roads might have many uses, the pathfinders had particular appreciation for their role in boosting recreational auto travel. Westgard, perhaps the best known of them, proudly asserted that "the preparation of dependable route maps all over the United States has in no small measure helped in their development and the desire to travel over them."[22]

With automotive pathfinders popping up all over the western states by 1910, new means through which to share the fruits of their labors appeared as well. Not only did guidebooks in many styles proliferate, but the pathfinders and their sponsors counted on their access to an assortment of newspapers and magazines. The public's fascination with the motor car, clearly a passion that had outlived the status of a mere fad, suggested that articles about autos and auto touring would find an ongoing readership, making such articles of interest to editors and publishers. To that end, therefore, periodicals such as *The Literary Digest* and *The Independent*, for example, would publish articles such as "Vacation Trips in America" and "The Banner Year of Tours Begins," which would circulate details of where to go and how to get there by automobile.[23]

Among American newspapers, a similar desire to capture the attention of the automotively inclined reader, matched with the interest of many local papers in promoting the Good Roads movement as a public service, fostered the appearance of articles about the horseless carriage. As early as 1911, for example, Bill Rishel filled the post of automobile editor for the *Salt Lake Tribune* in Utah, which also supplied Rishel with a car that became known as the "*Tribune* Pathfinder" to carry him on excursions all over the Rocky Mountain West. In that same year, the *Tribune* began to publish the information garnered during those expeditions in its columns, with the first piece headlined "Pathfinder Car Maps Out Utah Auto Routes." Within a decade, other western newspapers such as the *Denver Post* were publishing similar pieces, sometimes on a weekly basis in touring season, under such headings as "The Sunday One-Day Trip." Such articles would provide directions couched in the same form as the verbal guidebooks, with mileage marks and details about road grades and the drivability of each track. By 1920, such articles might be presenting travel information from a variety of other sources, ranging from the United States Forest Service to the Denver Motor Club and the B. F. Goodrich Travel and Transport Bureau.[24] Thus fully launched into a new phase of their familiar role as community boosters, many western newspapers were busily engaged in the cultivation of tourist travel down to the local level with their depictions of attractive nearby excursions—even as they might editorialize on behalf of projects, such as the designation of new national parks, that would attract new visitors to the region. In their advocacy of the horseless carriage's role in tourist travel, they also contributed to the enthusiasm for road building that produced both the private highway movement, as seen above, and federal highway legislation.

Consulting the newspapers that carried such articles highlights another development that, while unremarkable to our eyes, is worthy of substantive commentary. Besides the narrative descriptions that usually characterized any form of directions for driving, the articles themselves would also often supplement the verbal with the graphic in the form of increasingly detailed maps. Guidebooks of nearly any type, of course, had been susceptible to what one student has aptly described as the "impermanence" of the road and the surrounding landscape, especially in an era characterized by continued highway construction. Moreover, given the mass that many early narrative guides achieved, they were hardly handy tools for the driver or even the passenger to manage while the automobile was underway. At the same time, recognized touring experts and road scouts such as Bill Rishel in Utah found more and more inquiries directed to them, sent by motorists seeking to benefit from the hard-won knowledge garnered by the pathfinders in their travels.[25]

As a means of compressing great amounts of information into small packets to reduce the troublesome bulk of existing guides, the sheet map and its cousins, printed in bound atlases, proved an excellent solution. Bill Rishel, for example, claimed that he had begun sending out maps of his own creation soon after the turn of the century in response to requests from curious would-be motorists, pioneering the strip map that AAA would eventually adopt as the "trip-tik." Although many early road maps, especially those printed as illustrative material in traditional verbal guides, were closer to schematic drawings than modern road maps, they still incorporated at least as many if not more details than any narrative guide. The route books of the Touring Information Bureau of America, a guide which debuted in 1914, provided such information in their strip maps as the type of road the motorist would drive, which watercourses would have to be forded and which were spanned with bridges, what counties the motorist would cross, and which cities of what size the auto would have to navigate. Other guides from different organizations adopted similar approaches, dividing up the landscapes of individual states or the routes of privately sponsored highways into sections illuminated with maps as well as narrative discussions of highway directions and local communities.[26]

Maps made quick and notable headway among the traveling public as they began to appear in many different venues during the first decade of the century. Various public agencies grappled with this responsibility, acknowledging as Wyoming governor Joseph M. Carey did in 1911 that "no one can now contradict the fact that the automobile is to become an everyday feature on the public highways, both for pleasure and for business." As state highway departments and travel commissions began to appear, they began to produce versions intended for the motorist. One particular development on the eve of World War I, however, catapulted the highway map into the popular consciousness and the popular culture. When the Gulf Oil Company agreed in 1914 to print and distribute a map of the improved highways of Allegheny County, Pennsylvania, at the same time it was inaugurating its drive-in retail service stations, the age of the oil company road map had dawned. Within a year, three hundred thousand maps of New England and the Northeastern states had been distributed; by 1920, one source claims, a staggering sixteen million maps had been given away by Gulf alone.[27] Gulf's competitors, desiring to obtain the same sort of visibility that Gulf achieved with this bonanza of free advertising, soon matched Gulf's innovation.

In the wake of Gulf Oil's success, the petroleum industry discovered the value of the road map as a premium that might give one company or another just enough of a competitive edge to attract the patronage of a potential customer. In fact, probably without thinking of it in quite such specific terms, they had actually acquired another commodity to distribute: information. The facts and figures about one particular portion of the landscape, codified in graphic form and reduced to a 10 × 12–inch sheet, proved quite as compelling and just as integral to successful motoring as gasoline. The spectacular success of the oil company road map, however, should not obscure the fact that, in this same period, many other entrepreneurs also grasped the potential of information as another product with which to capture the attention of the consumer.

By 1920, organizations such as the American Automobile Association and the National Highways Association been supplying guides and maps (either their own or those created on contract for them) to motorists all over the United States for years. Meanwhile, pouring forth from the presses were other maps and guidebooks, under commission from the private highway associations, whose labors on behalf of the Good Roads movement have been chronicled above. Besides their enthusiastic support for the cause of highway construction, most of these groups also engaged in lively support of the concept of auto touring, especially if they could convince motorists to travel the route marked by a particular association and enrich the local businesses in the towns and cities along that route who had supported its creation. Still other guides for the traveler appeared under the sponsorship of a wide array of touring services or travel bureaus devised by organizations as diverse as the B. F. Goodrich Rubber Company, American Express, and *The Independent* magazine, united only by an interest in gaining the patronage of the motorist. The resulting deluge of guides in all forms but especially of road maps by 1920 guaranteed a thriving market for the commercial firms such as Rand McNally, General Drafting Company, and, later, H. M. Gousha that produced the maps for many of these enterprises to distribute. Even public agencies all over the West threw themselves into the process of producing and disseminating such information in bulk; by 1924, for example, Wyoming was distributing its first true highway map "around the state and the region to hotels, filling stations, chambers of commerce, and auto clubs."[28] Increasingly aware during the 1920s and 1930s of the economic value of tourism and eagerly determined to snag the largest possible share of each passing traveler's disposable income, westerners ranging from individual retailers of all kinds to civic associations, booster clubs, and business organizations produced a voluminous promotional literature that routinely emphasized the West's transformation into a national "pleasuring ground" accessible by automobile to millions.

The happy motorist, in the wake of such activity, certainly benefited from the bountiful harvest of information that appeared annually for his or her use in the two decades after 1920. As guidebooks, atlases, and roadmaps proliferated, other parties benefited from them as well. The travel guides, brochures, flyers, and related advertising sponsored by oil companies, motorist associations, chambers of commerce, and many other bodies highlighted not only the excellent roads in every part of the West but also the innumerable entrepreneurs just waiting around the next bend to ensure the traveler's comfort and delight. As more tourists were convinced in the early twentieth century that they could successfully and enjoyably travel by car, the resulting expansion in auto travel initiated a tidy symbiosis in which rising numbers of tourists nourished more and more purveyors of goods and services whose own propagation in turn facilitated even more travel, and so forth. Thus, the rise of the auto guide and the road map played a critical part in creating the infrastructure of auto travel that proved indispensable to domestic tourism throughout the trans-Mississippi West during the first half of the twentieth century.

Tourism on the Roads

Just as the increasing popularity of motoring for recreation encouraged the overhaul of western roads and inspired new means of navigating through the western countryside, the very existence of this new pastime inspired Americans to experience western landscapes from new perspectives. Though inevitably intertwined with other visions of how the automobile might be of use, the conception of motor touring soon after the turn of the twentieth century caught the eye of adventurous men and women who had already become confident operators of this new machinery. Eager to test the technological limits of their equipment and intrigued by the possibility of becoming new American pioneers, a first few hardy souls between 1900 and 1910 launched into breathtaking transcontinental expeditions. At the same time, in search of a means to express an often rudimentary but nonetheless pressing dissatisfaction with many aspects of life in contemporary urban-industrial society, other upper-middle-class tourists who motored through the countryside and then camped by the side of the road found in a sentimentalized image of the gypsy or the tramp quite a compelling identity to assume (if only temporarily). Such motorists often became (at least in their own view) the new "gypsies" or "vagabonds" whose journeys would be guided by nothing more formal than whim and happenstance. As geographer John Jakle observes, motoring of this kind offered "freedom of action, a kind of sociability and direct contact with landscape unknown to passengers of trains and ships." In particular, for those pioneering women at the opening of the twentieth century who were settling themselves behind the steering wheel, that "freedom of action" in the field of leisure bolstered the sense of independence in other spheres that the automobile could provide.[29]

Automobile tourists of all kinds, including self-described "motor gypsies," often expressed a particular delight in going, as one historian has phrased it, "off the beaten track" at the dawn of the era of motor touring. For them, reveling in their sense of independence from more orthodox forms of recreation and travel, the beauty and serenity of unspoiled countryside, the solitude of natural settings, and the escape from the burdensome character of most cities proved inescapably attractive. In the words of one Iowa excursionist, "I felt better for being out in the air. It was more recreation than any vacation I have ever taken." Another motorist, rhapsodizing just a few years later about his travels on the Pacific Slope, wrote, "The West is a wonderful country when it comes to the outdoor life—the mountains are grand, the fields beautiful, the water pure and more shades of green can be seen on these hillsides than one can image from a point 3,000 miles away." To go off the few familiar paths in most parts of the country before World War I, however, especially in the great distances of the trans-Mississippi West, also required a large measure of self-reliance. As the same Iowan observed about his 1905 excursion with his son, "What we don't know about running automobiles through mud . . . is not worth knowing," while another traveler, venturing around his home state of Wyoming four years later, wrote, "Highways, as we know them, were non-existent in those days. Roads? Yes. The state had plenty of roads, such as they were, but most of them for long and frequent stretches, were worse than none. Deep ruts; high centers; rocks, loose and solid; steep grades; washouts or gullies; stumps; sage brush roots; unbridged streams; sand; alkali dust; gumbo; and plain mud, were some of the more common abominations."[30]

Between the obstacles presented by such abysmal road conditions as well as the likelihood of frequent mechanical breakdowns and the absence of supply stops, long-distance auto tourists were regularly instructed by most experts (genuine and self-proclaimed) to carry an abundant load of necessaries. Such elaborate preparations, though frequently carried to extremes, did reflect prudent planning at the birth of the automobile age. Hauled along by one or more of the parties that made the first transcontinental drives between 1901 and 1908, for example, were ropes, buckets, blocks and tackle, axes, sleeping bags, water bags, spades, camp stoves, compasses, barometers, thermometers, cyclometers, batteries, first aid kits, rubber ponchos, tire chains, blankets, pith helmets, assorted spare parts, and a sufficient selection of fire arms to launch a small insurrection. Even in the wake of increasingly strenuous efforts to improve the nation's roads, long-distance motorists continued to receive urgent counsel not to be caught in the wide open spaces unprepared. One 1917 guide to auto travel in the "wonderland" of Utah and Idaho, for instance, recommended hauling, in case of breakdown, extra food and warm clothing, a spare tire casing and several additional inner tubes, and (whenever departing Utah to the east, west or south across deserts and mountains) an evaporative water bag, "an axe, shovel, 100 feet of rope, a three foot iron pin and a block and tackle." Four years later, a columnist in the *Denver Post* advised travelers headed for "remote places" to arm themselves with extra electric bulbs, spark plugs, and one or two extra tires—inflated and mounted on the rim—as well as additional inner tubes, tire patches and cement, a fire extinguisher, a tow rope, a supply of annealed wire, a pair of side-cutting pliers, and a roll of tape. And all auto travelers setting out for a voyage of any distance laid in outfits that would facilitate life on the road. Mary C. Bedell's impressive list of gear, published in her entertaining 1924 account of auto touring, *Modern Gypsies*, typifies both in scale and variety what was carried by the most dedicated motor campers: "tent, duffle bags, gasoline stove, Adirondack grate and a kit of aluminum kettles that nested, with coffee pot and enamel cups and saucers inside"—an array of equipment that added "four or five hundred pounds" alone to the weight of the fully loaded automobile.[31] A car so laden, puffing along western trails, bears a striking resemblance in the mind's eye to a hermit crab staggering across the ocean floor burdened with its house on its back.

In time, however, even the most cautious motoring tourists began to shed the most cumbersome portions of such paraphernalia, recognizing both the increasingly sturdy character of each new generation of automobiles and the ever more elaborate roadside infrastructure to tend to both machine and driver. After all, although the wanderlust that incited him or her in the first place provided the means to overthrow the daily drudgery long enough to renew one's physical and psychological energies, the motorized gypsy never really abandoned his or her place in conventional society. Moreover, while motoring represented a perfect escape from the stultifying clutches of many daily settings—"Thoreau at 29 cents a gallon," in one commentator's words—how could the gypsy caravan continue to wend its way through the countryside without someone on hand to fuel it at that or any other price?[32]

As exciting as the pioneering phase of motor touring seemed to some, therefore, its passing was mourned by comparatively few in light of the new comforts and conveniences whose appearance was hailed by many. By the middle of the 1920s, westerners could enthusiastically celebrate their continuing success in making the extraordinary routine. Writing in the inaugural issue of *Wyoming Roads*, the state highway department's publication, Sen. John B. Kendrick could acknowledge that the state had obtained, within just a few years, "transportation facilities that we could not possibly have enjoyed otherwise," a statement equally true of other "undeveloped and thinly populated Western states." Such facilities, Kendrick continued, made it possible for "the people crossing [Wyoming to] have revealed to them for the first time the many physical attractions of the state . . . an opportunity to glimpse the real beauty and charm of our landscapes," as well as the state's many marvelous natural resources, already being aggressively developed by its inhabitants. Writing with a similar tone of assurance, the Colorado Highway Department's magazine in the summer of 1927 declared the Centennial State a "Motorist's Paradise," unmatched by any other state in terms not only of its "scenic beauty" but also "a system of highways [that] permits the traveler to reach any part of the state in comfort and safety" (except, the article pointed out, during the pass-closing months of the winter). Brought into being by the "unceasing work" of public agencies ranging from the U.S. Forest Service and the state's highway department down to county commissioners, Colorado's "interstate roads" (those highways that had been designated as part of Colorado's share of the federal-aid system) had been turned into "veritable boulevards through the Rockies." Smooth, wide roads, built to accommodate the transmissions and sizes of contemporary automobiles, could guarantee that "motorists who remain on the principal highways need not be afraid of any difficulties" and that they could reach "all sections of the state." The motorist, such articles routinely argued, had wonderful opportunities, even in the states crowned with the high peaks of the Rockies, to play the gypsy.[33]

During the same era, merchants, chambers of commerce, and civic groups in communities all over the trans-Mississippi West saw free public campgrounds for the wandering motorist as yet another magnet to attract tourist dollars into their respective cities and towns, encouraging a spate of such projects. Wildly popular with motor travelers from the beginning, such camps soon developed a potent cultural life of their own. Many auto campers rhapsodized about the "great free masonry and democratic fraternity" that travelers would experience in the municipal camps, where people of all economic, social, educational, and geographic backgrounds would be thrown into association without regard for any distinctions or differences. Unfortunately, the burgeoning audience for this kind of recreational travel had continued to grow so rapidly that the free auto camp idea buckled in part under the weight of its own success. Even the most well-equipped camps were hard-pressed to cope with the pressure on their facilities, and less prepared facilities deteriorated into sanitation nightmares that became, in some instances, dangers to public health. Moreover, camps overrun with customers night after night created the same problems with destructive disturbances of the peace that had plagued private property owners in the early days of camping by the roadside. Especially among those poorer communities unwilling or unable to tackle the need for regular overhauls of everything from the parking spaces to the sewer pipes, turning municipal camps over to private enterprise became a very common solution to the problems that had arisen in trying to play host of the highways. In doing so, those towns and cities, in turn, swayed the course of the next phase of the American roadside: the birth of the motel.[34]

Just as many aspiring local boosters across the West had used the growing passion for auto-borne camping as a means of bolstering the economic underpinnings of their communities in the 1910s and 1920s, other like-minded individuals and organizations who saw tourism's possibilities for creating a new industry along western highways elaborated upon the many alluring splendors of western landscapes accessible by car. Following up on the seemingly irresistible power that western national parks had exerted upon motorists since the turn of the twentieth century, promotion-minded westerners sought to encourage all those who might come to the West to see *all* its wonders. Tens of thousands of pieces of advertising literature blossomed before each year's summer travel season, depicting the glories of western scenes. "High Spots of Colorado," for example, published by the privately financed Colorado Association in 1930, highlighted the many magnificent resources at the disposal of the automotive tourist. Motorists venturing, for example, to the vicinity of Colorado Springs and Pikes Peak would find excellent mountain highways climbing not only that peak but Cheyenne Mountain and making accessible such attractions as Cripple Creek, Seven Falls, North Cheyenne Canyon, South Park, the Royal Gorge, and "the never-to-be-forgotten Garden of the Gods." The brochure's author even boasted of "a veritable network of highways, bridle paths and street car lines" facilitating "an abundance of quick trips to scenic wonders and vacation playgrounds" all over the region. In a similar vein, *Salt Lake City: Seven Days in and around "The Center of Scenic America,"* which was frequently issued during the 1920s and 1930s by the city's chamber of commerce, not only celebrated the many alluring distractions in its vicinity accessible by auto but also pointed out some of the various hostelries available to entertain the weary sightseer. Enumerating a whole series of day trips from the City of the Saints, the 1937 version of this brochure described the Hermitage, "a picturesque mountain hotel, built of native timber in rustic fashion" in Ogden Canyon, the "picturesque and romantic Old Mill Club" with its "open-air dining and dancing pavilion" near Brighton, and the Pinecrest Inn, "an attractive mountain hotel" in historic Emigration Canyon, "in the midst of maples and evergreens and surrounded by rugged mountains."[35] Though stopped cold by the travel restrictions that emerged from America's 1941 entry into World War II, taking Americans off the road for the duration, such advertising reappeared with renewed vigor in the wake of the war's conclusion in 1945, reminding potential motor tourists once again that they could indulge in excursions by car with the greatest of ease. Indeed, by the midpoint of the century, even the lengthiest driving trips around the West had become so undemanding that narratives recounting such trips had mostly lost their allure for the reading public. By the time that the age of the Interstate Highway System began in 1956, the enthusiasm, excitement, or unbridled sense of adventure and discovery once so intimately associated with auto touring about the West had dissipated or found new outlets in more exotic recreational pastimes, just as travel writing found new avenues about the West to explore.

Those Who Toured

As much as we know about the enticements that drew Americans onto western highways, the tools that made their journeys possible, or about the roads themselves, we know rather less about the individuals who made up this traveling public. Lacking reliable statistics to document the number of motorists abroad in a given year, we must depend upon the same impressionistic accountings and sheer guesses that advertisers, local and state highway officials, and public and private tourist promoters cobbled together during these years to understand the scope and impact of this burgeoning populace. Thus, when the Lincoln Highway Association proposed in 1915 that twenty-five thousand cars had followed its route overland, or when travel writer Elon Jessup speculated that twenty thousand Americans had driven across the continent in 1921, we can only take such numbers in the context of the rapidly accelerating national passion for the automobile (as seen, for instance, in the rise of vehicles registered across the nation from over one million in 1913 to 6.7 million in 1919 and 17.5 million in 1925). Considering the steadily increasing numbers of auto travelers charted by the middle of the 1920s everywhere in the West—including private and public auto camps, state and national parks and forests, and highway traffic surveys—however, we can confidently conclude that auto touring had become an important national pastime by that point.[36]

Initially, of course, recreational auto travel, like the automobile itself, was anything but a choice of the masses. Even after excluding the cost of the automobile from the equation, the sums described in travelers' accounts for just maintaining and operating a working vehicle could mount up at an alarming pace during the 1910s and 1920s. When folded thereafter into the costs that various travelers recorded—for everything from food and lodging to the souvenirs and laundry that travelers inevitably accumulated—the amounts spent for oil, gasoline, tires, repairs, spare parts, and garaging could push the tab for a motor excursion of two weeks or more to at least five dollars a day. With a fortnight on the road thus perhaps costing as much as seventy-five dollars and a major driving trip to western national parks or the Pacific Coast perhaps reaching double that total by 1921, it is clear that motor touring remained most affordable for the upper reaches of the middle classes and above in the American socio-economic hierarchy. As Professor Marguerite Shaffer observes in her insightful *See America First*, at a moment when the average clerical salary stood at $1,505, a vacation that might absorb between 5 and 10 percent of that total probably outran the disposable incomes of very many Americans.[37] Over time, of course, developments as varied as rising wages, falling prices for used cars, cheaper roadside accommodations, and the ever-more common workplace benefit of two weeks with pay greatly widened the spectrum of Americans who could set off to see the country by motor. Nonetheless, for most of the period under question here, readers of these travel narratives should keep Shaffer's caution in mind.

If issues of cost kept lower-income Americans from routinely joining the ranks of the motor tourist, those expenses certainly played a part in preventing many if not most Americans of color from partaking of this pastime as well. Professor Albert Broussard, in writing of the African American migration to California at the time of World War II, concluded that the majority of those relocating from the South probably came by bus or train, because "after twelve years of economic depression, it was unlikely that the majority could have purchased automobiles." Even ownership of an automobile, however, could not insulate drivers and passengers from falling prey to the grinding bigotry that Americans of color routinely experienced in nearly every phase of daily life during these decades. Writing of African Americans in pre–World War II Los Angeles, the historian Douglas Flamming quotes from one woman whose family, on its journey by car from east Texas to southern California in 1924, resorted to car camping because of the lack of accommodations anywhere that would admit African Americans. As another historian astutely observed in writing about African American leisure and recreation, "without the freedom to stop at will, one dramatically confined the potential of the automobile. . . . The allure of the car was, and still is, largely embodied in the ability to go where you want, when you want, at the pace you want."

That being said, the anecdotal evidence at hand suggest that when economic and social circumstances permitted, these Americans took to the automobile with the same gusto as white Americans, leading one African American civic leader in the 1920s to complain that "the great outdoors calls [and black Angelinos] go in as many different directions as there are automobiles to take them," while the author of a 1933 article published in the magazine of the Urban League commented, "it's mighty good to be the skipper for a change, and pilot our craft wither and where we will. We feel like Vikings. What if our craft is blunt of nose and limited of power and our sea is macadamized; it's good for the spirit just to give the old railroad Jim Crow the laugh."

To meet the challenge posed by rampant discrimination in all types of roadside accommodations, publications such as *Hackley and Harrison's Hotel and Apartment Guide for Colored Travelers* and *The Negro Motorist Green Book* appeared in the 1930s, identifying those hotels, boarding houses, motor courts, and even private homes where African Americans could find shelter and, in Victor Green's words, "make traveling better for the Negro."[38]

By contrast, though American women of all colors also had their hands full throughout this period in surmounting barriers of all kinds, it is clear from many of the accounts gathered for this series that some white middle- and upper-middle-class women were able to seize various opportunities that the automobile and motoring as a pastime offered. Prominently represented among those individuals who made the earliest trans-continental drives during the first decade and a half of the twentieth century, they certainly helped to advance the interests of the automobile manufacturers who sponsored most of those excursions (between 1909 and 1916, for instance, the Maxwell-Briscoe Motor Company, the Willys-Overland Company, the Kissel Motorcar Company, and the Olds Motor Works each sponsored a woman's transcontinental drive). As the automotive historian Curt McConnell has noted, such expeditions emphasized the increasing reliability of these machines, highlighted the terrible roads on which they often had to run, and reminded the manufacturers themselves that American women could make up an important dimension of the market for their products. Moreover, as women motorists took to western highways in greater numbers before and after World War I, they established their claim on the driver's seat. In doing so, they demonstrated the kind of ingenuity, adaptability, competence, and independence that transformed such journeys into voyages of what Virginia Scharff describes as "personal liberation" as well as expeditions for the pleasure of touring. Foreshadowing the winds of social, economic, and political change already starting to sweep across the nation by 1920, these female motorists brought their own perspectives to bear upon all that they experienced and observed in making their way across the American West. In Scharff's view of the decade that followed, "women who were privileged to have access to automobiles availed themselves of the power of the machine to explore new territory." Although Scharff makes this point in the broadest metaphorical terms, the various travel narratives in this series written by women who literally did explore the West from behind the steering wheel reveal their particularly significant role in laying the foundations for the age of the motor tourist.[39]

Hard-pressed as we may be to know these motoring Americans *en masse*, however, we do have the opportunity to become very familiar indeed with those who took the time to compose the accounts that will follow in this series. Pragmatic, philosophical, facetious, pedantic, whimsical, zealous, joyful, or just plain dull: we will find all these aspects of the human temperament and many more on display in these commentaries. Through them, we may gain varied insights into a cherished American pastime as it unfolded in widely celebrated American landscapes, reshaping both the viewers and the viewed in the process. Though long neglected as a lens through which we may see the past, the tourists who participated in yet another "winning" of the American West during the early decades of the twentieth century have many stories worthy of the telling. What will follow in this series is a selection that will endeavor to make the past alive in the present and into the future.

Notes

1. James J. Flink, *America Adopts the Automobile, 1895–1910* (Cambridge: Massachusetts Institute of Technology Press, 1970), 88–104; the quotations are from pp. 88 and 100, respectively.
2. Regrettably, there is no comprehensive bibliographic guide to this literature, although Carey Bliss's admirable 1971 overview, *Autos Across America: A Bibliography of Transcontinental Automobile Travel, 1930–1940* (Los Angeles: Dawson's Book Shop), is an invaluable starting point for anyone seeking to track down this distressingly fugitive body of sources. Having begun this project with Bliss, I then widened my search by consultation of Michael Berger, *The Automobile in American History and Culture: A Reference Guide* (Westport, Conn.: Greenwood Press, 2001), Archibald Hanna, *From Train to Plane: Travelers in the American West, 1866–1936: An Exhibition in the Beinecke Rare Book and Manuscript Library, Yale University* (New Haven: Yale University Library, 1979), the extensive bibliography found in John Jakle, *The Tourist: Travel in Twentieth-Century North America* (Lincoln: University of Nebraska Press, 1985), and Michael Vinson, *Motoring Tourists and the Scenic West, 1903 to 1948* (Dallas: DeGolyer Library, Southern Methodist University, 1989), as well as examination of the relevant subject headings in the appropriate volumes of *The Reader's Guide to Periodical Literature.*
3. Emily Post, *By Motor to the Golden Gate* (New York: D. Appleton, 1916), reprinted by McFarland & Co., Inc., with annotations by Jane Lancaster in 2004; and Alice Ramsey, *Veil, Duster, and Tire Iron* (Pasadena: Castle Press, 1961), reprinted by The Patrice Press with annotations by Gregory M. Franzwa in 2005.
4. James M. Flagg, *Boulevards All the Way—Maybe* (New York: Doran, 1925); Lewis Gannett, *Sweet Land* (Garden City, N.Y.: Doubleday, Doran & Company, 1934); Dallas L. Sharp, *The Better Country* (Boston: Houghton Mifflin, 1928); and Frederic F. Van de Water, *The Family Flivvers to Frisco* (New York: D. Appleton, 1927).
5. For more details about the emergence of this important movement at the dawn of the automobile age, consult Flink, *America Adopts*, 202–205; James J. Flink, *The Automobile Age* (1988; repr., Cambridge: MIT Press, 1993), 4–5; John Jakle and Keith A. Sculle, *Motoring: The Highway Experience in America* (Athens: University of Georgia Press, 2008, in association with the Center for American Places at Columbia College Chicago), 34–39; Jakle, *The Tourist*, 101–19; Carlos A. Schwantes, *Going Places: Transportation Redefines the Twentieth-Century West* (Bloomington: Indiana

University Press, 2003), 114–28; and Bruce E. Seely, *Building the American Highway System: Engineers as Policy Makers* (Philadelphia: Temple University Press, 1987), 11–23. The quotation is from Schwantes, *Going Places*, 114.

6. The expansion of the Good Roads campaign may be followed in Flink, *America Adopts*, 204–205; Jakle, *The Tourist*, 121–23; Harold A. Meeks, *On the Road to Yellowstone: The Yellowstone Trail and American Highways, 1900–1930* (Missoula, Mont.: Pictorial Histories Publishing Company, 2000), 1–19; Frederic L. Paxson, "The Highway Movement, 1916–1935," *The American Historical Review* 51, no. 2 (1946): 239–41; and Seely, *American Highway System*, 24–45.
7. The quotation is from Flink, *America Adopts*, 205, while the ownership numbers are from Jakle, *The Tourist*, 121, and Schwantes, *Going Places*, 52; more detailed numbers, broken down by state, may be found in Flink, *America Adopts*, 74–78. Flink, *America Adopts*, 202–205, 208–11, and Schwantes, *Going Places*, 132–34, cover these events in useful detail, while Paxson, "The Highway Movement," 242–43, provides a brief overview that highlights the connection between these developments and the impact of World War I on the nation.
8. Seely, *American Highway System*, 46–55, discusses early efforts to implement the first highway-aid act and the influence it exerted upon state and local highway building. Jakle and Sculle, *Motoring*, 43–52; Jakle, *The Tourist*, 123–25; Tom Lewis, *Divided Highways: Building the Interstate Highways, Transforming American Life* (New York: Viking, 1997), 50–51; Meeks, *Yellowstone*, 38–40; and Schwantes, *Going Places*, 147–50, summarize Carl Fisher's activities and the era of private highway associations that followed in his wake.
9. While various histories of American motor travel such as Lewis, *Divided Highways*, and Jakle, *The Tourist*, describe Fisher's activities, the most in-depth discussions may be found in Drake Hokanson, *The Lincoln Highway: Main Street Across America* (Iowa City: University of Iowa Press, 1988), 5–13, 17–21; Joe McCarthy, "The Lincoln Highway," *American Heritage* 25, no. 4 (June 1974): 32–37, 89; Schwantes, *Going Places*, 146–50; Richard F. Weingroff, "The Lincoln Highway," Federal Highway Administration, http://www/fhwa.dot.gov/infrastructure/lincoln.htm (accessed April 18, 2006); and *The Lincoln Highway: The Story of a Crusade that Made Transportation History* (1935; repr., Sacramento: Pleiades Press, 1995), 9–20, although the latter should be treated with due caution since it seems to be the Lincoln Highway Association's history of itself. The Lincoln Highway itself has been profiled in unparalleled detail from Illinois through to California by

the late Gregory M. Franzwa in his multi-volume history and guide, *The Lincoln Highway* (Tucson, Ariz.: Patrice Press, 1995–2009).

10. Many of the names cited in this paragraph and the one immediately preceding it have been compiled through examination of the contemporary periodical literature and promotional materials; others have been drawn from a typescript list of "Named Roads" prepared in the 1910s or 1920s and now housed in the Vertical Files of the United States Department of Transportation Library in Washington, D.C. A copy of that list was supplied to the author by Professor Marguerite Shaffer.
11. The first quotation is from Edward Leo Lyman, "The Arrowhead Trails Highway: Southern Nevada's First Automobile Link to the Outside World," *Nevada Historical Society Quarterly* 42, no. 4 (Winter 1999): 269, while the second is from *Lincoln Highway* (The Pleiades Press), 227, and the third from Hokanson, *Lincoln Highway*, 20. This paragraph relies, as do its predecessors, upon the Lincoln Highway's own history and Hokanson, as well as Schwantes, *Going Places*, 140–44.
12. The efforts to the federal government to support highway construction during the 1910s and early 1920s are chronicled in Jakle and Sculle, *Motoring*, 39–43, 53–54; Schwantes, *Going Places*, 142–46; and Seely, *American Highway System*, 46–99.
13. Information about the 1929–30 Bureau of Public Roads survey is summarized in Malcolm M. Wiley and Stuart A. Rice, "The Agencies of Communication," *Recent Social Trends in the United States: Report of the President's Research Committee on Social Trends* (New York: McGraw-Hill Book Company, 1933), 1: 187; and a New Deal–era publication, S. R. De Boer and G. M. P. Dougall, *A Survey of Scenic and Recreational Resources of Utah* (Salt Lake City: Utah State Planning Board, 1936), 7, 8, as well as figures 4 and 5.
14. The quotations concerning Montana's highways are from *Her Majesty Montana* (Helena, Mont., 1935) and *Headin' for the Hills* (Helena, Mont., 1937). Both pamphlets are unpaginated.
15. Brief but useful references to the condition and extent of main highways in various Rocky Mountain states at the end of the 1930s may be found in Federal Writers' Project, *Montana: A State Guide Book* (New York: The Viking Press, 1939), 94–95; and Federal Writers' Project, *Utah: A Guide to the State* (New York: Hastings House, 1941), 133. The examples of travel advertising described in this paragraph are "Drive Covered Wagon Trails" from the Denver Convention & Visitors Bureau in *Time*, April 22, 1940, p. 44; and *How to see the Best in the West* (n.p., Standard Stations, Inc., 1940).

16. The first quotation is from Thomas F. Andrews, "The Controversial Hastings Overland Guide: A Reassessment," *Pacific Historical Review* 37, no. 1 (February 1968): 32; while the descriptions of the contents of "tourist guides" is taken from Robert G. Waite, "Over the Ranges to the Golden Gate: Tourist Guide to the West, 1880–1920," *Journal of the West* 31, no. 2 (April 1992): 103, 105. Other important sources for considering the evolution of guidebooks for western travelers are Ray A. Billington, "Books that Won the West: The Guidebooks of the Forty-Niners and Fifty-Niners," *American West* 4, no. 3 (August 1967): 25–32, 72–75; and Doyce B. Nunis, Jr., "California Why We Come: Myth or Reality," *California Historical Society Quarterly* 44, no. 2 (June 1965): 123–37.
17. John R. Eustis, "The Banner Year of Tours Begins," *The Independent*, April 5, 1919, p. 36.
18. The quotation about "shop talk" is from Warren J. Belasco, *Americans on the Road: From Autocamp to Motel, 1910–1945* (1979; repr., Cambridge: Massachusetts Institute of Technology Press, 1981), 36–37; the quotation about helpful residents is from Vernon McGill, *Diary of a Motor Journey From Chicago to Los Angeles* (Los Angeles: Grafton Publishing Co., 1922), 12.
19. The first quotation is from Winifred Hawkridge Dixon, *Westward Hoboes: Ups and Downs of Frontier Motoring* (New York: Charles Scribner's Sons, 1922), 17–18; the second is from Belasco, *Road*, 37. See also the section entitled "Motoring Difficulties" in chapter 5 of Jakle, *The Tourist*, especially pp. 108–11.
20. Roderick Clayton McKenzie, "The Development of Automobile Road Guides in the United States" (master's thesis, University of California, Los Angeles, 1963), 14; an example of such a guide is reproduced on p. 16 of McKenzie's thesis. Flink, *America Adopts*, contains a useful chapter on the origins of motorist organizations. The evolution of guidebooks, especially at a time before road maps, is also discussed in Hokanson, *Lincoln Highway*, 88; Meeks, *Yellowstone*, 24–26; John Nobel Wilford, *The Mapmakers* (1981; repr., New York: Vintage Books, 1982), 50; and Douglas A. Yorke, Jr., John Margolies, and Eric Baker, *Hitting the Road: The Art of the American Road Map* (San Francisco: Chronicle Books, 1996), 12–19.
21. McKenzie, "Road Guides," 13–14, 19–20; and Yorke, Margolies, and Baker, *Hitting the Road*, 12–19.
22. The significance of the highway pathfinder in the development and promotion of recreational travel as well as the development of western roads may be reviewed in Maj. Charles E. Percival, "Putting Big Business on the

Highways," *The Nation's Business*, September 1938, pp. 20–22, 64–67; Virginia Rishel, *Wheels to Adventure: Bill Rishel's Western Routes* (Salt Lake City: Howe Brothers, 1983); and A. L. Westgard, *Tales of a Pathfinder* (New York: privately printed, 1920). Meeks, *Yellowstone*, 56–62, focuses upon the circumstances of a specific named highway. The quotation from Percival is on p. 64 of his article; the quotation from Westgard is on p. 15 of his book.

23. See, for example, Hamilton M. Laing, "The Transcontinental Game: Motoring over Our Longest Road," *Sunset*, February 1917, pp. 72, 74, 76, 78, 80; Eustis, "Banner Year," 36; A. L. Westgard, "Let's Go: Here Are the Motor Trails from Atlantic to Pacific—And All Points Between," *The Independent* 98, no. 3678: 360–61, 379–80; and "Vacation Trips in America," *The Literary Digest*, June 3, 1920, pp. 124, 126–30, 132–33, 135–43, 146–47.

24. Virginia Rishel's biography of her father, *Wheels to Adventure*, contains a number of brief essays written by Bill Rishel about his activities as a pathfinder and a promoter of auto touring; for his connection to the *Salt Lake Tribune*, see the chapter entitled "Turn Left at the Red Barn" which also reproduces the publication of his first article in the *Tribune*. The *Denver Post* in the summer of 1920 printed a number of articles that are representative of the same sort of pathfinding and promoting, especially in their Sunday editions. See, for example, June 20, section 3, p. 2; June 27, section 3, p. 10; July 4, section 3, p. 8; July 11, section 3, p. 9; and so forth through the entire summer.

25. See McKenzie, "Road Guides," 24, for the remark about "impermanence" while Rishel, *Wheels*, 53–54, discusses the demand for information and Rishel's solution. The Lincoln Highway Association, of course, played an important role in the development and dissemination of early guidebooks, issuing its first official one in 1915 after having created a pamphlet for "Road Conditions and Directions" in 1914; see the discussion in *Lincoln Highway* (Pleiades Press), 115–18. As the association assembled more and more data for the motorist, the Lincoln Highway guide grew to encyclopedic dimensions; the fifth edition, published in 1924, exceeded five hundred pages, as may be seen in a modern facsimile edition: *The Complete Official Road Guide of the Lincoln Highway* (1924; repr., Tucson, Ariz.: The Patrice Press, 1993).

26. See Rishel, *Wheels*, 53–54; and McKenzie, "Road Guides," 29–38; a sample page from a 1918 TIB Road Book is reproduced on p. 35 of McKenzie's thesis. Other examples of highway guides from the period that make significant use of maps as well as narrative summaries of the road ahead include *Arizona Good Roads Association Illustrated Road Maps and Tour Book* (1913; repr., Phoenix, Ariz.: *Arizona Highways*, 1992), *The Complete Official Road*

Guide of the Lincoln Highway (1916; repr., Sacramento: Pleiades Press, 1984), and the 1993 facsimile from the Patrice Press of *The Complete Official Road Guide of the Lincoln Highway.*

27. The story of Gulf Oil Company's pioneering role is described in McKenzie, "Road Guides," 38–39, while further details, including the number of maps distributed by 1920, are supplied in John Margolies, *Pump and Circumstance: Glory Days of the Gas Station* (Boston: Bulfinch Press/Little, Brown and Co., 1993), 36; and Yorke, Margolies, and Baker, *Hitting the Road*, 34–45. Jakle, *The Tourist*, 110, mentions maps briefly within a broader context of growing distribution of information for use by auto tourists in the 1910s and 1920s, while John R. Waggener, "Putting Wyoming on the Map: The Story of the Official Wyoming Highway Map," *Annals of Wyoming* 75, no. 4 (Autumn 2003): 19–30, focuses upon the efforts of one particular state to create a cartographic guide for its visitors; the quotation from Wyoming governor Carey is from p. 20 of this article.
28. McKenzie, "Road Guides," chapter 2, highlights many aspects of this boom in the distribution of information. See also Jakle, *The Tourist*, 110; Margolies, *Pump and Circumstance*, 37; and Yorke, Margolies, and Baker, *Hitting the Road*, 39–45, for additional details about the proliferation of maps and guidebooks. The quotation about Wyoming's highway map is from Waggener, "Wyoming," 22.
29. Belasco, *Road*, 7–17, provides an excellent overview of the "gypsy" or "vagabond" mythology, as well as its origins and its impact on the early years of auto touring. The Jakle quotation may be found on p. 103 of *The Tourist.* Schwantes, *Going Places*, 23–25, 28, discusses framing western landscapes through the automobile's windows, while Lynne Withey, *Grand Tours and Cook's Tours: A History of Leisure Travel 1750–1915* (New York: William Morrow and Company, 1997), 324–36, provides further details about the rise of auto touring in the American West and the concomitant search for freedom behind the steering wheel. The rapidly changing relationship between American women and the automobile is traced with intelligence and verve by Virginia Scharff in *Taking the Wheel: Women and the Coming of the Motor Age* (1991; repr., Albuquerque: University of New Mexico Press, 1992), 51–88, 135–64, as well as by Georgina Clausen, *Eat My Dust: Early Women Motorists* (Baltimore: The Johns Hopkins University Press, 2008), whose examination of motoring women in Australia, Great Britain, and the United States during the first decades of the twentieth century helps establish the broader context for those who motored in the trans-Mississippi West.

30. The first two quotations are from G. B. Hippee, "A 1905 Auto Trip to Spirit Lake," *Iowa Heritage Illustrated* 80, no. 1–2 (Spring/Summer 1999): 27, while the lyrical ode to the West is from Fred C. Knapp, "Letter to the Editor: 'Automobiling' on the Pacific Coast," *Oregon Historical Quarterly* 75, no. 3 (1974): 289, and the description of Wyoming roads is from Calvin Wesley Williams, "Seeing Wyoming from a Studebaker EMF in 1909," *Annals of Wyoming* 51, no. 1 (1979): 137.
31. The details of the supplies assembled for the trans-continental excursions of 1901, 1903, 1904, 1906, and 1908 may be found in Curt McConnell, *Coast to Coast by Automobile: The Pioneering Trips, 1899–1908* (Stanford, Calif.: Stanford University Press, 2000), 37, 66–67, 97, 100, 102, 153, 157, 232–33, 272–74. Other details and quotations in this paragraph are taken from S. W. Ross, comp., *The Western Tourists' Auto Guide: Utah-Idaho America's Wonderland* (Salt Lake City: The Auto Guide Publishing Co., ca. 1917), 5; H. Clifford Brokaw, "In Going to Remote Places, Go Prepared for Emergencies," *Denver Post*, Sept. 25, 1921, Sec. 3, p. 4; and Mary Crehore Bedell, *Modern Gypsies: The Story of a Twelve Thousand Mile Motor Camping Trip Encircling the United States* (New York: Brentano's, 1924), 13.
32. The quotation about Thoreau is from Belasco, *Road*, 8, and appears to come from Elon Jessup's *The Motor Camping Book* (New York: G. P. Putnam's Sons, 1921), 4. Further discussion of the American susceptibility to automotive "wanderlust" may be found in Hokanson, *Lincoln Highway*, 31–32; Jakle, *The Tourist*, 103–104; and Schwantes, *Going Places*, 177–83.
33. The quotation from Senator Kendrick may be found in a brief essay entitled "Greetings" that appears in *Wyoming Roads* 1, no. 1 (September 1924): 2, while the description of Colorado as the "Motorist's Paradise" is from the title phrase of "Colorado Motorist's Paradise," *Colorado Highways* 6, no. 7 (July 1927): 3–5. The final quotation is from "What Colorado Has Received for Little Money for Highways," *Colorado Highways* 8, no. 2 (February 1929): 8. Articles presenting similar points of view include William C. Deming, "Federal Aid Highways and Wyoming Road Building," *Wyoming Roads* 1, no. 3 (November 1924): 7–8 and 17; F. E. Warren, "America's Good Roads," *Wyoming Roads* 1, no. 5 (January 1925): 2; Carl E. McStay, "West Urged to Unite in Defense of Federal Aid Highways," *Colorado Highways* 4, no. 11 (November 1925): 4–5; "U.S. Bureau Chief Urges Better Roads Thru Colorado Rockies," *Colorado Highways* 7, no. 4 (April 1928): 4–5; and "Editorial," *Colorado Highways* 8, no. 3 (March 1929): 2.
34. Belasco, *Road*, 76–79; Jakle, *The Tourist*, 158–60; and John A. Jakle, Keith A. Sculle, and Jefferson S. Rogers, *The Motel in America* (Baltimore: Johns Hopkins University Press, 1996), 31–34.

35. Salt Lake City Chamber of Commerce, *Seven Days in and around "The Center of Scenic America"* (Salt Lake City, ca. 1937), and The Colorado Association, *High Spots of Colorful Colorado* (Denver, ca. 1930).
36. The numbers cited in this paragraph are from Belasco, *Road*, 72, 74; Paul Sutter, *Driven Wild: How the Fight Against Automobiles Launched the Modern Wilderness Movement* (Seattle: University of Washington Press, 2002), 24; and Withey, *Grand Tours*, 334.
37. The efforts of various historians to assess the costs of motor touring and their implications for how widely this pursuit had spread include Belasco, *Road*, 42–43; Jakle, *The Tourist*, 117, 169; and Marguerite Shaffer, *See America First: Tourism and National Identity, 1880–1940* (Washington, D.C.: Smithsonian Institution Press, 2001), 364–65n76.
38. Albert S. Broussard, "In Search of the Promised Land: African American Migration to San Francisco, 1900–1945," in *Seeking El Dorado: African Americans in California*, ed. Lawrence de Graff, Kevin Mulroy, and Quintard Taylor (Seattle: University of Washington Press in association with the Autry Museum of Western Heritage, 2001), 195. The comment about the "allure of the car" is from Clay Williams, "The *Guide for Colored Travelers:* A Reflection of the Urban League," *Journal of American and Comparative Cultures* 24, nos. 3–4 (Fall and Winter 2001): 73. Other sources drawn upon here are Douglas Flamming, *Bound for Freedom: Black Los Angeles in Jim Crow America* (Berkeley: University of California Press, 2005), 225, 229, 259; Alfred E. Smith, "Through the Windshield," *Opportunity* 11, no. 5 (May 1933): 142, quoted in Mark S. Foster, "In the Face of 'Jim Crow': Prosperous Blacks and Vacations, Travel and Leisure, 1890–1945," *The Journal of Negro History* 84, no. 2 (Spring 1999): 141; and Cotton Seiler, " 'So That We as a Race Might Have Something Authentic to Travel By': African American Automobility and Cold War Liberalism," *American Quarterly* 58, no. 4 (December 2006): 1091–117.
39. The quotations from Scharff, *Taking the Wheel*, may be found on pp. 137 and 163, respectively; her chapters 5 ("Spectacle and Emancipation") and 8 ("Women at the Wheel in the 1920s") are particularly relevant to the relationship of women, leisure travel, and the automobile. Readers who wish for further information about pioneering women motorists should consult Clausen, *Eat My Dust*, 64–85; and Curt McConnell, *"A Reliable Car and a Woman Who Knows It": The First Coast-to-Coast Auto Trips by Women, 1899–1916* (Jefferson, N.C.: McFarland & Co., 2000).

Introduction to Volume 1

THE DAWN OF THE TWENTIETH CENTURY FOUND A GROWING number of Americans increasingly intrigued by the proliferating array of self-propelled vehicles pioneered by inventors, innovators, and tinkerers on both sides of the Atlantic Ocean. They began to experiment with this new mode of transportation in its many idiosyncratic (if not eccentric) forms. Although initially hampered in their earliest stages of development by everything from the nature of the terrain they had to traverse to the amount of power any individual model could produce, automobiles after 1901 rapidly established a significant presence in American life culturally as well as commercially. In various popular magazines (some devoted solely to the motor vehicle), article after article with titles such as "The Place of the Automobile" (1900), "The Promise of the Automobile in Recreative Life" (1900), "The Automobile and Its Mission" (1902), and "The Meaning of the Automobile" (1902) appeared, frequently reflecting the enthusiastic efforts of various authors to win new converts to a motoring way of life.[1]

Among the opportunities available for the automotively inclined, early promoters of the motor car often referred to what H. P. Burchell, in his 1905 essay "The Automobile as a Means of Country Travel," rhapsodically described as "this freedom, this independence, this being in the largest possible degree completely master of one's self [in which] that horrible fiend, the railroad timetable, is banished to the far woods [and] the steel rails, with their varying degrees of speed have ceased to be a necessity to the summer tourist[.]" As Burchell continued, "He can travel as slowly and sometimes as fast as he pleases and can run off the main road, here and there, visiting little-known places of historic or picturesque interest which would ever have remained to him as a sealed book had he been restricted to the undeviating pathway of the steam road."[2]

Even as we consider the allure that automobile touring exerted upon early motor-savvy Americans, however, the articles reproduced in the following section of this volume not only illuminate how auto touring took shape in the new century but remind us of the bumpy and often uncertain course that it followed in becoming a national pastime. While Henry Sutphen's 1901 article, "Touring in Automobiles," for example, asserted that "touring in itself is a pastime of which one may never tire," it also depicts a moment in time when almost every feature of the automobile, from whether it would run on steam, electricity, or gasoline to whether it would have three wheels or four, remained open to question. Though Hamlin Garland could describe a whirlwind 1902 motor excursion through the Wisconsin countryside that transformed driver and passenger into members of a new generation of "pioneers," Charles B. Shanks's account of a 1901 journey across the Far West come a-cropper in the Nevada desert and Hrolf Wisby's 1902 summation of a "practical automobiling outfit" demonstrated that the first auto tourists were of necessity mechanics, engineers, and road builders as often as they were recreationists. If Augustus Post's 1905 portrayal of "land cruising" through the countryside could promise the motorist "the power of the bird to swoop and soar and observe, with the mind of the man to speculate and understand," it could also comment wryly upon the "honest rustics of the constabulary and the local bench" whose adeptness at snagging motorists in their local snares would often "make the day's work profitable for all hands except the man who pays." And only the continued evolution of the vehicles themselves could make possible Philip Delany's "Frontiering in an Automobile" or Marcus C. Krarup's expedition "From Coast to Coast in an Automobile" at a time in 1903 when trails or paths of the most primitive kind stood in for roads across great swaths of the nation.[3]

Despite their renderings of the many difficulties that motoring Americans might encounter, however, these authors avidly endorsed the practice because of the spectacular rewards that auto tourists could reap. Commenting on the joys of "camping out with an automobile," for instance, Hrolf Wisby could observe that it would mean "modern man brought back to Nature on the latest vehicle of civilization [annihilating] the wearying consideration of time and distance," just as Philip Delany, in writing about his automotive "frontiering" through southern Colorado, could promise his readers that "you see, perhaps, the wildest and most natural places on the continent . . . the trails of Kit Carson and Boone and Crockett and the rest of the early frontiersmen, stretch[ed] out before the adventurous automobilist." Other essayists such as George Ethelbert Walsh, describing "Vacation by Motor Car," would applaud the possibilities of the "touring car" as "a moving camp" upon which "one can ride thru almost any part of the country and explore new regions." Even the less financially comfortable, he claimed, would be "so restricted in their vacation expenses that they cannot make arrangements to go touring for a few weeks" (though if such was the irreducible minimum of motor touring, then its likely audience still had fatter bank balances than the vast majority of Americans at the turn of the twentieth century).[4]

By 1907 and 1908, the published literature devoted to auto touring emphasized the growing practicality of the automobile as an agent of *transformation* as well as *transportation* across the nation. Not only would it allow more and more Americans (among those with the money to buy an automobile, at least) to achieve an unprecedented degree of personal freedom, but its dissemination among the population presented an unprecedented opportunity to find harmony with nature by "opening the countryside to the city dweller." The automobile had become "the gasoline camel of the American desert" even in wild places such as southern Nevada, carrying prospectors and miners about in their search for gold outside of Tonopah and

Bullfrog. It could carry travelers "cross-country" in competition with horse and rider. Moreover, it offered nearly unlimited scope for aspiring travelers to engineer their own adaptations of sleeping quarters, cooking gear, foodstuffs, and all the other essentials necessary for comfortable travel by automobile across whatever terrain or distance the travelers would choose.[5]

With the enthusiasm for overland migrations in search of leisure and recreation increasing by decade's end, therefore, Americans seeking enlightenment about what such adventures entailed could consult a growing number of books and pamphlets that could describe the challenges and the pleasures of expeditions on wheels. Whether writing about going "across America in a Franklin" or making a "world tour in a motor" that included a transcontinental excursion, various travelers shared their experiences.[6] Especially in singing so fulsomely the praises of motor adventures in search of unspoiled nature, but also in offering so many descriptions of the automobile's ability to carry Americans to so many parts of their own country where they had never been before, the essays reproduced in this volume certainly helped to foster the budding fervor for excursions across and around the trans-Mississippi West that would become such an important part of American tourism over the next five decades.

Notes

1. James J. Flink, *America Adopts the Automobile, 1895–1910* (Cambridge: Massachusetts Institute of Technology Press, 1970), 31–62, provides a very revealing discussion of the incorporation of the automobile into American society, while the essays whose titles are quoted here have all been reprinted in Frank Oppel, ed., *Motoring in America: The Early Years* (Secaucus, N.J.: Castle Books, 1989).
2. The quotations are from H. P. Burchell, "The Automobile as a Means of Country Travel," 273, as reproduced in Oppel, ed., *Motoring in America*.

3. The essays mentioned in this paragraph are Henry R. Sutphen, "Touring in Automobiles," *Outing: An Illustrated Magazine of Recreation* 38, no. 2 (May 1901); Charles B. Shanks, "Automobiling in the West," *Scientific American*, Supplement No. 1335 (August 3, 1901); Hrolf Wisby, "A Practical Automobile Touring Outfit," *Scientific American* 86, no. 9 (March 1, 1902); Philip Delany, "Frontiering in an Automobile," *Outing: An Illustrated Magazine of Recreation* 43, no. 2 (November 1903); M. C. Krarup, "From Coast to Coast in an Automobile," *World's Work* 8 (May 1904); and Augustus Post, "Land Cruising," *The Independent* 58, no. 2498 (June 1, 1905).
4. These quotations are drawn from Hrolf Wisby, "Camping Out With an Automobile," *Outing: An Illustrated Magazine of Recreation* 45, no. 6 (March 1905); Delany, "Frontiering in an Automobile," and George Walsh, "Vacation by Motor Car," *The Independent* 64 (April 16, 1908): 844.
5. This quotation is from William F. Dix, "The Automobile as a Vacation Agent," *The Independent* (June 2, 1909), 1259. Other articles referred to in this paragraph are Barton Currie, "Gasoline Camel of the American Desert," *Harper's Weekly* 51 (March 16, 1907); C. H. Claudy, " 'Cross-Country in an Auto," *Country Life in America* 12, no. 1 (May 1907); George L. Lawson, "Automobile Prairie Schooner," *Country Life in America* (June 1908); and Harry B. Haines, "How to Tour in an Automobile," *Scientific American* 97, no. 19 (Nov. 9, 1907).
6. L. L. Whitman, *Across America in a Franklin* (Philadelphia: Powers & Armstrong, 1906), and Harriet White Fisher, *A Woman's World Tour in a Motor* (Philadelphia: J. B. Lippincott, 1911).

"No system that employs gasoline as a fuel or motive power can ever be absolutely safe."

HENRY R. SUTPHEN

BARELY HAD VARIOUS PIONEERING VERSIONS OF THE SELF-propelled horseless carriage begun to populate the American landscape at the end of the nineteenth century than various authors set out to help potential users make sense of them. In this essay, for example, New York businessman Henry Sutphen surveys the progress made by inventors on both sides of the Atlantic in designing and manufacturing "practicable machines" that could serve the needs of leisure as well as labor. Describing in great detail the respective advantages and limitations of steam, electric, and internal combustion engines as well as the chassis to which the different kinds of engines were attached, Sutphen also evaluates their potential value for "an entirely new and fascinating amusement"—touring.

Having been exposed to the world of motor-powered recreation afloat after joining the Bayonne, New Jersey-based Electric Launch Company in 1892, Sutphen no doubt could write with a very experienced eye about all things mechanical, even if they were land dwelling rather than sea going. Beyond that perspective, however, Sutphen's article illuminates the early association of the automobile with comfort, convenience, and leisure. Characterizing it as an opportunity to pursue "the exploring of the particular locality in which [people] lived, but about which they had usually known little or nothing," Sutphen envisions touring as "a pastime of which one may never tire, provided only that we do not have to work so hard to obtain the pleasure as to be unable to enjoy it." Little did Sutphen and his peers imagine how far later generations of untiring tourists would follow this "amusement."

Touring in Automobiles

By Henry R. Sutphen

[*Outing: An Illustrated Monthly Magazine of Recreation* 38, no. 2 (May 1901)]

Several years ago the bicycle suddenly made a prodigious leap into public favor, a result largely due to the fact that it provided people of moderate means with an entirely new and fascinating amusement—the exploring of the particular locality in which they lived, but about which they had usually known little or nothing.

For the natural man, only one means of locomotion is available—his legs, and their radius of action is necessarily limited. Given the use of the four legs of a horse and we can of course go much farther afield, but the cost is at once tremendously increased, thereby placing this mode of locomotion out of the reach of the average citizen. But the bicycle rider can easily compete with the horse in the matter of distance covered, and the only expenditure is that of his own strength and energy.

And so everybody took up bicycle riding and enjoyed the novel sensation of becoming acquainted with the outlying country about his home. In short, it is the touring capabilities of the bicycle which account for its popularity.

Touring in itself is a pastime of which one may never tire, provided only that we do not have to work so hard to obtain the pleasure as to be unable to enjoy it. And to be popular, the cost must be moderate. The automobile of today offers itself as a factor in touring. It cannot be said that the ideal has been evolved, but the manufacturers have at least put practicable machines upon the market and each new model shows an improvement upon its predecessor. It is the history of the bicycle repeated, even in the matter of high prices and slow deliveries. But the manufacturers have learned something by their experience in the bicycle trade, and the development of the automobile should be proportionately hastened.

France and Germany have given most of their attention to the development of the gas engine or hydro-carbon form of power, while inventors in England and in the United States have worked more particularly upon the steam and electric types. Then there are the imperfectly developed alcohol and liquid air motors and half a dozen other forms of power that are still in the "blue-print" stage. For all practical purposes, our choice of a touring automobile must be made between the gasoline and the steam carriage.

Electricity is manifestly out of the question for touring purposes, its radius of action being absolutely limited, and its cost of operation comparatively high. The same objection applies to all similar systems, such as the widely exploited liquid air motor. The successful touring machine must be a prime mover, or one that develops its own energy from the raw fuel.

Gas and steam then are the alternatives, and how shall we decide between them?

Casting up their respective merits and demerits, we find that in the matter of first cost, the steam automobile has a decided advantage. But, on the other hand, the hydro-carbon vehicles are much less expensive to maintain and operate, and are therefore cheaper in the long run. In this connection, it may be remarked that the figures put forth by the manufacturers, as to the cost of operation, are apt to vary widely from those obtained by users in actual practice. Furthermore, one operator may get better and more economical results from a given machine than can another, presumably of equal intelligence. The personal equation enters here.

Safety is of course a paramount consideration. Both the steam and hydro-carbon systems use the highly inflammable gasoline or naptha as a source of power supply but the method of application is different. The steam automobile employs a gasoline flame to turn the water in the boiler into steam. This gasoline or naptha is carried under pressure in the fuel tank, and any leak or overflow is liable to start a fire which may do great damage to the vehicle, and result in serious injury to its occupants. In the popular view, it is the boiler that is the dangerous part of the steam-driven vehicle, but this is erroneous. A tube boiler, made by any reputable firm, cannot possibly burst, like a shell boiler. The most it can do is to blow or burn out a tube and a slight leakage of steam is the only visible result.

The hydro-carbon system, too, uses gas which is generated from gasoline within what is called a carburetor. After being mixed with air, it is drawn into the engine cylinder, compressed and exploded by an electric spark. The principle of expansion of gas to move a piston is the same as in the steam engine. But the gas engine dispenses with the boiler, or rather combines the boiler and cylinder in one piece. It is therefore a one-unit motor as opposed to the two units, boiler and engine of the steam carriage. No flame of fire comes near the gasoline itself, but great care must still be used in filling the fuel tanks. No system that employs gasoline as a fuel or motive power can ever be absolutely safe. The gas engine with electric ignition reduces the danger to a minimum, but it is still there. The manufacturers realize this defect and inventors are constantly at work trying to overcome it. What is particularly wanted is a successful kerosene oil burner for the steam automobile and the corresponding development of an internal combustion motor, using kerosene oil gas as its motive power.

In order to determine the best forms of power for long distance touring in England, the Automobile Club of Great Britain arranged last year for a thousand mile endurance run. During this test the hydro-carbon system made the best showing on the three points of reliability, speed, and low cost of operation. Following this example the Automobile Club of America intends to arrange for a five-hundred-mile endurance test run between New York and Buffalo, sometime during the coming season. This test will be open to all vehicles seating two people side by side, awards being made upon the following basis: Fewest stops, greatest carrying capacity in proportion to weight, and least cost for repairs. An average speed of twelve to fifteen miles an hour must be maintained during the entire run. This is the sort of experimenting that is certain to yield profitable results, both to the manufacturer and to the user of motor vehicles, and such a test is assuredly of more value than a dozen so-called road races. If the data for the New York–Buffalo test were at hand today, the tabulated results would materially assist the intending purchaser in determining which form of automobile is most likely to answer his purpose for touring on the average American roadways. In the absence of such data we can only draw our conclusions from private experience and theoretical knowledge.

With American roads as they are, the question of construction becomes important. The prevailing type of steam vehicles is too light to stand hard usage. The makers of gasoline machines have more generally realized the futility of attempting to put heavy motors on bicycle running gear and the present type of hydro-carbon vehicles is consequently more practical for touring use. But there is no reason why the steam automobiles should not be built to fulfill every requirement.

In the matter of repairs, the liability to breakdowns, and general efficiency, there is something to be said for both types. Both the steam engine and the hydro-carbon motors need careful and intelligent attention, if they are to give the best, or even satisfactory results. They are each liable to unexpected and annoying breakdowns, but it is certainly easier to locate the source of trouble in a steam engine than it is in a gas motor. In the first place, the steam engine is more familiar to us, both in theory and practice; and secondly, the gas engine is complicated by its electrical sparking apparatus, and electricity is a notoriously elusive fluid. The man who really and thoroughly understands the working of the petroleum gas engine must be a well-equipped mechanical engineer and something of an electrician as well. The old dictum that "knowledge is power" was never better exemplified than in the handling of a hydro-carbon motor. On the whole, when a breakdown occurs, the owner of the steam carriage has the better chance of reaching home under his own power. Locomotion is possible even with smashed water gauges and leaky tubes, but the gas engine will not run at all if there is anything radically wrong with its essential functions. And it is often a labor of hours to find out just what *is* the matter with a gas engine, let alone repairing it, with no tools at hand but a rusty spanner and a bicycle screwdriver.

In general efficiency, the steam vehicle has the advantage in ease of control and possesses decidedly greater flexibility of operation. The reversing process is perfect, since the locomotive link motion is used, and the engine can be started by simply letting steam into the cylinders. The gas engine cannot be reversed, and back motion can only be obtained by means of gearing. Moreover, the internal combustion motor will not start itself from a state of rest. The initial impulse must be given by hand or through some auxiliary mechanical device. The steam engine's speed can be governed with perfect certainty, either by throttling or by the cut-off, while the gas motor generally works best at a certain high normal rate, which must be reduced by gearing. Against this, the internal combustion motor is much less delicate in its fundamental working parts, it works on a one-unit system as opposed to the two units of steam or electricity, and, generally speaking, it can do rougher and harder work than the steam engine. Moreover, it needs but one fuel, gasoline, as against both water and gasoline which must be supplied to the steam engine. It is true that water is used for cooling purposes on all large gasoline motors, but the quantity is comparatively small, and its chemical purity is not so important as though it were to be used inside a boiler.

Of course the great difficulty confronting the manufacturer is not to make a machine that will run, but a machine that anyone can run. So far as possible, it must be automatic in operation and above all it must be virtually fool-proof. There lies the rub. The makers of the steam carriages have been especially ingenious in providing automatic governors for their machinery. If everything works perfectly, the water level, the steam pressure, and the fire are all looked after automatically, and the operator has only to manage his levers and enjoy the scenery. But it is not possible to wholly dispense with human intelligence and attention, nor even to substitute for it beyond a certain fixed point. The sooner that the owner of an automobile gets rid of the idea that machinery can be built and run on the "you press the button" principle, the quicker he is likely to arrive at his destination. To the ordinary observer, the familiar type of steam automobiles that go flying so swiftly and gracefully around our streets appear like very simple machines. A sprocket chain and a couple of levers is about all that he can see, and he vaguely concludes that the rest of it is in the box. But let him open that box and look within and he will see what is virtually a locomotive engine in miniature, with cylinders, valves, link motion, and all complete. Would he feel himself competent, after reading a dozen-paged manual of instruction, to mount the foot plate of "No. 999" and take the "Empire State" through to Albany? And a locomotive does not have to be steered.

A machine is a machine, whether it is employed to peel apples or to supply the motive power to a World's Exposition, and the best results can only be obtained by a thorough knowledge of its powers and an intelligent direction of them. To be a successful *chauffeur* one should be able to take his machine apart, clean, inspect, and assemble it again. The famous French automobilists pride themselves upon being practical machinists and the little knowledge that may come in so usefully on the occasion of a turn in the park is simply priceless when one is really touring. It is folly to start away from home unless you thoroughly know your steed. Look at a locomotive engine just after it has hooked on to its train and is about to start on a long run and you are pretty sure to see a man in overalls walking around the big machine with an oil can in his hand. One would naturally suppose him to be the fireman, such a prosaic job as oiling should be beneath the dignity of the engineer. But not so; it is the engineer himself and the regulations especially require that he shall perform this final grooming of his iron steed in person. And the reason is that he may at the same time thoroughly inspect the all-important running gear of the machine. The oil cups are not always placed in positions of the greatest convenience for the oiler's back; in fact, they are often quite inconveniently situated, the idea being to make sure that certain important working parts shall come under the eye of the engineer.

There is certainly a happy medium between the practice of the French engineers, who build their automobiles with as much machinery as possible in sight, and that of the American manufacturer, who tries to put all the working parts into the box. It is absurd to pretend that the motor vehicle is nothing more than a horseless carriage, even to its incongruous and useless dashboard, and consequently to ignore the fact that it is a real machine. It is equally ridiculous to unnecessarily expose delicate working parts to the deteriorating effects of dust and weather. The ideal touring automobile should be neither a park trap nor a road locomotive.

It is impossible in a general article to give more than the barest outline of what the amateur automobilist ought to know before he has earned the right to call himself a *chauffeur.* Accordingly no attempt has been made to discuss matters purely technical, such as the respective merits of two- or four-cycle gas engines, the mysteries of the "jump" and "wipe" spark, differentials, "flash" boilers, and the like. These things the layman must learn from practical and sometimes bitter experience. But some essential points in practice may be briefly noted. Brakes are a part of the construction that should be carefully looked after. The French law requires that every motor car must be fitted with at least two brakes, one of which must work directly upon the rim of the wheel. Of course, the latter would only be used in emergencies, as it is apt to injure the tire or even to strip it entirely from the wheel. But a shoe-brake upon the circumference of the drive wheels is the most powerful brake that can be devised and it is better to lose a set of tires than to be smashed up altogether. Speaking of wheels, brings up the question of wood versus wire. The later practice seems to be in favor of the wood wheel for medium and heavy-weight carriages. Its strength and elasticity are greater, it is not so liable to deterioration, and it is easier to keep clean. The tubular steel wheel is still a third type, but it is not in general use as yet. In a touring automobile, it is an obvious advantage to have all four wheels of the same size, as then the one extra tire carried will fit in any place.

Three or four wheels? The advocates of the three wheeler claim lighter draught, easier steering, and greater flexibility in withstanding severe strains. On the other hand, the four wheels afford much greater stability and the general verdict is decidedly in their favor. In this connection it may be said that a low center of gravity is essential in any automobile intended for work over rough roads. The absurdly high electric stanhopes, for example, are only fitted for park use and are none too safe there. A high carriage is absolutely unsuited for touring, for remember that you no longer have the weight and mobility of the horse to balance the imperfectly adjusted load.

In the use of the steam carriage it is important to keep the gasoline burner clean. The gasoline itself should be strained before being run into the fuel tank as any foreign matter will quickly clog the fireholes. The manufacturers all advise the use of "soft" water in the boiler. Otherwise chemical action is set up that quickly shortens the boiler's life. Still better results will be obtained by using only distilled water, but this is naturally impracticable when on a tour. But every farmer's wife knows the difference between "soft" and "hard" water. The water-glass is of course the chief object of solicitude on the part of the steam-carriage operator. The tell-tale however, is not always accurate, and it will not do to place implicit faith in its reading. The gasoline level in the fuel tank should be looked after with equal care and the spanner and oil-can should always be at hand to minister to loosened nuts and squeaky bearings. Extra large fuel and water tanks are obviously a part of any long distance equipment; also a well equipped tool box and plenty of extra parts.

On the question of pneumatic versus solid tires, the experience of the French automobilists should be helpful. Today ninety-eight percent of French motor vehicles are fitted with pneumatics, and the solid type has virtually disappeared. It has been found by experiment that (in France) the pneumatic tires cost ten francs less than the solid, and wore four months longer. Moreover, the life of the motive machinery was noticeably prolonged, particularly in the case of electric batteries. It was shown by experiment that twenty-five miles an hour was about the limit of safety for a car fitted with solid tires and running over a perfect road. At higher speeds, the vibration was so great that the motor was in imminent danger of wrecking itself. The same machine with pneumatic tires could be speeded up to sixty and seventy miles an hour with entire safety. It may be added that only the double tube pneumatic is used abroad, the American single tube being entirely tabooed.

The steering mechanism should be carefully designed, for upon its efficiency depends the comfort and the safety of the driver. A perfect steering device should call for a small expenditure of force on the part of the operator, and there should be adequate provision for taking off and distributing shocks due to sudden jars or obstructions in the course of the wheels. Moreover, it must act quickly so that, if necessary, the carriage may be turned within its own length. All of these requirements are mechanically possible and should be met by any good manufacturer. In this country the lever is generally used, while the continental manufacturers prefer the steering wheel. For high speeds, the wheel is undoubtedly preferable, and the later American models show that it is coming into favor over here for general use.

The sparking of gasoline motors is one of the minor perplexing problems and there are two general systems—dry batteries and the magneto or mechanical generation of the current. In the use of batteries there are frequent difficulties with the insulation, owing to careless wiring, and as there is no way of ascertaining the present degree of battery efficiency to guard against a sudden giving out, it is necessary to carry along an extra set. The magneto system has been adopted lately by one of the oldest and best-known American automobile manufacturers and as the result of years of experimenting with both types.

In the transmission of the power from motor to wheels, gears or belts may be employed. Each system has its good and weak points, but the solid gears in mesh are most in favor with explosive motor builders. With a motor, such as the steam engine, that can be effectually throttled, the difficulty of speed reduction virtually disappears.

In cold weather, freezing up is an unpleasant contingency, and in this respect the gasoline motor has the advantage over the steam carriage. With the latter, the water should be drawn off whenever the carriage is out of commission in the stable, and not infrequently during an unusually long wait while on the road. With the gasoline carriage, there is only the freezing of the water in the water-jacket to guard against, and this may be done by the addition of chemical compounds. Calcium chloride is said to yield exceptionally favorable results.

The ideal engine for automobile, and indeed any form of power work, would be the rotary, but the successful motor of that type has yet to appear. Parsons had succeeded in making his steam turbine marine construction, but the reciprocating engine still holds its own elsewhere. Innumerable patents have been taken out for rotary engines, but not one has proven itself commercially available. As compared to reciprocating motors, the rotary is either too heavy or it is less durable, or less economical, and the test of the actual practice is the only one worth considering.

It is fortunate that in this country the popular interest is rather in the line of touring than of racing. The latter is not an avocation or a recreation, but a pure game, and a mighty expensive one at that. It is the twentieth-century sport of kings and just as much beyond the poor man's purse as is a modern cup defender. Some of the successful French racing machines command enormous prices, simply on account of their triumphs on the road, precisely as with a winning racehorse. But touring is for all, and with the betterment of the public highways, it may be pursued at a very moderate cost. Already the idea has been broached of a national highway from ocean to ocean, with subsidiary branches in other directions. Just the other day the various automobile clubs in the East decided to undertake the work of putting up sign-boards along the common roads of New York and the neighboring States, and in general, the automobilists are taking up and carrying on the good work started and continued by the bicycle riders, for the improvement of public highways.

> "I go back with a knowledge of conditions and an experience such as no automobilist in this or any other country has gained."
>
> ALEXANDER WINTON

AS THE MINISCULE NUMBER OF AUTOMOTIVELY INCLINED Americans increased during the first years of the twentieth century, some of them pursued surprisingly ambitious goals for the fledgling machine. In the late spring of 1901, for instance, Alexander Winton, president of the Ohio-based Winton Motor Carriage Company, set out from San Francisco to cross the continent "from the Pacific coast to the Atlantic Ocean in an automobile" with Charles B. Shanks, a Winton sales manager and former journalist, as his passenger (and the eventual chronicler of the expedition). A man of unusual determination (at least as portrayed by Shanks), Winton pressed forward across mud flats, bridgeless rivers and streams, rock-strewn canyons, and snow-choked passes across the Sierra Nevada, finally coming to rest inextricably lodged in "bottomless sand" up to his vehicle's axles west of Winnemucca, Nevada. Writing of their travails in crossing northern California and western Nevada, Shanks describes a voyage that would put Odysseus to shame in their struggles to surmount Nature's unyielding obstacles. Although lacking the accoutrements of cowboys and Indians or stagecoaches and outlaws, Shanks's account does depict a series of wild landscapes little changed from the era of the forty-niners a half century before. Beyond such purple prose, however, Shanks ascribed their ultimate failure to "the utter absence of roads" in the Far West, a condition of course almost unimaginable to the modern reader. No doubt with the technologically inclined readership of *Scientific American* in mind, Shanks promises them insights into circumstances "the like of which automobile drivers in every civilized portion of the North American continent know not of . . . about automobiling in a section of this country where all kinds of climates and every condition of road may be encountered," a promise his concise but detailed article more than fulfills.

Automobiling in the West

By Charles B. Shanks

[*Scientific American Supplement*, No. 1335 (August 3, 1901)]

Covering the North American continent from the Pacific coast to the Atlantic Ocean in an automobile has been attempted by Alexander Winton, president of The Winton Motor Carriage Company, of Cleveland. That the expedition failed is no fault of the machine Mr. Winton used, nor was it due to absence of grit or determination on the part of the operator. Neither was the failure due to roads. The utter absence of roads was the direct and only cause.

Having been with Mr. Winton on this trip, I saw and experienced things the like of which automobile drivers in every civilized portion of the North American continent know not of, nor can an active imagination be brought to picture the terrible abuse the machine had to take, or the hardships its riders endured in forcing and fighting the way from San Francisco to that point in Nevada where the project was abandoned—where Mr. Winton had forced upon him the positive conviction that to put an automobile across the sand hills of the Nevada desert was an utter impossibility under existing conditions.

Rock roads and deep snow in the high Sierras were encountered and mastered, streams were forded and washouts passed, adobe mud into which the machine sank deep and became tightly imbedded failed to change the plucky operator's mind about crowding the motor eastward toward the hoped-for goal.

It was the soft, shifting, bottomless, rolling sand—not so bad to look upon from car windows, but terrible when actually encountered—that caused the abandonment of the enterprise and resulted in the announcement by wire to eastern newspaper connections that the trip was "off."

To those who are interested in knowing what was met and mastered during the days we were out from San Francisco; to those who wish to learn some facts about automobiling in a section of this country where all kinds of climate and every condition of road may be encountered in a single day, the experiences of the short trip will satisfy.

Our expedition left the government building in San Francisco and started across the bay for Oakland at 7:15 A.M., Monday, May 20. Left ferry foot of Broadway and got on road at 8 A.M. Turned off Broadway at San Pablo Avenue heading for Port Costa, distance thirty-two miles, hoping to reach there in time to catch the Sacramento River ferry to cross with Southern Pacific Express No. 4, which left Oakland at 8:01 with schedule to reach Port Costa at 9:15 A.M.

Instead of running the thirty-two miles, we clipped off forty-four between Oakland and Port Costa as a consequence of mistaking the road to San Pablo and going around by way of Martinez. Reached Port Costa too late for the No. 4 trip and had to wait until 11:17 A.M., when the transcontinental express (The Overland Limited) was ferried over.

All morning the sky, which during the three weeks preceding had been clear and bright, was heavy with clouds. Before the opposite bank of the Sacramento was touched, the clouds opened. And what an opening it was. Adobe roads when dry and hard hold out opportunities for good going, but when the sponge-like soil is soaked with moisture, when your wheels cut in, spin around, slip and slide from the course and suddenly your machine is off the road and into the swamp ditch—buried to the axles in the soft "doby"—then the fun begins.

Pull out block and tackle, wade around in the mud, get soaked to the skin and chilled from the effects of the deluge, make fastenings to the fence or telephone post and pull. Pull hard, dig your heels into the mud, and exert every effort at command. The machine moves, your feet slip and down in the mud you go full length. Repeat the dose and continue the operation until the machine is free from the ditch and again upon the road.

Tie ropes around the tires to prevent slipping. It may help some, but the measure is not entirely effective, for down in the bog you find yourself soon again and once more the block and tackle are brought into play. Slow work—not discouraging in the least, but a bit disagreeable, considering that it is the first day out and you are anxious to make a clever initial run.

After twelve hours' severe experience and the rain still pouring down, halt is made abreast of a lane leading to a ranchman's home. This ranchman is A. W. Butler. He came down to the road and replying to interrogations tells you that to Rio Vista, nine miles ahead, the road is particularly bad because of plowing and grading. Arrangements are made for our staying all night with him. The machine is run in his barn, we eat supper with intense relish, go to bed and get up early to find more rain, but a breaking up of the clouds with prospect of sunshine later.

Got upon the road 7:40 A.M. Reached Rio Vista and two miles further on to "Old River" at 8:40. Go east on the levee road, which is of adobe formation with steep descending banks on both sides. On the left side is the river; the opposite bank runs down to a thicket, beyond which are orchards. Slide off the treacherous road on either side and nothing short of a derrick and wrecking crew could serve to a practical and satisfactory end.

A few miles from the ferry, a tree had fallen across the road. Mr. Winton used the ax to splendid advantage and, after some delay, the road was clear, and we were going ahead once more. Reached Sacramento at 1:15 P.M., but delayed in California's capital city just long enough to take on five gallons of gasoline. One we went toward the Sierras, passing through Roseville, Rocklin, Loomis, Penry,

New Castle, Auburn, Colfax, Cape Horn Mills, and when darkness was fast approaching halt was made in the little gold mining town of Gold Run.

From Auburn the climb commenced, and when Colfax was reached and passed, Mr. Winton was busy with his skillful knowledge in crowding the machine up steep mountain grades, along dangerous shelf roads from which one might look deep into canons and listen to the distant roaring of rushing waters below.

Ordinarily there would be great danger in speed under such conditions—and there may have been risk to life and limb at the time, but I knew Mr. Winton, I knew him for his skill and that there was no call for nervousness with him at the wheel, so I sat back and enjoyed the scenery.

Reached Gold Run at 7:40 P.M., just in time to escape darkness and avoid going into camp on the mountain side. On such roads, or, rather, surrounded as we were by canons, operation in the dark could not be regarded as safe. Our run that day was 123 miles.

Next morning, May 22, at 6:45 o'clock, the ascent was recommenced. Up and up we went, winding around and turning in many directions—but always up. From Gold Run we passed along through Dutch Flat, Towle, Blue Canon, Emigrant Gap, Cisco, and on to Cascade. Roads became particularly rugged after leaving Gold Run, and when we reached Emigrant Gap the few inhabitants who make that their home told us fully what rock roads and snow deposits would have to be encountered between their station and across the summit down to Donner Lake.

It was the universal opinion that if the machine could stand the punishment sure to be inflicted between the Gap and Donner Lake, it would not be troubled at any point east of the Sierras, between Truckee, Cal., and New York City. Leaving Emigrant Gap, the game commenced in earnest. Unbridged streams were encountered and the machine took to the water like a duck in high spirits. Splash she would go in, and drenched she would come out. The water would many times come up as high as the motor and up would go our feet to prevent them getting wet.

When the New Hampshire Rocks were met, trouble seemed to be ahead. I asked Mr. Winton if he would put the machine to what appeared to me the supreme and awful test. "Of course I will," was the short and meaning answer, and on went the machine. One big bump and I shot into the air like a rocket. I was not thrown from the machine, however, and thereafter busied myself hanging on with hands and bracing with feet. At every turn and twist in the road, the rocks grew larger, and I wondered if anything mechanical could stand the terrible punishment.

The motor never flinched, its power never lagged, it pulled us through those rocks and up the stiff grades. Emigrants westward bound in the early days would never trust horses or mules to convey their wagons safely to the bottom of one particularly stiff and rugged grade which Mr. Winton caused the motor to ascend. Those early day pathfinders would tie a rope to the rear axle of the wagon, take a turn around a tree and lower it gently.

We at last got through the New Hampshire Rocks and began calculating what would be our fate in the snow immediately to be encountered. The Cascade Creek, swollen by the melting mountain snows to river proportions, caused a halt about one-half mile west from the commencement of what was expected to be bothersome snow.

The water in the stream was clear and sparkling, the current swift, and the bottom filled with huge sharp rocks. Mr. Winton pulled in the lever, the machine forged ahead. Splash and bump, bump and splash. Front wheels struck something big and hard, they went up in the air and when coming down, almost at the east bank, the right front wheel with a wet tire struck a wet slanting rock. The wheel was hard put, something must give way—and it did. The front axle on the right side sustained an injury, and after a lurch ahead the machine came to a sudden standstill.

Mr. Winton sent me to hunt a telegraph station. Walked east for about a mile until I could look up the mountain side and see the railroad snow sheds with some sort of a station in an opening. I climbed up through the snow, over fallen trees, broke passage through tangled bushes, and finally came upon a surprised operator, who asked what the trouble was. It was a little telegraph station for railroad service only, but the dispatcher took my messages and repeated them to the Gap, from which point they were sent, one to the Winton factory at Cleveland, asking for duplicate of part damaged, and another to L. S. Keeley, of Emigrant Gap, to come for us and our effects and take us back to the Gap, where we would wait for the repair parts. The machine was left alone in the mountain wilderness.

Arrived at the Gap and Mr. Winton soon developed uneasiness because of the enforced delay in the trip. Next morning he announced his intention of making a temporary repair and working ahead slowly through the snow.

On the following morning (May 24) at 7 o'clock, the repair had been completed. When darkness enveloped us that evening, the machine had covered seventeen miles. And such a day of battle. When it was over, we had reached and passed the summit of the high Sierras, the machine was hard and fast in a snow bank at the bottom of "Tunnel No. 6 hill," a treacherous descent, along which there was great peril every moment.

We walked back to Summit Station and stayed at the hotel that night. Next morning, aided by some kindly disposed railroad men who could handle shovels most effectively, the machine was dislodged.

Since the day in the snow banks, I have called it to Mr. Winton's mind. He says that the frightful experiences of that day, the abuse and hardship to which the machine was subjected, stay in his mind like the remembrance of an ugly nightmare. During the entire day, working up there among the clouds, we were cold and drenched. When it did not rain, it snowed or hailed.

On the 25th, after getting free from the snow bank and passing through a number of small deposits, we got to Truckee, where we took on fuel and went on to Hobart Mills, a delightful lumber town, where Mr. Winton decided we would stay during the following day, Sunday, and dry our clothes. Reached Hobart Mills in a terrific downpour.

The officials of the Sierra Nevada Wood and Lumber Company (the "company" owns the town and all there is in it) were particularly generous in bestowing upon us many courtesies and making the time we spent with them in Hobart Mills that of delightful remembrance.

Monday, May 27, started 6 A.M. from Hobart Mills, and that afternoon, toward evening, reached Wadsworth, Nev., the western gate to one of the worst patches of desert sand in that section. That day was another of rain. The early morning hours were bright, but when Reno, Nev., was left behind the skies changed from blue to white, then to a dark color and the clouds that had so quickly formed opened and spilled their contents about and upon us.

Reached Wadsworth splashed and covered with mud, wet through and hungry. Spent night at Wadsworth. Residents warned Mr. Winton about sand, more especially the sand hill just east of the town. Next morning we took on stock of rations and drinking water. That "sand hill," or rather the remembrance of it and the balance of our trip to Desert Station that day, are like the remembrance of another beastly nightmare.

All during the afternoon, it rained and the wind blew a gale, but the temperature was high and we did not mind. Had it not been for the rain and its cooling effect there on the sand and sage brush desert, I doubt whether we could have stood it.

The storm that day caused us to speculate largely as to whether some of the many bolts of lightning hitting close around us would not strike the machine, demolish it completely, and incidentally put the operator and passenger out of business.

But a kind providence was with us during the storm, and the lightning kept off. Getting up the Wadsworth sand hill, we cut sage brush and kept piling it up in front of all four wheels to give them something to hold to and prevent slipping and burrowing in the soft sand until the machine was buried to the axles and it became necessary to use block, tackle, and shovels to pull up to the surface. Got to the top at last, but found no improvement in sand conditions. It was the hardest kind of work to make the slightest progress, but at 5:45 in the evening halted at Desert Station, a place inhabited by D. H. Gates, section boss, his wife, Train Dispatcher Howard (his office, cook house, etc., were all combined in a box car which had been set out on a short siding), and a dozen Japanese section hands.

Passed the night comfortably, and when the road was taken next morning (May 29) at 6 o'clock, the sun was shining and Mr. Gates predicted no rain for the day.

We found the roads somewhat improved and on and on we went through that vast country of magnificent distances. We were in the country where rattlesnakes were thickest, near Pyramid Rock, of which one writer says: "This rock pyramid is alleged to be the home of rattlesnakes so numerous as to defy extermination."

When out of the machine and walking around bunches of sage brush care was exercised in keeping out of striking range of these venomous reptiles. Mr. Winton has some tail end rattles as trophies, but I was not so anxious to get close enough to kill the snakes and cut off their tails.

That day we plunged through four unbridged streams, and in one place where a bad washout had occurred, it became necessary for us to build a bridge before the machine would "take the ditch." We lugged railroad ties—many ties from a pile close to the railroad tracks some distance away. And they were heavier than five-pound boxes of chocolate, but we finally got enough and bumped the machine through and on its way.

Mill City was reached shortly before 5 o'clock. The Southern Pacific agent there said we could never get to Winnemucca (thirty miles to the east) that night because of the sand hills; the quicksand would bury us, he said. Another man who came up discussed the sand proposition with Mr. Winton and told him that there would be only one way in which "that there thing" could get through this thirty miles' stretch of quicksand. "How?" asked Mr. Winton. "Load her on a flat car and be pulled to Winnemucca."

"Not on your life," retorted the plucky automobilist; into the carriage I jumped, he pulled the lever and off we went. The course led up a hill, but there was enough bottom to the sand to give the wheels a purchase and from the hill summit we forged down into the valley where the country was comparatively level. Nothing in sight but sage brush and sand, sand and sage brush.

Two miles of it were covered. Progress was slow, the sand became deeper and deeper as we progressed. At last the carriage stopped, the driving wheels sped on and cut deep into the bottomless sand. We used block and tackle, got the machine from its hole, and tried again. Same result. Tied more ropes around wheels with the hope that the corrugation would give them sufficient purchase in the sand. Result: wheels cut deeper in less time than before.

It was a condition never encountered by an automobilist in the history of the industry. We were in soft, shifting quicksand where power counted as nothing. We were face to face with a condition the like of which cannot be imagined—one must be in it, fight with it, be conquered by it, before a full and complete realization of what it actually is will dawn upon the mind.

Mr. Winton said to me: "Do you know what we are up against here? I told the Plain Dealer I would put this enterprise through if it were possible. Right here we are met by the impossible. Under present conditions no automobile can go through this quicksand." I suggested loading the machine and sending it by freight to

Winnemucca. “No, sir,” he flashed back emphatically. “If we can’t do it on our own power this expedition ends right here, and I go back with a knowledge of conditions and an experience such as no automobilist in this or any other country has gained.”

When, after serious deliberation, he decided to abandon the trip he said: “If I attempt this game again, I will construct a machine on peculiar lines. No man who expects to operate in the civilized portions of this continent would take the machine for his individual service about cities and throughout ordinary country, but I tell you it will go through sand—and this quicksand at that.”

There is nothing more to tell. We left Mill City that night and rode into Winnemucca on a freight train. The machine, aided by its own power, had been hauled from its bed by horses and returned to Mill City, where arrangements were made to load it for Cleveland.

We left Winnemucca May 30, at 2:40 P.M. on a Southern Pacific passenger train, and arrived in Cleveland June 2, at 7:35 P.M.

"Between a kite and a Panama hat for automobiling there is but little choice, only a difference in the time elapsed before it flies off."

HROLF WISBY

ASSERTING THAT "AUTOMOBILING" HAD ALREADY BECOME "a healthful, pleasurable sport" at the beginning of the twentieth century, journalist Hrolf Wisby celebrated the rapid adaptations made by various manufacturers to the specific needs of touring by motor car. Applauding the choice of manufacturers to focus "all their mechanical ingenuity" on models that substituted "comfort and convenience" for their prior obsession with speed, he noted that driver and passengers would now find more and more designs that would accommodate everything from their limbs to their luggage. Unfortunately, Wisby continued, to date no experts or entrepreneurs had turned their attention to developing all the other accoutrements necessary to comprise a truly "practical" touring outfit. To that end, Wisby devoted the balance of his article to offering his own recommendations for everything from the proper clothing (kangaroo leather lined with "a strong, thick flannel") to rubber air mattresses, cookware, and suitcases. Especially for an age before car tops, side curtains, or even windshields, it seems likely that aspiring "chauffeurs" would understand and appreciate his appraisal of the value of "a seaman's suit of oilskin clothes [and] sou'wester" to turn aside the wrath of the elements. Moreover, Wisby urged his readers to be prepared for life's unpleasant contingencies by carrying everything from "a supply of drugs, medicines and plasters" to "a good six-shooter," the latter implement residing under the motorist's pillow at night for precautionary purposes. At the same time, however, he emphasized the notion that success in the pastime of camping by the side of the road would require the motor tourist to "make the machine your nomadic home for the time being" with all the necessary equipment to provide as many domestic amenities as possible. The truly well-prepared excursionist, he argued, would be the person who could "take along as little as possible and yet be comfortably fitted out."

A Practical Automobile Touring Outfit

By Hrolf Wisby

[*Scientific American* 86, no. 9 (March 1, 1902)]

Quite naturally touring has become a favorite pastime with those who patronize automobiling not as a fad, but as a healthful, pleasurable sport—a class of automobilists by the way that is constantly increasing, not only abroad but also in this country. In spite of the wretched condition of American roads, the successful long distance trips made by Arthur J. Eddy and a number of less-known chauffeurs have shown that extended touring in the United States is not only possible but probably more fascinating because of the additional obstacles that are continually presenting themselves to be overcome. In the vehicles also the demand for improved touring types can readily be seen, even by inexpert eyes, in the effort of the leading makers to produce a machine especially adapted for touring. Nearly all the standard 1902 models include a distinct touring type, and some of the largest manufacturers have made such types their specialty. The tendency in this direction has thus far had a beneficial influence, both in Europe and this country, on the style as well as the utility of the product. By dropping the racing requirements and centering all their mechanical ingenuity on the production of touring types, in which comfort and convenience must take precedence over the speed feature, automobile makers have at length succeeded, in the 1902 models, in turning out several types of touring vehicles that are decidedly superior to what was offered as a touring vehicle twelve months ago. At the present time, nothing so emphatically shows the rapid advance in automobile construction as the particular development of just this class of carriage. Bodies have become lower, wheel bases have grown longer, stouter and smaller wheels have taken the place of comparatively high wheels, and the consequent changes in the vehicle proper have been such as to afford more space for the feet, an easier seat, a handier position of the manipulating devices, and increased storage capacity not only for liquid fuel but for such luggage as may be necessary to make touring convenient and agreeable.

The proper vehicle is, of course, the most important consideration in a complete touring outfit, but now that such machines can be had at a comparatively moderate price, the difficulty of getting them at all has been reduced to the problem of selecting the best one. There are other items to be considered, however. There is really no such thing on the market as a practical automobile touring outfit. Nobody makes it; nobody sells it; and yet there is an unprecedented demand for it by experienced auto-tourists, that is, those who have tried to coax pleasure out of touring without the proper outfit to make it agreeable. Such veterans generally set about making their own outfits, but many wearying experiences may have to be suffered before they possess an outfit that is complete without being unwieldy.

Everyone is familiar with the black leather clothing worn by most chauffeurs. For all-around use, this is the proper and most practical clothing, and for long trips it is the only kind which has been found to be convenient and satisfactory.

Such leather clothing is usually made from calfskin, but the very best grade obtainable is invariably taken from the hide of the kangaroo—the skin being more pliable, and on account of its rather oily substance, it will shed rain a good deal easier than calfskin. The latest style leather clothing is lined, not with corduroy, but with a strong, thick flannel, especially manufactured for this use.

The proper automobile cap, with an extra long facemask and goggles combined, and a pair of earmits, ought to keep any head comfortable during fast going on cold days. The hands are best protected by fleece-lined buckskin gauntlets with cuffs wide enough to take the sleeve and hold it in.

As a rule, the novice chauffeur will do a great deal of thinking to make his initial tour a success, and generally he returns to his starting place—unless the railroad carries him—finding that he has been doing his most sagacious thinking on the wrong side of the problem. He thought of rain storms and took a mackintosh with him; he thought of a scorching sun and provided himself with a monster Panama hat; he thought of cold feet and added a footbag of furs to his inventory. Now, as a matter of fact, a mackintosh is a most irritating kind of garment when automobiling in a rainstorm. It has a tendency to fly up over the knees, interfere with the quick handling of levers, and is invariably stepped on or torn, on leaving the vehicle hurriedly. Between a kite and a Panama hat for automobiling there is but little choice, only a difference in the time elapsed before it flies off. Nothing equals a footbag for overheating the feet, and ensnaring them in such a way that if you leave the vehicle in a hurry, you are pretty sure of striking the ground head first.

In place of the mackintosh, which only affords partial protection, get a seaman's suit of oilskin clothes, which is sure to protect you completely under the most adverse weather and road conditions, while it is out of the way all of the time. Several of the contesting chauffeurs in the great New York–Buffalo Endurance Trial were only too happy to exchange their insufficient and impractical outer garments for an oilskin jacket, a pair of trousers and a so'wester to match.

Instead of the fur bags or similar contrivances for keeping the feet warm during the cold season, it is advisable to dress the feet so comfortably that they will be able to retain their natural heart even in frosty weather. The men employed in the ice-harvesting business on the Great Lakes have solved this problem in a very thorough manner. Adopt their footwear and you need never bother with furbags, soapstones, and such cumbrances. Briefly described, this footwear consists of a coarse, heavy-soled rubber, laced boot, into which is slid a sort of thick felt stocking. This arrangement affords a rubber covering to fight off dampness, a felt shell to fight off the cold, and a trouser-leg and a pair of woolen or flannel underwear under a sporting suit and a heavy-weighted sweater ought to give comfort, especially when a corduroy-lined leather coat is the outer garment.

Furs are not advisable for long-distance touring, whereas they yield much comfort during a few hours of driving and suggest an air of style not obtainable with more sensible clothing. Furs could be made preferable as an all-around winter garment if we would but learn from the Eskimos how to ventilate fur clothes, but there is no indication that we will ever take the hint.

During the summer season, instead of the ubiquitous Panama, the Japanese palm-leaf sun-hat will be found more practicable, since it will not fly off during the swiftest pace. The regulation auto cap, of extra light stock, would be the ideal headgear, if such caps could be had with the sweatband constructed in the same manner as that of the English army sun helmet—but hatters have yet to dream of this. A khaki suit with trousers cut on the cavalry order, so as to permit of canvas gaiters or leather leggings on the legs, would be one of the most practical things for summer wear.

Next in importance to practical clothing comes such luggage as the chauffeur may care to take along, either for his personal comfort or for camping by the roadside. The best of sportsmen in Europe are already beginning to patronize the "camping-out" idea.

To fit out an automobile for a long continuous tour, camping by the roadside, is equivalent to making the machine your nomadic home for the time being. There is nothing impracticable about it, for when a soldier is able to carry on his back his entire camp outfit in addition to his weapons, the smallest automobile on the market ought to carry everything needed to make its passengers comfortable in camp.

Breakables should be avoided entirely. Things that may be duplicated in any country store should not be given space unless "unknown regions" are to be invaded. Combustibles are to be discountenanced. A canvas tent on the military order with a folding center pole will house two people in good shape. A rubber air-mattress furnishes the best possible resting device. It is easily and quickly inflated, and can be rolled snugly to the size of a man's arm, taking up but a minimum of space. It is the best protection against ground moisture. An air cushion for a headrest, and an army blanket for bed covering, complete the camp bed. Before going to bed, be sure to lock the manipulating devices on your automobile so that no one may appropriate the carriage while you sleep. You might also place a good six-shooter under your pillow. You will sleep just as well, and it might come in handy. When you wake up in the morning, your breakfast is, or ought to be, in the basket you are carrying with you strapped to the stern body of the vehicle. Most of the basket outfits made for touring are most adorable objects of admiration, fit almost for a jeweler's showcase, but when you come to use them on the road your fancy is made to take many a sad shock. A better auto basket than any of those retailing from fifty to two hundred dollars can easily be improvised for a small amount of money. A wicker basket of the size of a small steamer trunk will do. Have a water- and dust-tight cover of rubber made to fit it snugly with leather mounting on the corners. Arrange straps on the inside of the lid to hold several plates, forks, knives, cups, saucers, etc., together with the necessary cooking utensils for making meals readily and conveniently. All such utensils should be of aluminum. A moderate supply of spices and groceries may be packed in a wooden box so as not to be mixed up with the other contents. If the tour is through a hunting or fishing region, the chauffeurs ought to be able to supply their own "table" by some skill with the rod and the gun. In fact, this would give a genuine zest to the entire undertaking, and afford the intrepid sportsman a solid feeling of having gone to the bottom of the matter. If the tour is through populated country districts, most of the camping is likely to be done in village inns, while the cooking, in such a case, would be entrusted to the innkeeper's "chef." To make an automobile camping trip a success, you must choose an out-of-the-way route that will compel you to camp out and "do" yourself.

Something that is almost always invariably overlooked in making up an outfit is a supply of drugs, medicines, and plasters. Accidents are liable to happen in a hundred unthought-of ways, and sometimes minor bruises and scars from slipping or falling become quite annoying from not being attended to promptly. A man not accustomed to use his hands for manual labor is practically doomed to hurt himself more or less during a long-distance trip involving the going into camp nightly.

A canvas folder with pockets for various-size bottles, boxes, and rolls, containing drugs and medicines, would in the majority of cases be found to be of practical use.

The personal effects of two passengers could easily be packed in two portmanteaus, as all that is needed, besides the clothes they are continually wearing, is changes of underwear and stockings, handkerchiefs, extra pair of shoes, and such little extra items as the taste of the chauffeur may fancy and the season of the year may require. The point should be to take along as little as possible and yet be comfortably fitted out.

Having followed this outline in the main, the intending auto tourist should take special care in packing his outfit. Careless packing will make the most ingeniously chosen outfit sound like a barrel of tin cans. Everything needed can be packed in three pieces. First, the rubber-covered basket. Pack the rubber mattress, tenting, and the blankets in that to prevent rattling of the eating and cooking utensils. Second, the portmanteaus with clothing, medicine, etc. Third, a canvas-incased rod and gun strapped together, and put in a cylindrical leather case with rubber covering.

“Now hold your breath for a wild ride.”

AN ENGINEER

ALREADY WELL KNOWN BY 1902 AS A PERCEPTIVE CHRONICLER of his native Midwest through such writings as *Main Traveled Roads* (1891), author Hamlin Garland wrote with great warmth in this *Harper's* essay of the serenity and beauty he observed along the “stately” Mississippi River as it flowed south, separating the states of Minnesota and Wisconsin. Rhapsodizing that “sunsets are more deeply purple and more mysterious in depth” from the “bold cliffs” above the river, he even characterized it as “in very fact a highway to the sunset into which Hiawatha might embark.” And Garland found an opportunity to immerse himself even more completely in the scenic glories of his home state as he set forth “whizzing about the country on the motor-car,” courtesy of a friend.

The trip that Garland describes, though brief in mileage, not only exposed him to magnificent vistas but to technological wonders that left him in awe of the automobile and the operator (“He seemed to know its power as well as its speed, and seemed not to fear that any jolt or jar would spring an axle or break a spoke”). Rattling across the Wisconsin landscape with such astounding speed (slow as a twelve-horsepower motor would seem to us today!), Garland mused about the character of his party as “pioneers,” breaking new ground in travel with every mile they logged. And like so many other early motorists, Garland clearly reveled in a feeling of freedom that characterized such a path-breaking excursion into the countryside.

Automobiling in the West

By Hamlin Garland

[*Harper's Weekly* 46 (September 6, 1902)]

From Lacrosse to Winona the Mississippi River scenery is at its best, and is compounded of bold cliffs, royal purple mists, and the sheen of a broad, swift, yet placid current. The bluffs rise from five to six hundred feet above the water's level and have a charm of outline distinctly their own, for they are not hills in the sense in which the rocky knobs of New England are hills. They are but the remains of the high prairie through which the waters of the past glacial streams have ploughed their way.

They are, therefore, not only stratified as to their ledges, but their slopes are prevailingly of wedge or pyramid shape—which gives uniformity in variety; and, furthermore, the fact that the observer is six hundred feet below the general level of the country gives a singular richness of color to every vista. Sunsets are more deeply purple and more mysterious in depth than from the plain, and the stately river often becomes in very fact a highway to the sunset into which Hiawatha might embark. The next artist who attempts to illustrate Longfellow's poem would do well to visit the upper Mississippi.

Notwithstanding the beauty of this river and its accessibility from St. Paul, Minneapolis, and other smaller cities, it remains amazingly lonely—for these are the days lying between the decline of the steamboat and the coming of the launch, between the passing of the lumber-raft and the coming of the care-free leisure of the carpeted house-boat.

For some years I have watched the slow growth of this esthetic appreciation at Lacrosse. It is only a few years since the first pleasure launch began to steal timidly about the islands. Now there are at least twenty, and every night during the summer and late in the autumn a fleet of these "poppers" laden with business men and their merry wives and children go forth upon the waters with great refreshment. The gorgeous coloring, the bold outlines, the coolness, the peace of the valley no longer go utterly to waste. Little cabins are being built along the bluffs like nests of swallows, and in the small towns (or near them) villas are to be seen with windows looking far to north and south, and the same pioneer who brought the first launch last year introduced the automobile, and developed the house-boat from a clam-digger's peripatetic shack to a luxurious summer home.

The house-boat has long been an institution on the Mississippi, but a rather shabby and sometimes a decidedly unsavory institution. It has been the floating home of those whose business made real estate an inconvenience. The inland pirates, log-stealers, clam-diggers, fishermen, and certain harmless but not very cleanly gypsies of the water have come and gone like troops of water-bugs in their patched and dingy little crafts, but it remained for a citizen of Lacrosse to show the possibilities of the idea. For several years I have enjoyed the hospitality of this friend's launch, and last year when he bought and began to refit a house-boat, he extended an invitation to share its pleasures. I was unable to avail myself of this kindness till a few days ago. As it fell out, I not only enjoyed the house-boat, but took part in some of the most exciting cross-country automobiling I have ever seen.

The house-boat was tethered to the shore near the little town of Trempeleau (a town yet to be famous for its beauty of site), and beside it, beneath the willows, stood a shining new auto, capable of carrying six people, while on the water-side a naphtha-launch glided to and fro as "tender." The boat was one hundred feet long over all, and twenty-four feet broad, and furnished with taste and discretion. It was completely screened with painted mosquito netting, and was deliciously cool and white throughout. It was indeed a floating bungalow, refined and lovely in every detail. The furniture was of rattan or hickory, the rugs of jute. The linen was spotless, and the table service simple but housewifely. As we sat that night round a pretty dining-table covered with fruit and flowers, and looked out upon the swift and silent rush of the great river, while the royal purple veiled the burning gold of the sunset, I felt that I was taking part in something vastly significant—the inauguration of a new and more resplendent reign of the Father of Waters, a return of his dominion over the souls of men.

For fifty years the raft, the steamboat, the railway train, have traversed this noble highway with little appreciation of its esthetic side. Business would have leveled these mighty walls if it could. Commerce would have straightened the shore-line into a steel-rod if it had been possible, but such deeds were not in the power of those who seek wealth, and as we gazed upon the dim peaks sentineling the gateways to east and to west, it was not difficult to imagine ourselves back to the days when the Sioux from Eagle Bluff watched the Chippewa gliding among the islands in his birch-bark canoe, so silent and lone it seemed. As I thought of the uses which have been made of small low-banked streams like the Thames, the Rhine, and the Charles, it was easy to predict that before another generation shall pass away, these noble reaches of water will be thick with pleasure craft, and these heights dotted with the homes of those who know the value of purpling cloud reflected in the bosom of a glorious stream.

These reflections were made even more definite as we went whizzing about the country on the auto-car, securing each moment new combinations of line and color. Here again we were pioneers. These woods had never before been traversed by a vehicle of such power and beauty as that in which we rode. This was especially true of the roads over which we whirled in going to Winona, some seventeen miles from the house-boat. This ride was the climax to a most inspiring outing—one enriching to my knowledge of my native State.

We left the boat at four o'clock of a sun-smit afternoon, with Mr. Blank himself at the throttle. The "machine" weighed twenty-four hundred pounds and had the power of twelve horses. Mr. Blank is not reckless, he is intrepid. He has invented engines, and could make a gasoline-launch if need were; we had confidence in him, and it was necessary, for we were not even able to keep the main road, and had hills, sand, mud, and rocks to contend with. For the first five miles the roads, though sandy, were comparatively level, and as we rushed along the farm lanes chickens rose like swarms of locusts from beneath our wheels; harvesters, smitten to rigid immobility by the flame of our scarlet chariot, stood like grimy scarecrows in the wheat; milkmaids hung from kitchen windows, dogs rushed out with startled outcry, while the children of assorted sizes, with frantic screams, shook hands and feet like jumping-jacks—the mothers clinging to the smallest ones as if afraid of the wind of our passing. It was superb! It was too exciting to be taken in silence; at every rearing lurch we of the trail emitted shrill whoops, for it had the rush and swing of a bucking bronco; but the calm, swift driver at the helm plied his levers and scanned the road with only a grim smile.

As we overtook a team, the nervous driver pulled aside, and his prancing horses dropped behind us too quickly to be really scared. If the driver were a woman, Mr. B. slowed up and I sprang out to help manage the horses, then leaped aboard and the wild ride began again. At Centerville we were sighted, word was passed, and the loafers came rushing out to gaze and spit and pass wise words, but we whizzed through with a reeling left turn which was like the swing of a pony rounding a steer. I began to understand the reason why an automobilist always goes like a man racing. It is like unto the joy of riding a running horse of incalculable power of limb and lung.

As the hills began, the engineer plied his brakes and his speed-regulating levers and ratchets with swift, unhesitating hands, till he resembled "the little man in the tin shop" of Riley's poem. It was beautiful to see the way in which we rose and fell over the ridges. His control of the car seemed marvelous to me. He seemed to know its power as well as its speed, and seemed not to fear that any jolt or jar would spring an axle or break a spoke.

From Centerville to Winona the road rises and falls along the base of a line of two hills, and the power of the machine was tested to the full, for the reason that a recent tornado had washed the hills to the bare rocks and flooded the valleys. The views of the great river to the left were magnificent as the sun westered, and we enjoyed them keenly, notwithstanding the uncertainties of the highway. We entered Winona over an astonishingly high bridge and rolled down to the Standard Oil depot just in time to pay a tribute of one cent extra on each of our seven gallons of gasoline. The salesman was just taking the fateful message from the telephone as we drew up.

Winona is a finely located town also, and is a thriving and cleanly place. Its citizens have autos of their own, and we did not fill a large place in the day's doings. We had made the run in a little less than two hours, including two or three stops. It took a half-hour to fill our tanks and get ready to return. It was just 6:30 as we started up the long incline of the bridge on our homeward course. Our engineer bent a little closer to his work. His engine was now well supplied with fuel, and he fully intended to draw upon it. His watchful passengers looked at each other significantly and nodded. "Now hold your breath for a wild ride."

With foot on the brake, left hand on the wheel and right hand manipulating the levers, the driver swept down the east slope of the bridge, while we shouted with joy in the superb vista to north and to south. The valley was filling with Tyrian-purple, the sun wallowing in murky clouds threw a dull orange film upon the smooth surface of the water, and the hills were topped with golden fields of wheat. The broad verdure of spring mingled with the russet of harvest-time.

Turning some mysterious screw, our charioteer let on still greater power and we retraced our devious way at a speed which made our coming seem slow. We took our mud-holes with a rush. The sloshing rise of the water was like the roll of soil before a plough-share. The same little boys stood to see us pass. The harvesters at supper rushed to the windows and doors, gazing with suspended action like cows with wisps of hay in ruminating jaws. The dogs came back with wilder clamor, but the chickens had left the road for their roosts. At Centerville we came into the good roads again, and for some miles ran at a speed approximating thirty-five miles an hour. We pulled into Trempeleau at ten minutes to eight, having made the sixteen miles in eighty minutes, and at 8:10 we were at the house-boat and seated before a delicious dinner of broiled chicken, brown bread, tomato salad, melons, peaches, and coffee.

As we reclined on the wicker couches on the forward end of the boat a little later, in the cool sweet gloom, listening to the lap of the wavelets on the bow, protected from all nocturnal insects, I thought of the burning heat of the city, and this boat-life seemed the farthest reach of comfort. The loneliness of the river again fell upon us—and though from a selfish standpoint I liked it, yet we could not but agree that such peace and beauty should go to heal the trouble and unrest of thousands rather than be the sole possession of a fortunate half-dozen like ourselves.

Mr. —— and his friends have shown some of the possibilities of this splendid river. With growing wealth and greater leisure the new generation are certain to develop every one of the esthetic capabilities of this region. Another generation will listen with unbelieving ears to the tales of the wigwam and the canoe, the sawmill and the boom.

“The farmer’s boy who drives a team today will need to know how to drive an automobile tomorrow.”

GEORGE LATHAM

ALTHOUGH STILL EARLY IN THE AUTOMOBILE’S INTRODUCTION to American life, George Latham’s 1903 observations about this new device’s developing role could include the flat assertion that it had already proved “a machine of great utility.” In doing so, Latham also offered a far-reaching assessment of the motor car’s place, both as a means of transportation and as a spur to industrial innovation.

Unlike the customary exegeses about the experience of motoring or the elaborations of the automobile’s technological components that constituted the majority of articles in this era, Latham instead chose to emphasize a broader perspective. Taking the automobile’s popularity as a given, he asserted its destiny as “a great industry” in which the United States would “surpass all others.” It would mean, he argued, “the opening of lucrative careers to hundreds of thousands of our future young men who are now schoolboys,” not to mention the constant improvements it would bring to travel of all kinds. In the light of rapidly rising manufacturing numbers and the total economic value of such production, Latham confidently concluded that a machine possessing such “utility” would have a substantial and productive lifespan in the United States. While unwilling to make more specific predictions about the automobile’s ultimate impacts, Latham proved sufficiently perspicacious in reading the motor car’s future that his careful appraisal deserves reproduction in this volume.

The Automobile and Automobiling

By George Latham

[*Munsey's Magazine* 39, no. 2 (May 1903)]

The interest and importance of the motor carriage not merely as a means of sport but as a machine of vast practical utility and as the basis of a great industry in which this country is destined to surpass all others

The daily newspapers recently stated that one of the principal American colleges had decided to include in its curriculum of technical science, the study of the automobile. The item was cabled across the ocean, translated into almost every European language, and heralded as another instance of Yankee enterprise. I have clipped out the original paragraph, together with some of the foreign comments upon it, and pasted them away among a collection of curiosities which I know will grow more interesting with age. It may not be in the next five years, nor even in the next ten years, but before the new century is out of its teens that little paragraph will look like ancient history, and whoever stumbles across it will wonder whether it was intended seriously or as a joke.

Some Significant Statistics

Five years ago one might have counted the automobiles in the United States on one's fingers. In 1903 more of the machines will be made here than in any other country in the world. And the industry is yet in its infancy. E. E. Schwarzkopf, than whom there is no better authority on the subject, has compiled statistics that show its growth during the past three years. In 1900 there were about eight hundred machines built in America, the average price being a thousand dollars, or eight hundred thousand dollars in all. In 1901 the output had increased to three thousand, while the price had been reduced to an average of eight hundred dollars each, making a gross valuation of two million four hundred thousand dollars. Last year eight thousand machines were made in American factories, at an average cost of eight hundred and fifty dollars, or a total output of six million eight hundred thousand dollars. This year it is estimated that at least twenty-eight thousand machines will be turned out, at an average buying price of nine hundred and forty dollars—making, in round figures, a total of twenty-six million dollars.

What this progress foreshadows for the future I will not venture to predict. For the present, however, it means an important factor in the wage-earning possibilities of the American people. It means the opening of lucrative careers to hundreds and thousands of our future young men who are now schoolboys. It means that the study of the automobile, which is now regarded as such a wonderfully progressive step when undertaken by a single college, will become as important and as thoroughly recognized as the study of the steam-engine is now. It means that the farmer's boy who drives a team today will need to know how to drive an automobile tomorrow.

Hostility to the Automobile

Automobilists are almost without exception enthusiasts. They are apt to be impatient with those who have not passed through the exhilarating experience which comes with the successful handling of a steering wheel for the first time. They chafe under the imputation of being considered dangerous citizens, and look upon the promoters of anti-speed legislation as unmitigated cranks. They should have patience. The present generation is no more hostile to the automobile than its great-grandfathers were, less than a century ago, to the railway engine.

Politicians who today make cheap capital out of their avowed hostility to the motor car will know better tomorrow. Their boys will teach them. The little gasoline engine, the crowning invention of the end of the nineteenth century, will make its way into the public schools even more readily than its predecessor, the electric dynamo. Its very simplicity and almost infinite utility will force it on the attention of young America. The great manufacturing States will see the necessity of educating their rising generation to the wonderful possibilities of the gasoline motor. The demand for expert mechanicians and chauffeurs, already far in excess of the supply, cannot fail to attract hundreds of young men whose ambition leads them above the role of ordinary laborer.

Is Automobiling a Fad?

"But it's a fad that will soon die out, like the bicycle," is the comment most frequently heard when one speaks of the great future of the automobile.

Against such a sweeping assertion it would seem almost useless to offer a logical argument. Still, where the assertion is made on what is believed to be reasonable ground, it may be well to show the falsity of such reasoning. The bicycle craze, or fad, as one may wish to call it, followed almost on the heels of another of its kind, the roller-skating mania. In both the essence of the craze was the same, namely, the gratification of a desire for swift locomotion. The little wheel of the roller-skate was the precursor to the solid rubber tire of the early bicycle. Expert skaters developed into expert bicyclists. Since the disappearance of the roller-skate and the decadence of the bicycle, many expert cyclists have in turn become expert chauffeurs, and some bicycle manufacturers have become famous as automobile builders. Hence, argue those who predict a short life for the self-propelled vehicle, the third-craze or fad will go the way of its predecessors.

Fortunately for the cause of the automobile, the one feature which was primarily responsible for the decline of the roller-skate and the bicycle does not enter into the sport of automobiling. That is hard muscular exertion. Grant, for the purpose of argument, that there is a possibility of comparison, however absurd, between the roller-skate, the bicycle, and the automobile—all being classed alike as fads. Let us carry out the comparison to a plain issue. Call it a six-day go-as-you-please contest, on a track, or wherever such a contest might be held. At the end of a few hours, at most a day, the roller-skate is down and out. A second day finds the bicyclist, if he has lasted so long, a nervous wreck. But at the end of the week the automobilist is for all practical purposes as fresh as when he began. He has missed no sleep, has had his meals regularly, his machine hums along as merrily as when it started, and is as fit as ever for another week's contest.

Compare the endurance of the three contestants, and you have the relative duration of the "fads."

The Utility of the Auto

There is a still stronger reason why the automobile has come to stay—its utility. We call the horse man's best friend, because he relieves us of the trouble of walking and is useful in bearing our heavy burdens. We eulogize "horse sense" because of the facility with which the animal's instinct can be subjugated to human intelligence. Yet whatever the horse can do, the automobile can do a hundred times better.

Where the horse would drop from fatigue, the automobile knows no weariness. Where the horse would slip and flounder over the impassable roads, the automobile will carry its human burden safe and dry-shod. Where the horse may "eat its head off" in fodder, the automobile only feeds when it works. When the horse may shy or bolt in spite of its horse sense, the automobile knows no terrors. Its fidelity is limited only by the intelligence of the man who guides it. It is the horse's best friend as well as man's. It relieves the horse of its burdens.

The Cost of Automobiles

"But why should automobiles cost so much?" I have often been asked. This applies especially to the high-priced foreign machines, which cost sums that seem to make automobiling almost impossible except for the very rich.

There is a story of a rich merchant who offered to give a poor man the cloth to make a coat. The poor fellow was grateful, but seemed dubious about the gift, gently hinting that a coat would need lining. The merchant readily promised the lining, too, but still the other did not appear satisfied; he had no trimmings. The merchant promised trimmings as well. Alas, his protégé had no buttons! When the merchant asked what the poor fellow did have, the answer was: "I have the buttonholes, at any rate."

Now, if that man had been a manufacturer of fancy-priced automobiles, he would have had a big capital to start upon. For the difference between a machine of twenty horse-power, costing, say, six thousand dollars, and one of forty horse-power, costing twice as much, is no more than the poor fellow possessed. It is merely a question of a smaller and a larger buttonhole. A machine of twenty horse-power has a cylinder of a certain bore. The width of the bore means the capacity of the cylinder itself, and the amount of gas and air that explodes in it determines the machine's rating of horse-power. Increase the bore, so as to allow a larger intake of gas and air, and there comes a bigger explosion, with a corresponding increase of power, and—but this is previously—a bigger check to raw when you pay for the machine.

Yet it would not be fair to bring against the automobile manufacturers in general any sweeping accusation on the ground of the charges they make for their goods. There are fancy-priced machines, but taking the business as a whole it is emphatically asserted that even with the demand outrunning the supply, as is the case just now, the net return is not a fair profit upon the capital invested. The remedy is not likely to be found in a general increase of prices to the customer, but rather in the cheapening of production by methods similar to those that are already in vogue with older industries.

For instance, the construction of automobile mechanism might not be more thoroughly specialized, certain parts now made by each manufacturer for himself being produced in factories devoted to one particular branch of the work. This would be possible, and would prove convenient and economical, if uniform standards were adopted throughout the trade. The same plan has been found advantageous in many other industries whose product is a highly complicated piece of mechanism, from the making of watches to the building of locomotives.

A machine of from sixteen to twenty-four horse-power is all that any man requires for touring. With such a car he can go as far as he likes over ordinary roads, carrying a supply of gasoline that should last him for two days at least. Where the roads are clear, he may spin along as fast as the average man cares to travel, and certainly as fast as is consistent with the admiration of the scenery.

Of course there are many enthusiastic automobilists who delight in possessing cars of forty or even sixty horse-power. That is their privilege, and they can afford to pay for it, just as some men choose to own fast horses for which they pay enormous sums.

On the other hand, where the automobile is not intended for touring, but rather as a substitute for the old-fashioned horse and buggy, a little six-to-ten-horse-power runabout will amply answer the purpose. And such a machine in constant use for city work, or in making short trips to the country, is cheaper in the long run even than a horse and buggy. Such an automobile is no fad.

“The whole of King Arthur’s court on bicycles could not have started the stir we created in that single automobile.”

PHILIP DELANY

ECHOING A LAMENT ALREADY HEARD IN MANY CORNERS OF the American West at the turn of the twentieth century, Philip Delany begins his article by observing that “romance is fast being crowded out of the life of the pioneer” by such modern devices as the automobile. Delany wastes no time, however, in pointing out that “the machine has its thrilling side too,” as seen in his description of a motor tour in the spring of 1903 from Colorado Springs to Santa Fe.

A banker and broker located in “the Springs,” Delany sets out with an acquaintance, W. W. Price, whose own automobile excursions had taken him to “many a Western cañon, pass and desert.” Traveling down the Front Range to Pueblo and then across country, along main highways and over mountain passes, they ventured to Walsenburg and Trinidad, on to Raton, New Mexico, and through Cimarron and Elizabethtown before finally motoring into Taos and eventually Santa Fe, thereafter returning to their point of origin in Colorado Springs. Clearly prepared to soak up all the sights along this route, Delany recounts the wild landscapes, forgotten Mexican adobes, and majestic Taos Pueblo that they encountered in their travels. Describing the residents of the pueblo (whom he names “Red Willow Indians” after the creek that flows by their home) as "a fine example of the early American aristocracy at its best," Delany further asserts that "they have lessons for modern American society."

Delany's narrative of this excursion, despite its brevity, highlights the many allures of recreational motoring already being grasped by a new kind of pioneer. In such explorations, Delany notes, the motorist could see "perhaps, the wildest and most natural places on the continent" and the peoples who inhabited them. With the automobile's ability to cover greater distances in far less time than any similar conveyance, "we crowded what used to take months to do in nine days." Above all, the traveler could now obtain an unprecedented degree of freedom, with "no beaten track to follow, no schedule to meet [and] no other train to consider; but he can go with the speed of an express straight into the heart of an unknown land."

Frontiering in an Automobile

By Philip Delany

[*Outing* 43, no. 2 (November 1903)]

Romance is fast being crowded out of the life of the pioneer; once he depended upon his own sturdy legs, or those of his broncho or burro—now he may, if he like, ride in an automobile, the latest pathfinder of the plains. The machine has its thrilling side, too.

To climb mountain passes with a thirty percent grade, to coast down rocky roads with only a few feet from wheels to the edge of an abyss of picturesque wonders, to swing along southern paths made famous by the Indians and pony express riders of only a few years ago, and along which a motor-car had never before been seen, this is an automobile trip that has exploring and sight seeing and excitement enough to suit the most adventurous spirit. Such a journey I took this spring with Mr. W. W. Price, who has, with an automobile, re-discovered many a Western cañon, pass and desert.

It took us two hours to run from Colorado Springs—our starting point—to Pueblo, past Pike's Peak and Cheyenne Mountain, most of the way over hot alkali plains, furrowed deep by cloud-burst and spring freshets. From Pueblo, taking supplies for the machine, we struck south across country. We were soon out of the world, drifting across a roadless land made more weird by the light which the moon threw over it. We were trying to locate the main highway to Walsenburg. For a time we crawled along where lines showed teams had once gone, until we came to a Mexican ranch of adobe houses; but the three big headlights on the machine discovered no one and we crept slowly away from the corral, the machine thudding sullenly under us. Then suddenly we blundered into the roadway and away we went at a rate of thirty miles an hour, transfixing with wonder a few Mexicans who were camping near by.

South from Walsenburg, the next day we swung past the Spanish Peaks, snow-white above the evergreens. Mountains were everywhere. They leaned in toward us threateningly through the clear air from all sides. Then down through Trinidad, toward Raton, New Mexico, the way wound around foothills, black with outcroppings of coal. From Raton we left the railroad lines, which had paralleled us, and pushed across the level plains, where cattle turned and ran in herds at the sight of a motor on the old Mexican land grant. After a night in an old adobe house in Cimarron we went down through the cañon, its rocky walls echoing in hollow calls the throbbing of the machine. As we hurried along, a fuzzy-coated burro walked out placidly before the car and nonchalantly jogged along, and the machine slowed down, necessarily, and followed the burro pace-maker. And so we were led into Elizabethtown, whose placer digging were the scene of a wild scramble in '68.

Having come in to Elizabethtown through a hole, we went out over a cloud. There are no other ways. The mountains surround it. The Indians call this pass "arrow stick in pole," it is so steep. Once at the summit, twisting and bending like a floundering whale, the car coasted down to the irrigated plain of Taos, where Indians, resting on their hoes, eyed us silently, and Mexicans saluted gracefully. Three miles beyond we swooped suddenly down upon the settlement of five-story, terraced houses of the Red Willow Indians. In their gaudy blankets they swarmed to the earthen housetops and watched us silently. But when, after much coaxing, we crowded the car with redskins and sent it dashing up and down at breakneck speed there were such war-whoops as city dwellers never hear.

These Indians believe that the Great Spirit has guided them to this promised land. They wandered here from the north, and we listened, standing with bare heads in an underground council chamber, to the recital in Spanish of the story of their faith. They are a fine example of the early American aristocracy at its best. They have some lessons for modern American society. In Taos, too, lived and lies Kit Carson, the hunter and trapper, scout and soldier.

From Taos we pushed through sand for many miles. The only living thing we saw was a gray coyote. But the desert is clean and sunny, which is something. At last we reached harder soil and green things growing. Indians greeted us on the way, and finally we came to the cliff dwellings of Pajorito Park, one of the many ruins of the great centuries-ago cities of the Southwest. One of the localities showed that 250,000 people lived there in houses, some of them five stories, or about seventy-five feet high. Irrigation, agriculture, industries, and arts were all parts of their daily life.

Running in to Santa Fé we passed wagons crowded with Indians, gorgeous in color, from bullet-headed papoose to squaw and buck. They all watched us stolidly, while the bronchos reeled and jumped with fright until we were out of sight. Then the bronchos probably received some attention.

Santa Fé is rich with history, and the road on to Las Vegas is rich with color and beautiful landscape. The wild green on every side is cut with clean white streams full of trout for the angler. The little Mexican adobe village of San José, which has scarcely changed in a century, nestles in the heart of this country.

When we went through San José I began to understand over again and in a new way Mark Twain's "Adventures of a Connecticut Yankee." The whole of King Arthur's court on bicycles could not have started the stir we created in that single automobile. We went through the place like the wind, the machine snorting, whistle tooting, while the poor inhabitants huddled into frightened groups out of reach. We were a kind of first thunderstorm to them.

We had a plunge in the Las Vegas Hot Springs and started north again along the old Santa Fé trail, meeting few people and seeing little that was new. One begrizzled old man, at an isolated shack, watched us so wistfully as he brought us some water that we half wanted to take him into the car and drive him into civilization, but he is probably happier as he is. From Raton it is back, over the same way we came, to Colorado Springs and home.

And so the machine is conquering the old frontier, carrying the thudding of modern mechanics into the land of romance. There are many pleasures in such a journey; you bring a new thing to an old people and they re-teach you old things that should never be forgotten. You see, perhaps, the wildest and most natural places on the continent; and there's a touch of adventure, for such a trip cannot be taken without some danger. We crowded what used to take months to do in nine days—nine hundred miles up mountain and down valley. The trails of Kit Carson and Boone and Crockett, and the rest of the early frontiersmen, stretch out before the adventurous automobilist. And when he is tired of the old, there are new paths to be made. He has no beaten track to follow, no schedule to meet, no other train to consider; but he can go with the speed of an express straight into the heart of an unknown land. And he isn't in much greater danger than the man who pilots his machine between the trucks and carriages of a crowded city street. It is only the beginning of automobile exploring and frontiering in the old West.

“We traveled in almost complete ignorance of what the next turn of the road would bring forth.”

M. C. KRARUP

THE SUMMER OF 1903 REPRESENTED A WATERSHED MOMENT for the fledgling era of motoring in America. During that season, three separate expeditions set forth from San Francisco heading east across the continent to New York City, a voyage that each party completed successfully. Although the journey of Vermont physician Horatio Nelson Jackson, his mechanic Sewall K. Crocker, and their canine mascot Bud is the only one whose story still has any traction in American memory (in large part because of the 2003 Ken Burns film, *Horatio's Drive: America's First Road Trip*, depicting it), each excursion involved its own particular adventures and achievements. Journalist Marcus C. Krarup's account of the trip in which he participated, for example, follows Krarup, driver E. T. (Tom) Fetch, and their part-time companion N. O. Allyn on a passage that carried them across the Sierra Nevada, Wasatch, and Rocky Mountain ranges, through the desolate empty spaces of Nevada and Utah, over innumerable gullies, gorges, rivers, and streams, and into long soggy stretches of the Great Plains before reaching the Mississippi River and crossing out of the West. Wedged in among spare parts, supplies, and baggage, Krarup and his colleagues clung to their twelve-horsepower Packard steed as it bore its 3,000-pound load steadily eastward.

Having written frequently about the automobile for other periodicals including *Outing* and *Horseless Age* during the years immediately preceding this experience, Krarup brought both a competent knowledge of the motor car and an author's skill to the telling of the tale. Moreover, Krarup had prepared a series of dispatches during the trip that were published in *Automobile* throughout the summer and fall of 1903. Unlike quite a few writers before and after him who portrayed early motor travels, Krarup proved sensitive not only to matters mechanical but picturesque as well. Perhaps since "the motor never fagged" and Krarup and his fellow voyagers soon developed "perfect confidence" that it would never falter or fail, he could afford to include in his gaze not only "steep, tortuous and narrow shelf-roads" or "unbridged ravines and washes," but also scenes possessing "the grandeur of desolation and loneliness." On the other hand, like most of his peers who wrote about such long-distance travels, Krarup devotes nearly all his attention to his party's encounters with landscapes west of the Mississippi, in recognition not only of the progress achieved by eastern states with their road building but also the formidable challenges present throughout the West to the auto traveler.

From Coast to Coast in an Automobile

The story of the fastest motor-car trip across the continent— a novel device for climbing sandhills, coasting down tortuous shelf-roads, crawling over gulches in twelve-foot jerks— adventures in mountain, desert, and prairie, ending with a wild night dash to New York

By M. C. Krarup

[*World's Work* 8, no. 1 (May 1904)]

Until last summer, nobody had succeeded in traveling across this continent in an automobile. Then, however, thanks mostly to improved construction of automobiles, three motor-car expeditions toured from San Francisco to New York.

The writer participated in the trip, which followed the most direct and central, but also most problematic, route between San Francisco and Denver. We finished the trip in the shortest time of the three parties and with more regular progress from day to day. Mr. E. T. Fetch was the chauffeur for the entire distance and Mr. N. O. Allyn accompanied us from Reno, Nevada, to Colorado Springs, perched on the spare tires and the baggage piled behind the seats.

Starting on June 20th, in the evening, we traveled eastward through California, Nevada, Utah, and Colorado to Denver, and after a rest of four days continued the journey, passing through Omaha, Chicago, Cleveland, Erie, Buffalo, Rochester, Syracuse, and Albany, finally reaching New York City on August 21st. The same twelve-horse-power car, weighing with baggage and three on board about 3,000 pounds, was the conveyance throughout. Interruptions due to failure of the motor or driving mechanisms were unimportant and brief.

We traveled in almost complete ignorance of what the next turn of the road would bring forth, depending upon information picked up at our nightly lodgings for finding the road or trail that would take us with least inconvenience to another stopping place, fifty or a hundred and fifty miles away. But a certain sense of adventure in mere transit through rough, uninhabited sections, even at a moderate gait, soon gave place to perfect confidence that the automobile could be relied upon for extra mileage when necessary.

We knew that even though we had strayed from the shortest road or had been misinformed as to difficulties, it would take us into some port for the night. Fatigue of muscle or mind was of very small consequence, except where ravines or "dry washes" frequently crossed the mountain or desert trail and necessitated constant use of the change-gear and the brakes. The motor never fagged, of course. After strains which would have completely exhausted the best of horses, it was as ready for a gay spring as ever. From this fact sprang the exhilaration of motoring over rough and roadless country.

The climb from Placerville—the "Hangtown" of pioneer days—to the summit of the California range of the Sierras, in June was a pleasant procession over the old stage-road of the "Forty-niners," which is still kept in fairly good condition. Following the picturesque American River closely for a day's journey, we enjoyed scenery to our heart's content, with halts for meals and rest at excellent road-houses strung along the route at intervals of a dozen miles, as far east as the famous summer-resort of Lake Tahoe. The climb is long, however, with only brief respites from steep grades calling for low gears, and the abundant supply of cold water along these mountain roads is a convenience to assist in keeping the motor from overheating under its hard work. A greater surplus of power than we had and a motor fan—now so commonly used—would have been of advantage.

Crossing the Sierras we had to keep constant watch, with eye and ear, for the passenger-stages, mule-drawn freight-wagons, and even pack-horses, coming in the opposite direction. The bends of the road are continuous and often sharp. Timber and jutting rocks bar the perspective. The splash of the turbulent river in many places drowns the tinkle of the bells on the lead mules. Suddenly confronted with an automobile, the animals would probably take fright and jump over the edge of the road. Indeed, a stageful of passengers were overturned in 1902 when a steam-car driver ventured part of the way toward the summit. Accordingly, we were anxiously enjoined to time our passage so that the four-house stage coming down from Lake Tahoe "full of women and children" would meet us at one of the way-stations. We did not mind observing the precaution, as these stages come down the mountains at a clip of about twelve miles an hour.

From the summit of the Sierras in California, 7,300 feet high, there is a sharp descent by a serpentine road down to the basin occupied by Lake Tahoe and the Truckee River. The drop—for such it would seem to the novice—is one of 800 feet in two miles of winding road. Down this the car slid in nine and one-half minutes under brakes. After crossing the valley, the road rises again, now in Nevada, to the second summit, and from here it falls through Daggett's Pass to the broad Carson Valley 2,400 feet below. The descent is as steep as the first and three times longer. The valley was visible from the pass as a misty triangle studded with barely discernible ranch-buildings and poplar groves—a veritable bird's-eye view. The road was carefully laid out and sandy.

These long descents over steep, tortuous, and narrow shelf-roads, with nothing but space on one side and mountain on the other, were the first initiation on this trip to something unusual. Over the last, the Kingsbury Grade, the brake-rings became so heated that we stopped three times to cool them, once at a very picturesque spring 1,200 feet above the valley.

At Wadsworth, Nevada, our troubles with sand began, and I can almost add, ended. Repeatedly assured that we could never get the car through the sand, we approached a sandhill outside of Wadsworth with many misgivings. We were comforted when the means we had devised for such emergencies proved effectual. It consisted of two strips of canvas six feet wide and twenty-four feet long. Where the sand is round-grained, loose, and dry the driving-wheels of a car can get no hold, but spin around as in water or slimy mud. Our strips of canvas, laid on the ground for the wheels to run over, held the sand together, and then the motor-power was sufficient to drive us ahead. In this manner the two strips, each laid down three times, took us over Wadsworth hill, much to the astonishment of a number of citizens who had assembled there with a team of horses and stout tackle to help us. Our experience soon taught us that bad sand exacts about eighteen times more power per lineal foot than a 20 per cent hill with good footing, but we ceased at Wadsworth to worry about sand, knowing that the canvas would serve its purpose.

Our next obstacle was more stubborn. Most of the 300 miles through the Humboldt River Valley, the soil is a sandy, alkaline marl which "washes" very readily, and the road consists of two ruts inclosing a ridge overgrown with stout sagebrush. Frequently the ridge is so high that the low-built car cannot be driven ahead. We found that the sage-bushes could be mowed down under the axles by the weight of the car, but when the differential casing struck the ridge and the rear wheels were lifted off the bottom of the ruts, it required a lifting-jack and ingenious manipulations to wiggle the car back to a footing. We wrenched the car in efforts at getting out of the ruts to avoid a high spot in the ridge ahead, and we had many a sudden drop in attempts to ride the ridge and straddle the rut. Then we drove many miles beside the trail, where the old sage bushes grow as thick as an arm and up to man's heights. A tarpaulin stretched under the car for protection of the mechanism against dust and mud was soon whipped to shreds, and when that was gone all the paint on the axles and casings underneath the car quickly disappeared. Our shovel was strapped there with its hickory handle exposed. Before we got through Utah, its long fiber was whipped loose, too, and a new shovel had to be bought. Sometimes twigs and pulp of sage accumulated in the quadrant in which the gear-changing lever moves and interfered with the management of the car, necessitating frequent cleanings. But these, after all, were merely trifling vexations.

Between Mill City and Winnemucca the most direct trail was described to me as a succession of sandpits extending for about twenty miles, with the sand a little worse than any other in the State of Nevada. It was here that an automobile in 1901 had come to a final halt. But another road led over a spur of the nearby mountains through Dun Glen pass. This route we chose, although it involved a rise of 1,500 feet followed by a steep descent over a rugged mountain-side. Through the pass we met roaming flocks of cattle and horses, which all but barred the way by their curiosity. The descent had the grandeur of desolation and loneliness. Even by this route we did not escape four miles of deep sand when the plain was reached again, but fortunately at the worst places the sagebrush at the sides had been laboriously cut down and spread in a thick layer over the trail so as to ease the load for horses. This helped us.

Easy driving had been promised us beyond Wells, where the Humboldt River begins from a number of circular water-holes or craters. But it was just in this waterless portion of Nevada and in the adjacent portions of Utah that innumerable gullies and ravines crossed the trail with such wearisome repetition that about 2,000 movements of the gear, clutch, and brake-levers were required in one day to nurse the car into and again out of ditches. Often when the car stood almost on end in a dry gulch about six feet wide and three feet deep, the headlight would graze the opposite bank. In proceeding to get across, one of the front wheels would be lifted from the ground while the other was swung around till it struck the panel of the hood—a contortion for which even our flexible car was never intended. The same section of the trip had many forbidding grades, more than twice as steep as any in the Sierras or the Rocky Mountains.

These hills we climbed in installments. The motor was set going at full speed, running idle. Then the clutch was applied, causing the flywheel momentum to jerk the car upward some ten or twelve feet. Then the brakes were quickly clapped on while Mr. Allyn and I chocked the rear wheels with stones. The process was repeated till the top of each hill was reached. One at Fenelon, Nevada, required perhaps a dozen jerks. Another, leading up to the Promontory Range at Lake Utah, required even more. It was scaled in full view of a number of railroad men, who cheered the performance from a distance by a chorus of locomotive whistles. Their professional sympathy was with the motor.

Through Corinne, Brigham, Ogden, Salt Lake City, and almost to the heart of Utah, at Provo City, the driving is free from all difficulties. The main road runs in the shadow of the eastern range of the Wasatch Mountains and compares favorably with eastern highways. From Provo we made our way through Spanish Fork Canyon to the crest of the main range of the Wasatch Range and over Soldiers' Summit to Colton. Here we were informed that the wagon-road through Castle Gate had been washed away in a recent freshet. The only other way to get to our destination for that day—the town of Price—was to follow a devious course skirting the Uintah Indian Reservation and then to tack back to Price through Soldiers' Canyon, a piece of road which had a national reputation for roughness. It turned out to be the most difficult piece of ground, for an automobile, between San Francisco and New York. A crevasse to the left, and a dilapidated wall or slope of tumbled-down rocks of enormous size to the right, forced the car to proceed absolutely in the wagon-trail without deviation, and the ground between the ruts was obstructed by huge stones. These we could not straddle as do the high-built freighters' wagons that ply in astonishing numbers over this remarkable thoroughfare to the Fort and the mining regions farther north, but by piling smaller stones in the ruts we forced the wheels themselves to lift the car over the bigger stones in the middle. Two miles of this occupied us for three hours, but Price was reached at nightfall, to the utter astonishment of the inhabitants. The next day was set aside for rest.

Besides a repetition of all the difficulties already experienced, the route from Price, through Woodside, Green River, and Thompson Springs to the Colorado line presented also a few surprises. Quicksand in Price River at Woodside detained us for three hours. Driftsand piled in banks further delayed our arrival at Green River till half past ten o'clock at night. No vegetation was visible the rest of the way to Thompson Springs, and the fifty additional miles of Utah were covered at night to avoid the heat of the day. The ground here abounded in ravines, or *arroyas*, of the most malignant description.

A change for the better came with our entrance into Colorado. The trail became a road—the beginning of a State highway which was continued thence to Denver; not a broad, macadamized avenue by any means, but a narrow strip of ground blasted out of rock for mile after mile, where necessary, and following the steams—first the Grand, then the Eagle, then the Homestake rivers—to the continental watershed at Tennessee Pass. The territory of unbridged ravines and washes was behind us; two ruts with unsubdued nature between them was no longer the only thoroughfare. Nevertheless, the first few miles of the Grand Canyon road did more damage to the pneumatic tires than all of the desert and plains. Sharp ledges on the stiff grades gouged chunks of rubber from the casings, and at Grand Junction it was considered best to put the new unused reserve tires on the rear wheels.

About six and one-half miles west of Rifle, there is a shelf road, mostly clay, descending about 200 feet in one-third of a mile. Soaked by rains off and on during the day, and by a thunder-shower which overtook us just there, this grade called for chains around the tires to safeguard the descent. Even with this precaution against slipping, we found it necessary to walk beside the car and put it sidewise when the wheels, floundering in the messy clay, showed signs of sliding too close to the outer edge. But it was a comfort that a comparatively small muscular effort was sufficient to direct the sprawlings toward safety. The car slid to the side almost as readily as forward.

Above Glenwood Springs, the canyon of the Grand River narrows down to a gorge. The river, the railroad on the south side, and the wagon-road on the north side, fill all the space between the cliffs. Indeed, frequent blasting had been needed to make the canyon hold all three. Above is the "mesa," rough table-land devoted to stock-raising and some agriculture by irrigation. The road is so narrow and many of the bends are so sharp that speed above ten miles an hour is out of the question. Where the Eagle River flows into the Grand, the road turns at right angles upon a bridge. Five minutes before our arrival at this point, another automobile had come from Denver in the opposite direction, carrying its owner, Mr. G. W. Woods, and two other men, bound for Mr. Woods's ranch on the mesa north of Rifle. At this point they had been spilled. The men were congratulating themselves on their miraculous escape from injury when we reached the spot, and were surveying the wrecked car with more curiosity than discomfiture. The steering mechanism—after much previous fast driving—had forsaken them, with the result shown in the illustration.

Our own steering was not quite so reliable as it had been, for the breaking of a brace-rod for the front axle—in Utah—had caused the left front wheel to "toe out" a trifle. This was later remedied in Denver, but meanwhile it was giving us some apprehensions on the slimy roads by which we had to climb to the elevation of the Tennessee Pass, 10,418 feet, the following two days. The rain which pursued us reduced one day's journey to twenty miles—from Edwards Post-Office through Minturn and Gilman to Red Cliff. We had chains around the tires all the time, but they soon wore through at the most exposed links. They were pieced together with leather straps, and other links were exposed thereafter.

Just beyond the Tennessee Pass, where water begins to run to the

Atlantic Ocean, the car slipped into the Tennessee River by a false move. The stream's identity was not clear to us then, however, as it is there only a foot wide. A mile farther on the way to Leadville, it carries a large volume of water from the snowtopped mountains which flank the pass at a distance.

Gasoline of low grade, not over 68° Baume, had so far been used throughout, as no other was obtainable, and the high altitude in conjunction with this fuel had somewhat reduced the power of the motor. The cooling water boiled and evaporated far below the ordinary boiling point, 212° Fahrenheit, and the rarefied atmosphere could neither carry away as much heat nor fill the cylinder with as complete a charge for combustion as lower down. But these drawbacks really proved of minor importance. They interfered hardly at all with the continuance of the trip from Leadville to Buena Vista, then over the Park Range, through the South Park district, and through Ute Pass to Manitou and Colorado Springs, though the elevation over the largest part of this distance is between 8,000 and 10,000 feet.

When going on a cliff road along Arkansas River, however, the inner front wheel struck a stone which had tumbled down from above and the resilience of the tire caused the whole front portion of the car to bound to the right. An inch farther would have meant something serious for which not even the gorgeous aspect of the multi-colored cliff at that point could have compensated. The incident was the first of its kind, as we usually watched closely for stones in the tracking localities where they might spell trouble.

East of Denver, where some repairs were found advisable—especially of worn bearings—travel in ruts was resumed for a while. Cattlemen had fenced in large blocks of land, without regard to the section-line roads, and the opening of gates became irritating, not only on account of their number, but particularly because they were nearly all fastened with barb-wire rings pulled very taut over the posts. These results in lacerated gloves and scratched hands. Grasshoppers were swarming, too, and the sharp sting when they struck one's face while the car went at some speed was annoying when repeated. The ruts made by narrow-tired vehicles were barely far enough apart for our wheel-gauge. They turned steering into an operation requiring continuous and conscious effort. Beyond Fort Morgan a network of irrigation ditches, all brimful of water, held us captive for an hour in vain attempts to find an exit one early morning. We were then trying the plan of starting before sunrise, about four o'clock in the morning. A farmer, just out of bed, finally showed us the way out of the labyrinth, but not till we had criss-crossed over a square mile of soggy meadows and taken the depth measure of several ditches. This was in the upper South Platte River valley, where so much water is drained from the river that the towns below, Julesburg and Ogallala, get none. At North Platte the supply is renewed not only in the river, but unfortunately also on the roads.

From this place to Columbus, Nebraska, our travel was amphibious. Stretches of excellent road alternated with temporary lakes and mudholes, in which the car was swamped, the wheels spinning around in the sticky mud with no propulsive power. We had to use boards, fence-posts, brushwood, chains, the shovel, the jack, and strong pulls on the front wheels to get out of these predicaments. Only once—near Clark, Nebraska—was the motor disabled. The water had entered the carburetor, and we had to employ horses to drag the car out. Fast in the mire seven times in one day was the record for that disagreeable trip along the Platte River, but the mudholes which were successfully rushed or laboriously traversed on the low gear ran into the hundreds. The front wheels were very useful as feelers in those days. With the rear wheels on *terra firma* we drove the front wheels cautiously into the water or mudhole, in confidence that we could always back out so long as the rear wheels had a firm hold.

Our intimate acquaintance with diluted road material did not improve our appearance, and arriving mud-splashed at hotels we were not always welcome guests until the hotel people learned how far we had come.

The western portion of Iowa offered a repetition of these experiences, and the farmers were not always cordial. In two or three instances they responded with much rudeness to our greetings. Our relations to the population from now on were not so pleasant as in the far West, but the road conditions continued to improve. The traveling, as such, was devoid of all incident and interest from Wheatland, Iowa, far into New York State, where the tires began to give out, and where heavy rains had drenched the roads, especially through the Mohawk Valley. From Clinton, Iowa, to Chicago is an almost uninterrupted stretch of good macadam. Sandy or hilly roads in Indiana, Ohio, and Pennsylvania which had been looked upon as "bad" seemed very acceptable highways after the roadless sections in the West. The mud through which we arrived at Albany after a long day's drive, though ten inches deep in places, after all had a firm bottom.

When we attempted, however, to drive from Albany to Poughkeepsie the same night, we undertook too much. The night was very dark and the post-road was very muddy and very crooked. The oil lamps were in bad order and went out periodically. At every cross-road there is a quadruple guideboard. These had to be examined by matchlight. The slush, the darkness of all but the first ten feet in front of the car, lack of sleep, and nervous strain in general, produced a sense of insecurity that became quite intolerable on some of the steep hills. Part of the time it seemed impossible to determine whether we were in the road or beside it. Everything lay in a dull glare before us; and this condition of the overtaxed sense Mr. Fetch termed "road glare." When Hudson was reached, about two o'clock in the morning, we stopped, and the car did not get to Poughkeepsie till the next day at one o'clock, and then proceeded immediately to New York under escort from Peekskill.

A wild night drive into the city, following close upon the heels of a leader and guided solely by his tailboard light, terminated the transcontinental trip in a cloud of dust, which is nearly always the penalty that the motorist pays for the civility of escort.

“There is not the slightest excuse why a chauffeur should not know . . . as much about the country lying in advance of him as a military commander for purposes of seeing an army through.”

HROLF WISBY

AS THE POPULARITY OF USING THE AUTOMOBILE GREW among Americans in the first decade of the twentieth century, aspiring motor campers found no lack of advice on the printed page about their particular pastime. Numerous writers such as Hrolf Wisby (whom we have already encountered) produced copious amounts of suggestions, recommendations, and prescriptions, intended to ensure successful excursions into untamed landscapes. Striking out to bring enlightenment to the ignorant, Wisby for instance observed archly that “there is as much difference between touring in the ordinary way, and camping out with your machine, as there is between a stroll down the avenue and a cross-country tramp.” After all, he continued, “few know anything about camping,” which meant that the experiences and insights of self-proclaimed experts such as Wisby would be indispensable (at least in their own minds) in demonstrating how best to combine the joys of camping with the advantages offered by motorized transportation.

Wisby’s admonitions to the reader did indeed focus upon a host of practical proposals, beginning with the necessity of preparing intricate, customized maps of each route with the aid of lots of tracing paper and continuing through how to choose the right vehicle with sufficient power and space to meet the challenges of road and trail. Like nearly every other author who discussed the possibilities of motor vacations in the woods, he also dilated at some length about the array of supplies and equipment he considered essential for any successful automobile voyage. Running the gamut from chains, rope, a jack, a spade, and an axe to blankets, tent, hammocks or pneumatic mattresses, and a number of inclement-weather garments, Wisby's shopping list included tools for emergencies and conveniences that furnished creature comforts. He proposed a full assortment of kitchenware, binoculars, a camera, a lantern, and plenty of hunting and fishing gear to allow the motor camper to enjoy the moment and also remain as self-sufficient as possible. At the same time, in case of the most dire contingencies, he even recommended carrying a telegrapher's key or telephone so that the camper could tap into civilization's web of overhead wires in case he had to call for help. Wisby's outdoorsman (references to women in such settings being as rare as the proverbial blue moon) thus would have the most up-to-date technology at hand as insurance while at the same time setting forth, in Wisby's words, to bring "modern man . . . back to Nature on the latest vehicle of civilization."

Camping Out with an Automobile

How to make a road map—the car and its equipment—the camp kit and how to pack it—sport en route

By Hrolf Wisby

[*Outing* 45, no. 6 (March 1905)]

There is as much difference between touring in the ordinary way, and camping out with your machine, as there is between a stroll down the avenue and a cross-country tramp. Everybody is familiar with touring in its usual aspect, but few know anything about camping out, and still fewer attempt it. A little experience and a good deal of forethought will enable you to "live with" your auto and make a decent showing, even if you don't combine the qualities of a woodscraftsman and a scout. In a little while you will want to be distinguished from the mere tourist, as the voyageur from the ordinary traveler.

Automobile camping stands apart from any other branch of the sport. It is neither touring nor racing. It is modern man brought back to Nature on the latest vehicle of civilization. It is closing in an embrace with mother earth, yet not locked with her in the compass of a day's slow tramp, but free to roam, to camp, and to change your ground at will, to surmount the obstacles of the open country, to annihilate the wearying consideration of time and distance. It is terrestrial man gifted by an almost aerial mobility—a gift of his own ingenious flying, even more remarkable than the nomadic roving of Bedouin sheiks.

The first thing to do is select your route carefully. The chart will not tell you everything. Some judgment is necessary to map out the probable daily mileage in advance in order to reduce the area of desirable camping ground for each day to the smallest possible radius. The actual picking of the camp must, of course, be done on the spot. Nevertheless, it is convenient for the chauffeur to know when he is traveling over favorable ground for this purpose, and no special facilities are required to make this advance knowledge accurate and reliable.

Most of the big automobile clubs the world over publish good maps, and the topographic charts of the various States are of great aid in judging the lay of the country.

With this equipment, which can be absorbed in any large library, you can construct a set of handy maps for use when under way. Take a good, plain geographic map. Place over it a transparent tracing-paper, say of an "onion" finish, and thumb-tack the corners. Trace with black ink the rivers, railroads, towns, etc., of the country you wish to pass through. Trace with red ink the route you decide to take in passing through. Then take a topographic map and trace, in the same manner, mountains, hills, elevations and valleys; in short, the build of the land you are to enter. If your tour includes travel in but little known regions of this country, provide yourself with a tracing of a survey map such as the U.S. Geodetic Survey issues, which will give you what accurate information is available in advance. The data gleaned from these three maps should enable anyone to make up a driving chart, its object being to show at a glance the combined information contained in all the other maps. To be practical, such a chart must be simple—a sort of ready-reference résumé of all needed road and camping information. Stake out your route in a heavy, red line. Everything that crosses this course is of more interest to you than what runs parallel with it; hence, note all railroad (——), highway (——) and river (· · · ·) crossings, towns (C), farms (O), and wayside houses (X). Note only unusually high grades and low drops of the road, thus: Gr. 30 percent or Dr. 20 percent. The topographic maps will give you every boulder, peak, and bush in the country, but all you want to know is, "How long does this forest I am traveling through continue?"—or "How long must I camp in this treeless country before I strike woods and shelter?" Forests, and even the nature of forests, are easily indicated on the map by various symbols (¶ † ‡), but instead of massing them to show the size of the forest, as is usual, simply draw the outline, say, for a pine forest with symbol (†), for a hardwood copse with (‡), and for miscellaneous woods with (¶). A carefully planned map will give you a correct idea not only of the route, but of how far you must travel to obtain the best available camping ground before night.

The size should not be larger than an ordinary handkerchief, and after pasting the map on chart canvas it should be rolled around a paper or wooden cylinder, placed in a waterproof box with a glass pane, so that the chauffeur may have it continually before him and turn the cylinder as he progresses over the route shown on it. This arrangement will obviate that most wearisome operation of a long-distance trip, of having to stop to consult maps—a very exciting performance when it rains or blows—or to consult "people you meet," who, as a rule, don't know any more about the country they live in than the average New Yorker knows about New York. There is not the slightest excuse why a chauffeur should not know, for his particular purpose, as much about the country lying in advance of him as a military commander for purposes of seeing an army through.

Next comes the choice of a proper vehicle, which for an extended trip of this order had better not weigh much more than half a ton. If the party numbers eight persons, two 1,200-pound cars with one horse-power behind each one-hundred pounds, and each carrying four passengers, would be far more preferable than a big high-power car of double capacity. Not only will the traveling be more commodious, but in case of breakdowns or accidents, the uninjured car can tow the other. The cars should be of the same model and make, so that the spare parts and accessories carried can be used to equal advantage for both.

For summer travel a tarpaulin roof on a frame, supported by four stanchions, and with side curtains, would give you entire protection from sun heat and rain showers. The same arrangement can be used for winter travel with an addition of a windshield in front. It is better to have the shield made in two sections, and folding vertically in the center, so that both panes are placed at angles with the wind pressure, in which position they are also better protected against the shocks of a jolting and jumping car front. Personally, I am in favor of no protection overhead or in front, for the most scorching sun that ever shone can be defeated in a Japanese palmetto hat, a suit of karki, and the wind pressure of the ordinary touring gait, while proper fur clothes, hood, and face-masks will enable anyone not too enfeebled to face the blasts of a winter storm. The leather upholstering of the car will not suffer the least from an extended tour if well-fitting covers of enameled oilcloth are used. Less than two dollars' worth will protect every square inch of leather in a tonneau car. Dirt, mud, and dust is readily removed by a few wipes with a cloth, or the covers, which are entirely waterproof, may be cleaned in a brook, and thus you are always sure of a clean and sanitary seat.

Besides the usual outfit of tools, spare parts, tires, etc., for making wayside repairs, an auxiliary kit is required to make camping possible and comfortable. If you intend to cover rough country, encase the bottom of the car in a detachable sheet-iron covering built in several sections. Have it fit snug and tight to prevent rattling and resist shocks. Nothing but iron will do, as you must be prepared for "roads" that are simply too deep ruts, with a stony ridge in the middle on which the car bottom will drag at intervals. You must also take into account stretches of open country, bristling with tough vegetation like sage brush, which has been known to wear to a shaving the wooden handle of a spade strapped under the car body.

Take with you enough rope and chain to go around all four wheels. Sometimes you may need all four lengths of chain to pull the "other" car out of a dilemma. For this emergency, carry detachable links to join the chain lengths into one, and use the road as a pulling strap at either end of the chain. Thus a degree of resiliency is established sufficient to prevent both rope and chain from breaking. Carry also a small jack for lifting the car-body to admit of repairs, a spade, an axe, and in winter, a wooden shovel or two. You will find them very useful when you least expect trouble. For summer camping, bring along a military canvas tent. If you roll it in the army regulation style, you will be surprised to see how small a bundle it makes. Have the poles made folding, the same as the legs of a surveyor's or photographer's tripod. To provide against dampness under foot, a floor covering is best made out of the kind of flexible enameled oilcloth used for dashboards and carriages. It is absolutely waterproof, won't crack, and can be kept clean and sanitary simply by wiping. For a hamper covering, this material is also preferable. Right here let me warn you against stuffing your clothes in hampers. You can't use them if you do, without a tailor to press them, and the tailor is never there when you want your clothes. Pack your clothes in a trunk and send them ahead by rail to some point of interest on your route where you can stop over and dress a bit. Don't take along with you in the car any other or any more clothing than you need for actual travel and camping. Plenty of underwear and stockings is alike indispensable during any season, but for summer a light karki suit, with a long leather coat for cool nights, and an oilskin suit for rainy weather is really all you need unless you wish to add overalls for doing repairs. A pneumatic mattress and an army blanket is all the bed you would want, and the outfit rolls up snug. To my mind a hammock makes a handier and more comfortable bed for summer sleeping, and where trees are wanting it may be slung inside the tent on the poles, provided these are made strong enough. But even where there are no trees, sleeping in the open in a hammock can easily be accomplished. Here is an arrangement that will accommodate three sleepers: put three hooks on the side of the automobile, one in front, one in the middle, and one in the rear. Fasten the rear ropes of the hammocks to these hooks and lead the head ropes through the tent opening and secure them around the center pole. The heads of the sleepers will be quite close together and on a higher level—affording better sleep—than the feet, which will be at least a yard apart, and thus easy getting in and out of each hammock is provided. This shows what three hooks, properly used, are good for. For winter travel you, of course, dispense with your tent in favor of the sleeping-bag. If you can't get what you want at the stores, make your own bag. The outer covering should be waterproof. Rubber is too heavy and bulky, and unless you know of something better, I would again suggest a heavy grade of enameled oilcloth. This material will also prevent bugs and vermin from entering the bag, and, unlike rubber, does not "draw" the skin. The body of the bag can be made out of a high grade horse-blanket with an inside lining of flannel, or simply a pure flannel blanket, than which nothing is warmer. It might not be amiss to let the neck of the bag continue into a hood for the head—simply oilcloth lined with flannel. This scheme enables you to remove your cap during your sleep, and thus obviate the headache this headgear often produces in a tenderfoot, while you have all the comfort of a loose-fitting hood.

A cheap and quite efficient method of improvising a sleeping-bag on the spot is to fasten together with safety pins two pieces of enameled oilcloth, roll up your blanket and slide in. I should think that stunt would make 10 degrees below seem a small drop to any man sleeping in the open. When I stopped at Dyrisfjordur in Iceland, in 1888, I saw Fridthjof Nansen, who was then preparing to cross Greenland with a kit so simple and small that even I, who was at that time a naval cadet, questioned its efficiency. He had no fur clothes at all, but wore a thick gray woolen suit of a special weave, the jacket being double-breasted and buttoning on the side, not in front. His sleeping-bag was of the same material with a light canvas cover, which did not protect nearly as well as the oilcloth cover suggested above. "*Mine ski er mit baal,*" he explained, meaning that he would use his skis so well he should need no other warmth.

The automobile camper cannot depend upon exercise to keep him comfortable—hence his kit must be the heavier.

To get the proper benefit of a sleeping-bag, leave your fur garments in the car, remove your boots, and keep on only your underclothing and ordinary traveling suit, both of which should be made of wool. When you have bagged yourself in this manner, effect a change of stockings, and you will not be likely to suffer from cold feet. If a strong wind is blowing, go to work with the wooden shovel and pile up a foot of snow right in the face of the wind. Lie down in your bag under the lee of this snow wall and you will be entirely comfortable. In fact it is warm to sleep out in the snow in this fashion, whereas canvas overhead makes you chilly, and besides it is liable to blow away or burst under the weight of snow. When you wake up in the morning, just remove the hood and rub your face and hands vigorously with the snow. This will give you splendid circulation. Leave soap alone and don't wash. In extreme cold, soap will only crack your face. To "equip" your face for the rigors of fast traveling in a freezing atmosphere, rub both face and hands with Vaseline, and keep on rubbing until every pore is fed and closed. You may then wipe with a rough towel, and whatever dirt is on your face will come off in the towel, enough Vaseline remaining in the pores for protection. You are now fit to jump out of the bag. Before dressing, however, wrap yourself in a blanket and skip around in the snow with bare feet for five or ten minutes. If you keep your feet going you won't feel the cold in the least, and it will give you a start of warmth and comfort that will last all day. Now slip into your fur garments and boots, and light the camp fire. With the first sip of fragrant coffee you will be quite comfortable, and at peace with all the world, even if the thermometer says thirty below.

The common kind of fur coat is not so good but what it can be improved. The open front is a mistake. It is of little use except to get at the inside pockets, and inside pockets are a mistake. A fur coat opening on the right side with clasps unbuttons readily with the right hand. Big pockets sewn on the outside will make unfastening unnecessary, except for donning and doffing the garment. Go a step further and appropriate the century-old experience of the Eskimo in building fur clothes. Dispense entirely with buttons and clasps. Shape the coat like a turtleneck sweater. Make it loose-fitting all over, and especially over the waist. Cut it off at the hips. Make the trousers out of the same fur, with the hip-lining somewhat lower than the ordinary, so that the coat will just overlap it. This design will afford extreme mobility of body, also in the waist, where the space provided by the loose overlap of the coat will supply ventilation—a most important thing, without which any garment is unsanitary and soon ceases to yield and retain warmth. Under each armpit insert a single row of, say, four circular eyelets, and sew over them, on the inside, a strip of cheese cloth. This will prevent chills around arms and shoulders from stagnant sweat, and it will add to the wearer's comfort. Snap-buttons could, of course, be provided on the right shoulder and on the side of the neck, to make the jacket slide on easier, but it isn't necessary if only the neck is wide enough to put the head through. First insert the arms in the sleeves and then draw the jacket over your head as you would a sweater.

The Greenland Eskimo is so particular about ventilation that he leaves an open space at the waist—through which his skin shows—between the coat and the trousers, which fasten about the lower half of the loins with a strip of raw-hide.

Your portable kitchen must contain nothing at all likely to rust or tarnish. Aluminum utensils are far away the best. Nothing, however, will replace steel knives and forks, and if you wrap them in oilcloth after cleaning, they won't tarnish. Traveling in a treeless country means that you must have a gasoline stove to be replenished from your car tank, but in most instances you should be able to enjoy a camp fire. For personal protection carry a revolver, and for "picket duty" bring with you a good hardy dog that you can also use in hunting, and let him sleep in the car. A shot-gun and a rifle should enable you to bag whatever seasonable game you may locate, and an outfit of fishing-tackle will come handy evening winters, when you may have to emulate the Indian, and fish through the ice. Presuming you are a fairly good sportsman, there will be periods during such a tour when you should have no difficulty in supplying the camp with all needed provisions. In fact, the shooting and fishing end of such a trip, in conjunction with the camping feature, is the very sport that lends zest to it. You can camp on the tin-can plan, but it isn't very exciting.

The proper way to pack is one of those little side issues that most tourists do not stop to consider, and which, for this reason, causes needless worry and work. The baggage is usually stowed with no discrimination between the things needed constantly and the things wanted only occasionally. This means unpacking a lot of things you don't want, to get at what you do want, every time anything is wanted. Bags, satchels, suit-cases, etc., are useless, and take up too much room. Bundles alone are satisfactory, but labeling them won't do because you have to hunt for the label, which is liable to get torn or lost. Provide yourself with a dozen different colored pieces of oilcloth. Use white pieces for packing underclothing, black pieces for clothing, red for footwear and outerclothing. Pack your charts in yellow, your ammunition in blue, and your kitchen utensils in green oilcloth. Divide up the other colors to distinguish the rest of your kit, and pack what you need constantly in the hampers, which had better be lined inside and outside with heavy enameled oilcloth. It is much easier to remember the contents of a bundle by color than by number or location.

Opportunities for appropriating and improving the ideas carried out by experienced voyageurs will suggest themselves to the ingenious camper.

Here is a good idea originated by an Englishman and improved upon by an American. The latter is a New York business man and known to me personally. In tramping the Alps he ran across an apparition resembling a peddler, which on close view proved to be mainly an alpenstock with strings tied to one end of it, and at the other end an English scholar of Socratian simplicity. On each string dangled a small bundle done up in paper, the total number of bundles representing his entire pack. He could readily unpack any one of these bundles, and put his hand on what he might want, without disarranging the rest of his baggage. That was his scheme. A few weeks later my American friend was fishing salmon in the Loch Lomond with a Scotchman, who considered himself weather-and-worry-proof in a triple-ply raincoat. A shower came up. The American, who was dressed in an ordinary outing suit, produced a yard and a half of enameled flexible oilcloth, and cut an aperture in the middle of it with his pocket knife. Putting his head through this aperture he had in effect the protection of a Mexican poncho. A gooseback could not shed the rain better than this oilcloth cape, which was comfortable because it hung loosely and provided ventilation. Another piece of oilcloth, the size of a handkerchief, pinned to his cap, transformed it into a waterproof headgear. He didn't look pretty, but he felt pretty good. After the shower, which left the American dry and cool, and the Scotchman wet, hot and swearing, the former suggested luncheon. The Scotchman's fare was almost as water-soaked as himself.

"Have a bite with me?" suggested the American, unclasping his belt, from which various strings depended holding small parcels wrapped in oilcloth and all marked 8:10 A.M., the hour of starting. The Scotchman, who supposed the parcels to contain only fishing requisites, was hugely elated to find in some of them a choice assortment of sandwiches as fresh and palatable as could be desired.

"Suppose we sit down," remarked the American, removing his improvised mantle, which, spread upon the wet grass, afforded a dry seat to sit on and a clean cloth to feast upon. At the price of less than thirty cents my American friend had succeeded in providing himself ingeniously with raincoat, rain-hat, a dry seat, a clean tablecloth, and rain-proof kit, each separate part of which could be got at without disarranging the other parts—the alpenstock scheme was out-done.

If you go out automobile camping, you will have to go out afoot shooting and fishing a bit, when it will pay you to adopt the oilcloth idea, which you will find entirely practical.

The care practiced in packing your camp-kit properly is, to some degree, a waste of effort, unless at the same time, you provide for a proper distribution of the separate parcels.

For a party of three traveling in a tonneau with seating capacity for five—and this is an ideal proportion of room to occupants for just such a trip—I would suggest a handy disposal of the outfit mainly in hampers. Besides the usual arrangement over the rear wheels, an auxiliary hamper could be strapped on the outside of the tonneau door, which should contain nothing but the "emergency" wardrobe, such as oilskin clothing, rubber boots, etc. When a shower or a dust-storm springs up, the third man traveling in the tonneau simply reaches over, empties the auxiliary hamper and deals out the clothing. You avoid the irksome stop or slow-down at the very time when you may want to use all possible dispatch to gain shelter. Directly under the forward end of each side hamper is a space, in most machines of standard make, extending to the dip of the rear wheel dash, which could very well be utilized for an auxiliary hamper. An oblong pattern, measuring twelve inches wide and thirty inches long, would fit most cars of 1,200 pounds size. It should be fastened at top and bottom in a readily detachable manner, so as to permit access to the machinery, part of which it will necessarily hide from view when in place.

Leaving one seat in the tonneau for the occupant, the other seats could be either removed and replaced with specially made hampers, or a large hamper fitting into the vacant space, and extending the height of a man's shoulder when sitting, could be placed upon two seats, leaving a double seat for the occupant and the camp dog or "mascot." This hamper should be divided vertically in three compartments to make the contents "get-able." You probably will not be able to get just the shape of hampers you want at the stores, but any maker of wicker-ware and reed furniture—there are plenty of them in the business directory—will build you any desire pattern for a slight extra charge, if you furnish dimensions and measurements. Thus equipped, your machine will carry two regular side hampers horizontally, two auxiliary placed vertically under them, a fifth—the "emergency" hamper—on the door, and a sixth filling half the inside tonneau space. There is enough variation in the shape of these patterns to permit of your packing your whole outfit in wickerwork and oilcloth—a decided advantage. Tent-poles, spade, and shovels being detachable, you can strap them to the car body in line with the chassis rail after inserting them in cases of heavy oilcloth. The guns and fishing rods, similarly encased, go under a double strap on top of the rear-wheel hampers. There should be room on the tonneau floor for the pneumatic mattress when deflated and folded four times. The tent canvas rolls up snug in a corner, unless you travel "omnibus" style, when you may stow it on the roof. Consign your portable kitchen to the vertical hamper on the left, and your kitchen utensils, etc., to that on the right. Dispose the balance of your kit among the other hampers as already indicated.

For a trip of this kind, a searchlight is almost indispensable, not only for examining the road-bed but for the timely locating of such obstructions and dangers as cannot be detected without it. You may drive along a well-kept country road for miles without mishap, and, when you least expect it, suffer the experience of a friend of mine, whose face was horribly lashed by brushing full speed against a row of low-hanging willows. He was watching the road intently when it happened, and his lamps threw no light on the danger overhead. In some parts the farmers have the cute habit of putting up a rail or a board fence across the road as a warning in case of a broken bridge ahead or similar accidents, and while the "warning" works well enough in the daytime, it becomes a menace to night travel, as such a fence is usually not detected until you are climbing it. A searchlight will enable you to spot the fence in advance, and as you return upon your tracks, you can manipulate the flash left and right to pick out a cross-road or devious route. When two machines are doing the trip together, and cross-roads puzzle you as to the right course to follow, let one machine remain at the crossing while the other goes ahead scouting. The scout can signal "All right—come on" by three flashes of his searchlight, either by revolving it thrice in a circle, by turning it off and on, or by fanning a cap before it.

If you combine the instinct of the sportsman with the touring spirit of the automobilist, it is not at all unlikely that successful camping and hunting and fishing may take you out into the open where roads are not and the chart is a vacant space. Suppose you lose your way in the wilderness, that you have a serious breakdown, that your provisions give out, and starvation faces you. Suppose—for this has occurred more than once—that all this trouble happens under the shadow of a telegraph pole, humming with the busy talk of faraway cities. What wouldn't you give for a chance at that wire for a minute or two? Don't you think it would be just as well to carry along a small Morse instrument, and learn just enough of the code to tell the nearest operator that you are in trouble? Be a little circumspect, however, and don't do it too often, that you may not be mistaken for a "wire-tapper." Also, don't in your hurry and worry forget to pay the tolls for your "steal" at the nearest telegraph office. While you are about it, you may as well supplement your ticker with a modern portable telephone—a miniature pattern of internal 'phone will do—for in many districts the upper wire in the farmers' fences is part of a rural telephone exchange, through which you can call up pretty nearly a whole community—from a team of horses to pull you out of a hole, to the sheriff and his posse and the doctor and his bandages, for automobiling, like all true sport, has a delightful degree of uncertainty.

“So when the roads in places began to resemble a Hackensack meadow struck by a tidal wave . . . and the cold, pitiless rain was trying to extinguish in the boys any remnant of vitality . . . there were lots of cheerful idiots . . . to console them with the opportune advice: ‘You ought to have started a month later.’ ”

FROM HELL GATE TO PORTLAND

ALTHOUGH INDIVIDUAL MOTORISTS OR PROFESSIONAL WRITERS generated many of the earliest writings about the automobile’s potential uses or about the experience of being behind the steering wheel, American automobile manufacturers became increasingly frequent contributors to this growing literature. In a number of instances, they not only sponsored automobile excursions or competitions to demonstrate the power, speed, or resilience of their machines, but they then produced the written record documenting the particular event. Thus, the Oldsmobile Company prepared and distributed a pamphlet profiling a race it sponsored between two of its own cars from New York City to Portland, Oregon, in the summer of 1905 (the 1931 reprint of which is included here). Planned in conjunction with the latter city's Lewis and Clark Exposition and a national Good Roads conference scheduled to take place at the exposition grounds, this expedition represented precisely the kind of event that manufacturers hoped would rivet the attention of potential owners.

Determined no doubt to stir up the maximum public interest, Oldsmobile established challenging conditions for this race against the calendar. While commissioning two experienced professional drivers, Dwight B. Huss and Percy F. Megargel, to pilot the two vehicles involved (and offering the added incentive of a thousand-dollar cash prize for the driver who arrived first in Portland), the company selected two standard seven-horsepower runabouts from its stock and required that their departure from New York be no earlier than the beginning of May, leaving them less than fifty days to reach Portland in order to arrive by the opening of the Good Roads conference. Following a route selected by James W. Abbott, a representative of the federal government's Office of Public Roads, each driver and his single companion had to be prepared for unknown road conditions, mechanical difficulties, and the vagaries of weather and terrain. Despite their frequent reliance upon the Union Pacific Railway's right-of-way to guide them across empty spaces, both parties struggled to keep their bearings. Moreover, once each automobile had crossed the Mississippi River, it had to surmount every challenge from bottomless mud holes and roadless prairies across the Great Plains in Iowa and Nebraska to sage brush–encrusted trails and rock-strewn passes across Wyoming, Idaho, and Oregon, piercing both the Rocky Mountains and the Cascade Range to complete its journey. Both survived the journey, though, reaching Portland within a day of each other, with the wining vehicle (driven by Huss) having arrived after forty-four days in transit.

Incorporating accounts by both drivers with an introduction that provides a context for their travels, *From Hell Gate to Portland* highlights the encounters of cars and drivers with territories as yet unprepared for the automobile. Proposing that "one who follows carefully the story of this race will get a fairly accurate idea of the road conditions of this country, and will be impressed with the need of a concerted good road movement," the author of the introduction directs the reader's attention to the landscapes of the Far West as described by Huss and Megargel. Beyond their comments about the trials and tribulations of the road, however, both men also found much to remark upon about the farms, ranches, homes, and towns scattered all over the region. While crossing the plains of Nebraska, for instance, Megargel notes that "we encountered vast tracts of original prairie land without fencing of any kind, and every few miles we found herds of cattle, usually looked after by one or two cowboys mounted on fiery little ponies." West of Laramie, horse- or mule-drawn "prairie schooners" hauled along the trail. And on many evenings, western hospitality treated these motorists to "right smart" meals ("to use the term generally adopted in the West as an expression of praise"). Following the adventures of Huss and Megargel aboard "Old Scout" and "Old Steady" thus exposed readers to a West that still seemed thoroughly untamed, if not downright wild.

From Hell Gate to Portland

The Story of the Race across the American Continent in Oldsmobile Runabouts, Told by the Men Who Rode and the Man Who Looked On

[Detroit: Oldsmobile Motor Co., 1905; reprinted 1931]

Foreword

While the Lewis & Clark Exposition was drawing the attention of the more or less indifferent East to the golden, romantic shores of the Pacific during the summer just passed, a notice appeared in the automobile publications calling for volunteer drivers to compete in a race across the continent from New York City to the Exposition grounds at Portland, Oregon, for a cash prize of $1,000, the machines to be seven-horse power Oldsmobile Runabouts of standard make, and each driver to be accompanied by one companion.

Hundreds of applications were received. They came by regular mail, by registered mail, by special delivery, by telephone, by telegraph and in person. On May 5, Dwight B. Huss, of Detroit, and Percy F. Megargel, of Buffalo, were selected. Both Huss and Megargel were experienced drivers, having taken part in the New York–St. Louis tour of the previous year and other endurance runs. Huss had made a name for himself by his fine work in the English endurance run of 1903, where he had carried off the gold medal with a four and one-half-horse power curved dash runabout.

Two stock seven horse power runabouts were selected, and before leaving New York a name appropriate to each was selected and conspicuously placed on the familiar curved dash. On May 8, the start was made from New York City, Dwight B. Huss driving "Old Scout" and accompanied by Milford Wigle, of Detroit, while

Percy F. Megargel, driving "Old Steady" was accompanied by Barton Stanchfield, of Lansing, Michigan.

June 20, the opening day of the National Good Roads Convention in Portland, was set for the date of the arrival of the winner. In the following pages are set forth both by word and by picture some of the most interesting incidents of the contest. One who follows carefully the story of this race will get a fairly accurate idea of the road conditions of the country, and will be impressed with the need of a concerted good-road movement. The journey was replete with exciting incidents, the final dash over the Cascades and down Seven-Mile Mountain forming a fitting climax to the undertaking. The winners drove Old Scout triumphantly to the Exposition grounds within the hour set for the opening of the convention, the 4,000 miles having been covered in exactly forty-four days, a most creditable performance, and one which made Huss and Wigle not only the heroes of the Good Roads Convention but of Portland and her visiting thousands.

How the Man Who Watched Viewed It

The plan of a transcontinental race was first proposed by James W. Abbott, at that time special agent for the Rocky Mountain Division of the United States Office of Public Roads. Mr. Abbott was actively interested in the success of the National Good Roads Convention, and the idea of the race appealed to him as a means of drawing the attention of the country to Portland. The route to be traveled was laid out under his direction and advice, and starting with the racers at New York, Mr. Abbott followed them from point to point by train, taking accurate data regarding road conditions and other information which he found valuable in his work.

Writing for the *Automobile*, Mr. Abbott says among other things: Of that vast stream of infatuated Argonauts which in 1849 poured in ever-swelling tide across prairie, plain, desert, and mountain to the new-found gold diggings in California, was one Hosea B. Horn. With beneficent purpose to enlighten those who might follow him through the mysteries and hardships of a then unchartered trail, after he had reached the goal of his pilgrimage, he published a most intensely interesting and valuable little book, which he entitled "Overland Guide from U.S. Indian Sub-Agency at Council Bluffs on the Missouri River to the City of Sacramento, California." In his preface, dated Sept. 1, 1850, he says: "The distance from place to place is accurately shown, and each camping place particularly pointed out, so that the emigrant may know as well in the morning at what point he must camp as he does in the evening, thus saving many a mile's drive over a bad road in the dark. All the mineral and other poisonous waters near the road are carefully pointed out, and the distances from each to pure water given, so that whoever pays attention to it need not lose their teams, as hundreds did this as well as last season, for the want of such a book as this." And so he gives the route with great particularity, distances from point to point, and total distances from "Council Bluffs Agency Ferry, Wheeling, Clark & Co., proprietors of the Ferry," to Sacramento, California.

There is going on today a movement toward the Pacific, involving more people than the gold excitement allured, even when the frenzy was at its height, and destined to be equally as important in epoch-making history. I believe the time to be close at hand when the automobile is to become a factor in this movement, and when information regarding route and actual conditions will be as cordially welcome as was the very opportune little volume here referred to.

The recent transcontinental race was by no means undertaken merely to exploit the merits and virtues of a simple and inexpensive little car. A more important purpose was to bring vividly to public attention a clearer knowledge about all phases of existing transcontinental highways. In the limited space of such an article as this, it is manifestly impracticable to give in minute detail all the information which might be desired, but an effort will be made to cover the subject partly in detail and partly by suggestion of fruitful sources of information.

The goal of the trip was the annual convention of the National Good Roads Association, called to open in the auditorium on the grounds of the Lewis and Clark Centennial Exposition at Portland, Oregon, at 2 P.M., June 21, 1905.

The first question to be decided was the route to be taken. There are many gateways between New York and the Pacific, and it was by no means a simple question to say in advance with minute particularity what line should be traversed to bring the winner to his journey's end within the time allowed.

Our latter-day prophet, Hosea, said in his introduction: "Council Bluffs is the natural crossing of the Missouri river, on the route destined by nature for the great thoroughfare to the Pacific. This was the road selected by Nature's civil engineers, the buffalo and the elk for their western travel. The Indians followed them in the same trail; then the traders, next the settlers came." While Hosea, with pardonable license, may have claimed for the buffalo and the elk an initiative in trailblazing which precedes the dawn of history, it is a remarkable fact that the "civil engineers" who came two decades after Hosea with the iron trail adopted the location of their alleged prototypes. The desire for a railroad line to the Pacific carrying the nation's commerce to the Orient, which had been a fascinating dream for nearly fifty years with the American people, was realized at last, and when the dream came true Hosea's prophecy was fulfilled.

It was clear that the proper route to Portland should cross the Missouri River at Council Bluffs, where splendid steel bridges long since displaced the ferry of Wheeling, Clark & Co., which had been such a source of revenue in those primitive days.

Horn's book mentions eleven ferries across the Mississippi, but from the advertisements which the thrifty author published, it is evident that in his time the principal crossings were at Dubuque,

Davenport, and Burlington. It also seems evident that these three routes converge at Des Moines, from which place there was one main road to the ferry crossing. For the automobile trip, the Davenport crossing was selected, the route followed being practically that shown on the Mendenhall map through Aurora, Geneseo, and Moline, into Rock Island, and crossing through the Government reservation.

The start from New York had been made on May 8, from which date forty-four days would elapse before the opening of the convention. That date for starting was suggested by the writer, assuming that the route to be traversed would be a little in excess of 3500 miles, and that 80 miles a day should be allowed, so as to safely cover all the contingencies of a trip about which there were so many uncertain factors.

On the eighth, ninth, and tenth, climatic conditions were reasonably propitious, and Buffalo was reached far ahead of average schedule time. Then the heavens opened and the floods came down. For more than a thousand miles the roads were just such as history tells us they had in England till long after the reign of Queen Elizabeth. Instead of being discouraged and hopeless over the conditions which this trip developed, let us rather take heart and, seeing how the country roads of England today are like the driveways in a park, let us rather have faith in a time to come, when even Iowa shall see the truth as it is and know that comfort and economy in highways are not incompatible.

Of course, when anything goes wrong there are plenty to say: "You might have known better. Had you been guided by the light of such intelligence as is happily exemplified in us, you might have escaped this pitfall into which you have blundered so heedlessly." So when the roads in places began to resemble a Hackensack meadow struck by a tidal wave, with bays and inlets, capes and islands never found on the maps, and the cold, pitiless rain was trying to extinguish in the boys any remnant of vitality which had survived the trials by immersion in mud and water, there were lots of cheerful idiots, dry and warm themselves, to console them with the opportune advice: "You ought to have started a month later."

This was a subject to which I gave very careful thought and study throughout the entire trip. My conclusion was that no mistake whatever was made in the time of starting, in view of the date fixed for the meeting of the convention in Portland, but that if the trip were not subject to any time limit, it would be better in the average year to defer starting at least until the middle of May. That would allow another week for an Eastern winter to relax its final hold, and for the roads to become settled, dried, smooth and inviting.

In setting the time for a transcontinental trip, the controlling feature which will be ignored only at imminent peril is that great chain of mountains rising far up into British Columbia and running for fifteen hundred miles until it shades down and disappears in the desert of Southern California. Through Oregon and on to the north this is known as the Cascade range, because the mighty Columbia, the father of Northern waters, cut its way through it to the sea, and while passing Mount Hood, one of its majestic, snow-mantled peaks, the river goes merrily tripping and dancing in its gentle fall over the famous Cascades. In California it is known as the Sierra Nevada, the Spanish for Snowy Range, because the snows of heaven fall and gather on it to greater depths than on any other mountains on the continent of commensurate height and latitude. Woe be to the man who presumes to cross this range in an automobile sooner or later than the time when nature is pleased to invite him. This varies in different years.

A fair average date of opening for the Cascades is about June 1, and for the Sierras about July 1. There is generally a storm about the time of the September Equinox, in which snow gathers in great drifts upon the mountaintops along this range. Ordinarily this storm is succeeded by ideal weather. The snow melts away and a sort of Indian summer with autumn tints and golden haze comes to charm the traveler and lull him to unguarded confidence.

Sometimes far into October he can cross the passes on either the Cascades or Sierras with exhilarating delight. And sometimes they close with this equinoctial storm and stay closed, and the traveler, who in presumptuous desperation, should attempt to cross these huge snow banks in an automobile would come to grief, as they do in Arctic regions when winter prematurely shuts them in with ice.

Excepting for this range, any time during the period from the middle of May to November 1 can be selected with warranted assurance for a transcontinental trip in an automobile. We happened to encounter very heavy storms in May. In the latter part of June of this year, there were greater floods still in Nebraska and Iowa.

But if the boys were all right as to time of starting, there was one serious mistake made. In their zeal to make progress, they traveled through storms for which they ought to have laid up. It is an awful hazard to health, vitality, and machinery to try to plow through rain and mud as they did at times, and in my judgment the ultimate resultant of progress was loss.

The road which we intended to take west from Omaha to Granger followed the railroad very closely, always keeping it in sight. The boys pulled out of Omaha on a balmy, beautiful afternoon, with high hopes and cheering prospects. With roads as they expected to find them, Cheyenne 500 miles away, should easily have been reached in three days. There were neither heavy grades nor deep sand to impede progress. In settled weather, with roads dry, good time is just as attainable between Omaha and Cheyenne as between New York and Buffalo. Such good luck was not to be. By noon the next day, they not only found themselves in pouring rain, but they discovered that they were entering a rain belt where the elements had been acting with great freedom for a couple of weeks. It is said to have been the custom on the roads of England during the Middle Ages for the hapless traveler to seek the highest ground as he journeyed across the country, trying to avoid being engulfed altogether. And so it was with the boys. They see-sawed from ridge to ridge, and back and forth across the Platte River. It was no use. The harder they tried, and the more recklessly they defied the mud and rain, the worse things got. Instead of reaching Cheyenne on May 20, as they had expected to do, it was late at night on May 31 when Old Scout reached there, and Old Steady was still a day behind that.

A few miles west of North Platte, the Sand-Hill region of Nebraska is reached. That doesn't mean steep hills, but it means a sandy soil through which water drains more readily than it does through the black prairie soil of the corn belt farther east. North Platte is on the dividing line between the farming country which thrives without irrigation and that where it is a *sine qua non.* When we reached there, Julesburg was a bog hole, and the mud in the roads axle deep for wagons. Men who had lived in that country for thirty years, who appeared to have the fear of God in their hearts and to be not prone to lies, asserted that never before had such rains been known in that section. The innate selfishness of the human heart could never be more typically illustrated. They all persisted in viewing this unprecedented downpour from the standpoint of its effect upon the ranch and the range, and without commiseration for Huss and Megargel.

At North Platte the aboriginal civil engineers of Hosea had exhibited that fallibility in location which has not lacked analogy in the practice of the human species. The trail which they outlined continued to follow the Platte River in its general course for 400 miles to its junction with the Sweetwater, and then it followed the Sweetwater 125 miles farther up the gradual and at least imperceptible slope of the South Pass; and when the very indefinite line had been passed where the waters divide, one half flowing down toward the Atlantic and the other half toward the Pacific, this trail of the buffalo and the savage had led the fur trader down a fork of the Green River for a distance before it again turned to the northwest.

There are no more thrilling pages in American history than those which tell of the trails to the far west. The early movements westward were naturally by water. Men could move themselves and their belongings that way more easily and with more security against the treacherous savage. When Captain Meriwether Lewis and William Clark in 1804 sailed up the Missouri on that perilous mission from President Jefferson, they found that French traders had preceded them for many hundred miles. They sailed on up the Missouri, along the eastern border of what is now the state of Nebraska, through what are now South and North Dakota, and on through the Montana of today well toward its northwestern corner. Then leaving the river after it ceased to be longer navigable, they crossed the Indian's "Shining Mountains," and after almost incredible perils reached the headwaters of a northwestern fork of the Columbia. Finding this impracticable for their purpose, they abandoned it, and, crossing the Bitter Root Mountains, passed over to the head of the Clearwater, which they followed down to the Snake, and that on down to its junction with the main Columbia, and still on down that majestic stream to its mouth, where they found at last the western ocean, which they sought.

At North Platte the river which the old trail followed turns to the northwest, but the railroad follows a more westerly direction, and soon after leaving Cheyenne crosses the front range of the Rockies by a grade naturally very easy and now made extremely light by a tunnel. The ease of this pass is apparent from the fact that it took the boys less than five hours to make the nearly sixty miles across it and down to the town of Laramie on the plain at its feet. Although Cheyenne is 6,050 feet above sea level, the rise toward it is so gradual as to be hardly perceptible, even from the train.

The arrival of Old Scout at the door of the Administration Building of the exposition and the delivery by Huss to President H. W. Goode of the letter from Manager Melville E. Stone, just on the minute set for the opening of the convention, was one of the most spectacular incidents which ever came under my observation.

It was the first automobile that ever crossed the Cascades to Portland. Was it not as important an epoch in the history of Oregon as the arrival of Hunt at Astoria already alluded to?

A mighty transformation scene is being enacted in the Northwest. The people are learning a little about it through this beautiful Lewis and Clark Exposition. That the automobile will be strictly in it as a factor, who will deny?

How Huss Tells It

"It didn't worry me much, at the time, that exciting ride down Seven-Mile Mountain in our descent of the Cascades, when a slip or the loss of control of Old Scout meant a plunge down hundreds of feet to almost certain death, nor did, for that matter, the thousand and one incidents and accidents of the 4000 miles of almost unknown roads, but to write about it, that's a different proposition.

"I can get up a good case of worry just at the thought. Megargel now, is up to this sort of thing. He knows how to make you see things by the use of his pen. Wigle and I saw things all right, and did a few, but we were pretty busy most of the time with our minds, pretty intent cutting down the miles and avoiding the unexpected, but if you insist on our story, you will have to hear it in the only way I can tell it—the way it happened.

"When we left New York City on May 8, at 9:30, on a bright Monday morning, our spirits were high, and the way looked easy ahead. In fact, the way through New York and pretty well into Ohio was easy. It was not until we had left Omaha behind that Wigle and I began to realize what a trip across the American continent means.

"The drive to Chicago, which was made in seven days, was a familiar one to me, as I had covered the same route last year with the St. Louis tourists. A two weeks' rain just before we crossed Illinois, Iowa and Nebraska, made the roads of those states soft and sticky beyond description. Only those who have driven over the 'Gumbo' roads after a rain can understand the difficulties we encountered.

"We rode in mud up to the hubs at times, and I have seen the wheels many a time with so much 'Gumbo' sticking to them that they would weigh 250 to 300 pounds each. All through these states, and in fact until we reached Omaha, Old Scout and Old Steady stuck pretty well together, neither one caring to have the other get very far out of sight.

"I am not going to try to describe that fight through the mud belt—one continuous nightmare of mud as it appears looking back now. On the trip to Omaha both machines had carried as light baggage as possible, each having about 200 pounds' weight aboard besides the drivers. At Omaha we equipped for the wilder country ahead, taking on extra tanks for desert driving, sand tires, firearms, and cooking utensils, all of which increased the weight materially, so that when the machines left Omaha, each had a load of practically four full grown persons. The farther west we traveled the more interesting grew the country. On May 31 we reached Archer, eight miles from Cheyenne, at 8:30 in the evening, and were met by an enthusiastic crowd of automobilists. We reached Cheyenne at 10 o'clock. If you had seen that procession come into town, you would have smiled. You would have seen Old Scout towing another car, besides carrying two passengers in each rig.

"We will not mention the name of the car, because it might cause some hard feelings. The next night we spent at Laramie, which we left in the morning in company with a White steamer bound for Goldsmith. We left the town at 8 A.M., taking a northwesterly course. Then we ran up against a small river.

"The only thing to do was to cross, so Old Scout took a flying leap and managed to get over, but not so with the steamer, as she stopped in the middle and her fires went out. Rope and tackle were used and in an hour she was on dry land. In the next four hours we had forded four streams. We got as far as Medicine Bow at 7 o'clock, and just outside of the village we ran into the first sinkhole on the trip, and Old Scout dropped almost out of sight.

"We got a man to help us out, and with the aid of our tackle got on land just as darkness overtook us. I hired a man to watch the car and Wigle and I went back to the village to bed. Old Scout stayed out in the cold. We left Medicine Bow next morning at 4:30, thinking we would make a long run that day. At 1:30 o'clock we were at a small station on the Union Pacific, just 35 miles from our morning start. I don't want to say much about the roads between these points, because it takes more than a pen to describe them. I don't know how Old Scout ever lived through it, but she did. We forded five big creeks, driving over rocks and stones and so much sage brush that Old Scout's radiator looked like a badly twisted piece of tin. At last we found the railroad, and we both swore to stick to the Union Pacific the rest of the trip. The everlasting sage brush was one of the worst nuisances we had to contend with.

"We left Sage Tuesday morning bright and early, after having had a good night's sleep at the section boss's house. We took the main road along the railroad and drove about five miles, when the road left the railroad and started off through the sage brush. As we could see no other road, we were sure we had the right one. We drove two hours and landed up against a large ranch down between some mountains.

"We asked the distance to Cokeville and found we were farther away than when we left Sage. We were both very much disgusted, as we had to go back over the same trail to the railroad. After skirmishing around in the sage brush for some time, we found the tracks and arrived in Cokeville at noon, having covered 50 miles, and going only 15 in the right direction. We had dinner and left for Soda Springs.

"We chased up and down hill all the afternoon, and managed to get to Soda Springs at 7 o'clock at night, covering about 75 miles. We left Soda Springs at 6:30 Wednesday morning and got nearly to McCammon, where we found a bridge out and a river too deep to ford. We had to turn back, and after going through several lanes, crossing fields of sage brush, and fording two creeks, we found a bridge and crossed at the river.

"It was in making this detour that Old Scout had a narrow escape. We were on a very steep hill—so steep in fact, that it was impossible to hold the car—and we shot down the hill and over a 12-foot embankment into a ditch. Our good luck was that the ditch was dry. Wigle and I had a hard time getting the car out, and were surprised to find it still hanging together. The front axle was so badly bent that the wheels were on a slant of fifteen degrees. We drove 30 miles in that condition to Pocatello, where we spent part of the night and Wednesday forenoon getting things straightened. We found we had one advantage with our bent axle—the wheels fitted the 60-inch track, while before, ours being 56, would not.

"We left Pocatello at 2:30 Thursday afternoon and drove to Ross Forks, the roads being very good. After leaving here, we had gone but a short distance before we were hub deep in the sand, and Old Scout gave a few grunts and stopped. As we had carried sand tires, we thought this was a good chance to test their efficiency. After the tires were on, we started and the way Old Scout performed with them was a wonder. We had six miles to go and were only 30 minutes going. We arrived in Blackfoot at 6 and decided to stay all night, as the next station was 60 miles across the Great Snake river desert.

"On June 10 we pulled into Boise, Idaho, at 4:30 in the afternoon, after a pleasant ride of 90 miles. The roads were an improvement, and really were the best we had had since leaving Chicago. We were met by a big delegation headed by a Mrs. Taylor, and were escorted into town. That wasn't enough—they gave us a banquet and the keys to the city. The banquet was most enjoyable. Three days before, we were in a cloudburst and as a result of the drenching, I suffered from a severe cold. And as we appeared to have a safe lead on Old Steady, who we lost shortly after leaving Omaha, we decided to rest here a day or two.

"After we left Boise, I felt in good fighting trim, and on June 15 we reached Ontario, Oregon. Here we were met by James W. Abbott, the good-roads man, who had started from New York at the same time we did, and had headed us off at difference points by railway. He gave us all the information possible regarding the

Oregon roads, and it was meager to say the least. The day before we reached Ontario, a large touring car arrived from Portland, having come up the Dalles 100 miles by boat, there being no road that way.

"The chauffeur reported incredibly bad roads until he struck the one we were to follow. From that point he came along with little trouble. This encouraged us, and we left for Burns in high spirits. As a matter of fact, we found the roads through Idaho and Oregon the best west of Chicago. The run across Oregon was an exciting one, and on the Cascades we encountered one or two experiences thrilling enough to last a lifetime.

"It was on Monday afternoon when we began the descent of the Cascades following the Santiam road, which necessitated the descent of Seven Mile Mountain. So rapid was the descent that it was impossible to hold the car. All brakes were set, the rear wheels were sliding, and Wigle, who was holding to the rear, was dragged nearly seven miles. I held my breath as well as the steering lever, and expected every minute to be dashed down into the canyon several hundred feet below. This was by far the most exciting adventure of our trip.

"Tuesday night was spent at Lebanon, and Wednesday morning we reached Oregon City, where we were met by a delegation of local autoists, representing the Portland Automobile club, under whose escort we ran into Portland, reaching there at exactly two minutes to one, just one hour before the opening of the National Good Roads Convention, to which I had been appointed delegate by Governor [Fred M.] Warner, of Michigan. Our reception was wildly exciting, and the streets were packed with cheering people. We were taken to the Portland club for lunch and then to the exposition grounds, where I delivered to President H. W. Goode of the exposition the message which I brought from Manager Melville E. Stone, of the Associated Press. We were then escorted to the convention hall, where I presented my credentials as a delegate, and the message from Mr. Stone was read. It was as follows:

New York, May 5, 1905.

Hon. H. W. Goode, President Lewis & Clark Centennial Exposition, Portland, Ore.:

Dear Sir—I have a peculiar pleasure in complying with a request that I send you a greeting, to be conveyed by automobile across the continent.

The century which has just passed was chiefly notable as the century which developed inter-communication. It was the century out of which came the ocean steamship, the railway, the telegraph, the cable, the telephone, wireless telegraphy, rotary and perfecting printing presses, stereotyping, news gathering associations and the newspapers.

But nothing could better illustrate the progress of 100 years than a comparison of this new expedition by a twentieth century motor car from the Atlantic seaboard to the land 'where rolls the Oregon,' with that other expedition of Lewis and Clark, which meant so much for our common country and the world's civilization.

With all good wishes, I am sincerely yours (signed)
Melville E. Stone.

"After the reading of the message I was called upon for a speech, which was a harder job possibly than this one. Like most trying things, I felt better after it was over, and our first day in Portland closed with a triumphal parade through the streets and exposition grounds of the Portland automobile club, headed by Old Scout. We went to bed that night mightily pleased with ourselves for having made the first automobile trip across the continent from the Atlantic to the Pacific, and for having made it in the very creditable time of 44 days, or 40 days of actual running time."

As Megargel Tells It

Leaving Albany at 7 o'clock on the morning of May 9, we had anticipated getting into Syracuse in ample time for dinner, after lunching at Utica. It had rained in the night harder than we had supposed, and the roads were full of mud and water. Owing to the mud guards having been stripped from both Old Steady and Old

Scout, we were soon covered from head to foot with mire, while our baggage and supplies, strapped on the rear deck, were almost unrecognizable when Syracuse was finally reached.

In the tour to St. Louis last summer, the tourists encountered just one day of rain and mud and the schedule for that one day was about seventy miles. Our run from Albany to Syracuse was nearly three times that distance and the mud was unusually deep, yet the way those two little seven-horse power runabouts plowed through on high speed surprised us all.

Huss and Wigle beat us into Syracuse, and we found them at the Yates when we pulled in, their car, Old Scout, being washed at a local garage.

We witnessed two very fine exhibitions of horsemanship that went a long way toward making up for some of the very bad driving we had been encountering ever since leaving New York. In the first instance, a young girl was driving two horses hitched to a milk wagon. When the animals commenced to balk at the sight of the automobile, she stood up in the wagon and the way she laid on the whip left the horses no room to doubt that they were handled by a master. The result was that they passed our runabout without further misbehavior.

In the other case, a man was trying out a colt. The animal attempted to back up, but the whip was used so vigorously that he changed his mind and went past the car. We met one team that was driven by a drunken man, and also passed the usual number of drivers who, upon catching a glimpse of the automobile, turned into the plowed field.

All four overlanders are so sunburned already that they can scarcely wear collars or gloves.

Leaving Syracuse at 6 A.M., Wednesday, May 10, Old Steady resumed its way westward, following Old Scout, which Huss had managed to get out of the garage some thirty minutes earlier.

Both cars got lost in the swamps, although they were on different roads, and they got to Rochester about the same time, Huss coming in by way of East Avenue and our little car by way of Monroe Avenue. Both crews took dinner together at the Whitcomb grill and started for Buffalo at the same time.

The engine of Old Scout seemed to run a little better than mine, and Huss steadily drew away until a long freight train coming between us separated us for the balance of the day. Huss managed to get lost again, and we arrived at Jayne's garage, on Main Street, Buffalo, some thirty minutes before Old Scout. W. G. Jaynes, who handles the Olds in Buffalo, had a crowd of automobilists awaiting us and a supper at the hotel followed.

Huss, in Old Scout, led us out of Buffalo by about ten minutes. As usual, both crews lost themselves and traveled many more miles than were necessary. In fact, after making numerous turns, Old Steady struck a section of the country where automobiles appeared to be unknown. A small boy on his way to school, whom we stopped to ask about the road, was frightened and commenced to cry violently. Soon after, a girl, after taking one look at the begoggled, mud-covered tourists, gave a yell and started down the road at top speed. When she saw we were overtaking her, she made for the side fields, falling several times before she finally convinced herself that we were not really after her. The next youth we met dived bodily through a barbed wire fence and streaked across the fields at top speed.

Both cars arrived in Erie at about the same time, Old Steady suffering from a punctured tire. It rained hard before dinner was finished, and we donned rubber coats and put on the tire chains.

An early start on May 12 enabled us to cut down Old Steady's lead to such an extent that we overtook Huss loading up with gasoline at the Ohio Oldsmobile Co. garage in Cleveland.

The roads from Cleveland—yes, from Conneaut—to Clyde were in terrible shape—low speed a large part of the way and numerous mud puddles of uncertain depth to ford. At Bellevue water was flowing on the city pavement level with the curbs, and on the country roads, especially in the lowlands, the wheeling was most difficult. Hundreds of acres that hard-toiling farmers had plowed and planted were immersed under several feet of water, and at one point we ran a quarter of a mile without seeing the road at all, the water in some places coming above our axles.

Both cars together once more on May 17, and both crews quartered at the same hotel, after the shortest day's mileage since leaving New York, and the hardest work. Illinois mud, even when taken at a racing gait, brought our mileage down to 64 miles for the day, and we worked tooth and nail ever since 5 A.M. It is now 10:30 P.M., and we have just arrived in Geneseo.

Old Steady has run like a top all day—never missed an explosion, and the way she pulled Stanchfield and myself through mud that hid the hubs from view on more than one occasion, has caused the Oldsmobile to rise greatly in my esteem. And with one quarter of the distance between Portland and New York covered, and both cars on even terms, it is still anybody's race.

Since leaving Chicago we feel that we are getting into western country, and the horses we meet now are only half broken as a rule and cut up badly upon sighting and automobile, bucking and kicking being indulged in to a considerable extent.

The mud all day had been that sticky, thick, black mud that only Illinois and Missouri can boast of. To get through it, we were obliged on several occasions to use block and tackle. The water in our tank boiled, but the engine never faltered, although every one of the four wheels was so stuck up with mud as to render the spokes invisible. The cars and occupants were so covered with mud when we arrived here tonight that we were hardly recognizable.

We ran into Davenport today, May 18, in time for dinner, and found an enthusiastic crowd of automobilists, including a number of ladies, awaiting our arrival. We were escorted from Moline across the Mississippi river into Davenport, and after refilling our tanks, washing the mud off the radiators, and partaking of a hearty luncheon at the restaurant kept by Mr. Robertson, secretary of the Davenport Automobile Club, we left town under escort.

This morning's run was one of the most difficult we have yet undertaken. It was through the lowland along the banks of the Rock River, the waters of which frequently overflowed, and sometimes for long distances the roadbed would be covered with water, to what depth we could only guess. At one stage of the morning's trip the water flowed into the car and we got our feet wet, yet the engine never missed a stroke. Now the question we are asking each other is, how could this happen without wetting our carburetor? The apron under the car is the only thing we can think of that saved us from getting stranded.

Immediately upon getting into Iowa, the black, sticky mud that had been clinging to our tires and ourselves disappeared, and a yellow clay soil composed the roadbed. It was hard and made pretty rough going, but we were able to use our high speed again, and that readily compensated us for the jolting we received.

We found a bridge down this afternoon, and were obliged to resort to block and tackle to get Old Steady back in the road.

We have just arrived at the hotel here after passing entirely through the town, and half a mile into the country, without knowing we had come to Brooklyn.

All day May 19, the wheeling has been most difficult, as the roads were badly cut up when soft and have since hardened, with the ruts deep and narrow, and the soil for the most part is of yellow clay. We fell behind about an hour today, owing to our radiator coils being so covered with mud that our cooling apparatus failed to perform its work. We got under the car, and with screwdriver worked industriously picking the mud from the pipe for more than sixty minutes. During this time Old Scout secured a lead of some fifteen miles.

The inhabitants all through this section are watching the race with interest, and take pains to inform the occupants of the rear car just how far in advance the other machine is, as we pass through their towns. The horses all through Iowa cut up badly upon the approach of an automobile. One old farmer with long whiskers of the Populist variety, for whom we had stopped our car to get his horse and mule combination past, was highly indignant at "an automobile from New York being on his road," as he termed it. "Do you know the law in this state compels you fellows to run your machine into the field until we can pass by?" said whiskers. When we informed him we knew of no such law, and that our automobile was not afraid of his team, even if they were scarecrows, he wanted to "lick the two of us," as he put it. We found several bridges down today, and had to resort to our block and tackle in hauling Old Steady through the muddy river beds.

Wherever we stop our car, it is at once surrounded by an enthusiastic crowd of spectators who continue to stare at the mud-stained, battered Oldsmobile, until we eventually haul out of town. One motherly old woman who passed us as we were working on our car by the roadside exclaimed: "You poor fellows, I am awfully sorry for you." Despite our hard trip, both Stanchfield and myself are enjoying excellent health. In fact, I think I have gained about three pounds on the trip thus far, and as our car left New York carrying some forty pounds more live weight than our rival, if this increase keeps on we shall be sadly handicapped by the time Portland is reached. Stanchfield reminds me as I write this that we still have the desert to cross.

Seventy-two miles was the best we could make today, May 20, and the going was the hardest yet. The roads are full of ruts made by narrow wagon tires cutting deep into the roadbed when the ground is soft. Our tires suffered more from the run today than during all the 1500 miles previously traveled. The front tires are now worn through both rubber and canvas on either side, and our rear set has fared little better. Anyone who has ridden a few miles over roughly cut-up roads can imagine what seventy-odd miles of such riding will do to tires, machine, and tourists. We trailed Old Scout all the morning, caught them at noon, and passed them when one of their rear tires went flat some miles out of Des Moines.

One of the worst mud holes thus far encountered was the Skunk River bottoms, several miles east of Altoona. Huss and I agreed to help each other across, or neither of us would have ever reached the other side. First, one car would plunge into the water and mud until stuck, then we would rig our blocks and tackle, attach it to the car axle and bring the other end back to the car still on dry land. By all of us pushing, and the free car towing, we managed to work our way across a swamp that everyone told us was impassable. All of us worked in water and mud nearly waist deep. My rubber boots were not nearly high enough to escape wet feet, as the water simply poured in over the tops, and when I reached Des Moines, I was able to pour several quarts out of each boot after nearly an hour's work in pulling the boots off. The other boys, clad in low shoes and leggings, made no effort to escape with dry feet, and all were soaked within a few minutes. The water was so deep that at one time all of the four wheels were out of sight, and a stream flowed freely through the flooring of the wagon, soaking everything, filling the carburetor with water and short circuiting the battery.

Yesterday, May 23, when running into Omaha, we encountered for the first time a road machine at work on the Iowa roads. Road machines in the west differ from those used in the east; this machine, instead of being hauled by two or four horses, was drawn by no less than sixteen. What is true of road machines is also true of farming implements. In the west the farmer does not follow a single furrow plow to which one or two horses are attached, but sits on a big four- to six-furrow implement to which from four to eight horses are hitched. It is nothing new to see single fields of 100 acres, and they are often only one of numerous such fields comprised in an Iowa or Nebraska farm.

Iowa seems to be a great horse- and cattle-raising country. Each farmer raises from twenty to a hundred horses a year and several times that many head of cattle, while pigs are too numerous to mention. There are hundreds, yes, thousands of pigs on every farm, I believe. These droves of ham and pork chops occasionally block the road so that we are obliged to slacken speed and blow the horn for a long distance before we can get a clear road.

That ill feeling against automobilists that one encounters so frequently among the farmers in the east is lacking out here, and every farmer met with is your friend, no matter how badly you scare his horses or how much damage his nag does before you finally get past him on the road. There is no difference, however, in the nature of the horses. Some do not even prick up their ears at the approach of our machine, while together go through a series of rearing, kicking, and bucking that would do credit to a Wild West show. In passing horses on the road we have to be extremely careful, as several have kicked most viciously at our car and its occupants.

We laid over here in Omaha today to purchase such supplies as were deemed necessary for the second 2000 miles of our tour. The cars were washed and the wiring gone over, arrangements were made with a laundry for a relay of clean clothing, maps were studied carefully again, and such information collected from those who have been over part of our trail as we thought would prove valuable in reaching our destination.

Both crews have provided themselves with firearms, but should we encounter any hostile foe, whether he be wild animal or bad man, the others will have to be able to shoot straighter than I can with the big 38-calibre revolver I purchased for the trip.

It has been almost impossible to secure any accurate information concerning roads ahead of us. We spent the night of May 26 at Palmer, Nebraska, and before going to bed located Old Scout at Grand Island, a point equally far west but on the main line of the Union Pacific, while we were on a little branch line used mostly for shipping cattle and hogs.

Before reaching Grand Island, we were unfortunate enough to crash through a bridge, part of which has been washed away. The fall broke both side springs of our car, the strut rod on the front axle, and bent both the front and rear axles. Stanchfield succeeded in making temporary repairs which enabled us to travel some fifteen miles into town, where much valuable time was lost getting Old Steady into shape again.

We left Grand Island about daylight on the morning of May 28, with the rival car about forty miles ahead. After industriously plugging along all day, we reached Kearney at five o'clock in the afternoon, and spent the night. We took advantage of this stop to readjust our tire chains, and, getting an early start on Monday, we headed for Cozad, which place we finally reached about 8:30 in the evening, having passed through mud holes, buffalo wallows, and alkali pits that seemed impossible for any automobile to force its way through.

Men and women encountered in this part of the country are all good horse drivers, and although the animals they drive are as a rule only half broken and have never seen an automobile before, they seldom take to the cross roads or cornfields at the sight of our machine, as did many of the farmers we met in the east. We meet many people riding horseback—men, women, boys, and girls—all riding astride. I have not seen a side saddle since leaving Chicago, though I have seen many women riding.

Game is very abundant all through Nebraska, jack rabbits and cottontails being seen by the score, while quail, wild doves, prairie chickens, and many large birds with which I am not familiar are found in numbers. As we go westward, the little square wooden houses are becoming scarce, and those of sun-dried brick are taking their places.

Leaving Cozad, we encountered vast tracts of original prairie land without fencing of any kind, and every few miles we found herds of cattle, usually looked after by one or two cowboys mounted on fiery little ponies. The riders, as a rule, rather enjoy the antics of their animals as they buck and pitch at the sight of the automobile, and wave to us gaily as we pass them. The ranchmen all treat us well, and when a stop is made for adjustment or oiling, they flock around us in numbers if a ranch happens to be in sight. Good hotels are very scarce in this section.

Nebraska is a great place for snakes, and wolves are also very plentiful. When we were at Lodge Pole, on Wednesday night, a farmer living in the hills twenty miles to the north came in and reported the loss by gray wolves, of eighteen head of cattle and two horses. The barking of coyotes kept us awake all that night; it was a distinctly new sound to me, and I have not yet become accustomed to it. I killed my first rattlesnake just before reaching Lodge Pole. He was a whopper, measuring more than six feet, and having seven buttons to his rattle. The Stone hotel at this little place was kept by a former resident of New York State, and it is needless to say that he put himself out to look after our wants. In our long run from Lodge Pole to Cheyenne, a distance of 140 miles, we passed through six towns, three of which boasted a population of less than twenty-five persons, and the largest village encountered was Sydney, with some 900 inhabitants. We repeatedly ran through prairie dog towns. In fact, about every five miles we would strike one of these dog villages, comprised of from two to five hundred mounds. The dogs would congregate on the tops of their houses until Old Steady would be almost upon them, when they would scamper down into the regions below.

Gasoline has commenced to come pretty high, while the quality goes in the opposite direction. There was a time in Ohio when we could get fuel at 15 and 18 cents a gallon. Now it is 30 to 35 cents a gallon, and every hundred miles farther west it is reported as being a few cents more. Water, too, is a very scarce commodity, and it is sometimes ten miles before we come to a well or a stream—quite a contrast to our run through Illinois, Iowa, and eastern Nebraska, when we ran day after day with the water up to our hubs.

For several days we have been wearing our revolvers in plain sight, with our belts bristling with cartridges, as do many riders we meet along the road.

We arrived at Laramie, Wyoming, Friday, June 2, thus reaching the summit of the Pacific Slope. Snow-covered mountains were in plain view, and the wind coming from their direction very strongly reminded us of the icy blasts encountered on the streets of Buffalo or Rochester on a winter's day when the wind is blowing off the lake. The soil here is sandy, with long stretches of small gravel, which would make most excellent roads if there was enough travel to grind it down. The ranches of Wyoming are not so pretentious as those in Nebraska; the buildings are not nearly so large nor so well constructed.

Leaving Laramie, we passed many parties traveling in prairie schooners to and from the east. These schooners, usually a single wagon drawn by two or four horses or mules, with one or two saddle ponies and a cow tied behind, are visible for miles, their big white canvas bow tops glistening in the sunshine, and we often pass as many as half a dozen of them traveling together.

We spent Saturday night, June 3, at Terry Fee ranch, and left Sunday morning for Elk Mountain. Several hours were lost pulling our car out of a creek which we had attempted to ford but which, too late, we found too deep. However, we reached Elk Mountain Sunday night.

Since getting up into the mountains, I had wondered how so much snow could remain on the ground, but about ten miles out of Elk Mountain I no longer wondered, for we ran into as fierce a snowstorm as one experiences in the east in mid-winter. It lasted only for a few moments, but we were not prepared for snowstorms, and with the wind whistling around our heads and the snow blowing in flurries about us, we felt the cold keenly.

Sage brush was about the only thing we could see today, and this morning we struck an unusually large brush, which, catching in the radiator, tore one of the copper pipes in two. Luckily, we carried some pieces of small hose, which enabled us to make temporary repairs.

It was almost impossible to follow the trail after leaving Elk Mountain, and we lost it once or twice. Finally, however, we succeeded in working our way out of the mountain wilderness, sticking to the tracks of the Union Pacific until we reached the coal-mining town of Hanna, a place of about 1000 inhabitants, one hotel, several saloons, and two or three stores. Here we replenished our supply of gasoline, paying 45 cents a gallon.

From Hanna to Rawlins, a distance of about forty miles, the traveling is very good as a rule, and when we finally reached Rawlins, we were most agreeably surprised to find in the Ferris Hotel a modern building, well equipped, and supplying an excellent table. Once more we are occupying a room with connecting bath, and, having removed the alkali dust, both Stanchfield and I feel civilized again.

From the best reports, our rival, Old Scout, is about 100 miles in the lead.

Misfortune seemed to attend Old Steady after leaving Rawlins, and her progress toward the Land of the Setting Sun depended solely upon the efforts of one man—the writer—and his continued good health. Poor Stanchfield collapsed with mountain fever at Diamondville on June 10, and we had to put him to bed in the Daly hotel. He began to feel ill at Opal, but as there was no doctor there and no fit hotel accommodations, we kept on, Stanchfield riding on the baggage on the rear of the car, wrapped in all the rubber coats we had. When we reached Diamondville, he could stand it no longer, and, after getting him to bed, I spent the rest of the day looking up a doctor. I finally managed to catch one at Kemerer, ten miles distant, and brought him to Diamondville in Old Steady. He was one of those nervous little men filled with his own importance, and knowing it all at a glance. He looked "Bart" over, prescribed a hot bath, hot lemonade, plenty of blankets, and no air in the room. Then he said his bill was $10, and wanted to know who was going to pay it. An automobilist is looked upon as an easy mark in the far west, just as he is in other places.

Stanchfield has a bad attack of mountain fever (we are nearly 8000 feet above the sea level here), aches in every bone and muscle, has a burning fever with intermittent cold chills, and was most miserable when I left him, to push on alone. The fever has not bothered me yet, but I shall breathe easier after passing Fossil, for from there down the altitude lessens with almost every mile.

After leaving Rawlins, where my last letter was written, on the morning of June 6, we had to return to that town and spend the night there as a penalty for our own thoughtlessness. Ever since leaving New York, we had been using No. 4 Mobiloil for both cylinder and transmission, with excellent results, but we neglected to stop at the railroad station in Laramie for the supply shipped there, and, running short of oil, we bought a small quantity of so-called gas-engine oil at a store. We filled both the cylinder reservoir and the transmission. When we reached Rawlins, we received a consignment of Mobiloil, and, unthinkingly, poured it on top of the other. We pulled out of Rawlins the next morning at a good rate of speed, everything working finely, but when we had gone about five miles, the car faltered and stopped. When we tried to start the engine, we found the cylinder stuck, and with visions of a ruined cylinder and other complications, we took off the cover of the crank case. When the two oils mixed, they had formed a paint-like solution that the heat of the cylinder transformed into a hardened, sticky gum, and as the piston of an Oldsmobile fits the cylinder within 3/1000 of an inch, the coating of gummed oil soon stuck the piston.

Well, I walked back five miles across the cactus plains to Rawlins, hired a team, and went back for Old Steady. We worked most of Tuesday night, and until 10 o'clock Wednesday morning cleaning out the engine. Gasoline, kerosene, and lye had no effect, and not until we resorted to muriatic acid would the gum dissolve.

Stanchfield showed some ingenuity in fixing a piece of sheet-iron from the front axle to the rear part of the radiator pipes to protect the radiator from the sage brush and greasewood bushes, which the car is obliged to straddle continually on the trail.

After leaving Rawlins, we struck into what is known as the Great American Desert—a stretch of sandy country in which absolutely nothing can grow except sage brush, greasewood, and cactus. There were no ranches, cattle, or horses for many miles westward, and in fact, hardly a living thing but jack-rabbits, prairie dogs, and rattle-snakes. Water is very scarce there, and long lines of tank cars stand on the sidings of the Union Pacific, and when the water supply of one of the infrequent small towns along the railroad gives out, these cars are sent to a neighboring town to borrow.

Despite the hard going, we got to Point of Rocks, Sweetwater county, at 9:30 P.M., having covered the 100 miles from Rawlins sine 10:30 A.M. For the last twenty miles we had to resort to our sand tires to make any progress at all. Without them, the rear wheels would sink to the axles in the soft white and red sand.

The population was exceedingly sparse, the various sidings, all of which bear names, having not more than three inhabitants each, and the larger settlements a maximum of twenty-five. Our bunk Wednesday night was in the Union Pacific freight house. We had ham and eggs for supper; in fact, our meals at every stopping point for the last 400 miles had been ham and eggs. We got to Granger, in Sweetwater county, on June 8, just one month from the day we left New York on a trip we expected to accomplish in thirty days, and still we were 1000 miles from Portland. Had the weather been at all favorable, I think we could have made the run in one month.

Last Friday, June 9, we got caught in a storm such as occurs only in the Rocky Mountain districts. Suddenly the sky grew black, then we had thunder and lightning, followed by such a terrific hailstorm that both of us crawled under the car in the mud to save ourselves from the chunks of ice nearly two inches in diameter that descended in torrents. After the ground was covered about two inches deep with hail, it commenced to rain, and after every clap of thunder the amount of water coming down seemed to double in volume. We had discarded our tire chains for the sand tires to cross this section. We did the best we could with rope, but every little rivulet had been transformed into a raging mountain stream, and the first one we attempted to run engulfed Old Steady and pretty nearly swallowed up the crew. We half waded and half swam to the shore, leaving the car with just the top of the seat above water. For some hours we waited for the storm to abate, but the longer we waited the higher the water rose.

Sighting a sheep ranch in the distance, we walked to it. At first the place appeared to be deserted. The house, a long, low, log structure, chinked with mud, was occupied by pigs, chickens and lambs; the dooryard was one of the foulest smelling places I have ever been in, and everything about the place was filthy to an extent one could hardly conceive. Eventually we found the owner, Lone John, in the barn, with more pigs, chickens, sheep and a team of his broncos.

He seemed glad to see us, as company is scarce in this part of the world, and immediately commenced to tell us of his troubles, which were numerous. He was at war with several of his neighbors, and kept a loaded gun at hand at all times. He had just been released for cutting open the head of one of his neighbors with an axe, and he regretted the fact that he had not killed the man. Despite his grievances, he willingly threw the harness on his horses, and telling us where we would find the wagon, and to use his team as we saw fit, went out to round up his flock of about 500 sheep and about half that number of lambs. We drove the broncos down to our stranded machine, and, attaching a line, soon pulled it out of that creek, and through four others before we got it to the ranch.

The Lava Mountains of Eastern Idaho seemed to swarm with eagles and other large birds. Today I counted at least twenty eagles, some of them so tame they would sit on the ground not twenty paces from the road while Old Steady thundered past with its muffler wide open. There is a law protecting eagles, and the birds seem to know it.

The different altitudes did not affect me until nearing Soda Springs, when, after pumping up one of our tires, I suffered from a violent bleeding of the nose. The slightest exertion causes a person to pant violently, while harder work causes one not accustomed to the mountains to bleed at the nose, mouth, and ears. The mountain peaks around us are all snow-capped, and every few miles I pass the remains of huge winter snowdrifts, which even now are many feet deep. The houses are few and far between, and are usually constructed of logs filled in between the cracks with mortar or dried mud. The roofs of the houses and stables are covered with long poles, straw, and mud. They nearly all leak to some extent when it rains, but are effective in keeping off the sun's scorching rays.

The scenery along the route from Soda Springs to McCammon was grand. Massive rocks and high piles of lava greeted the eye on all sides, while the trail ran along through a narrow pass between overhanging mountain peaks. Snow covered the higher points, and

I occasionally ran across a drift alongside the road. A number of sheep outfits, immigrant wagons, and considerable cattle were frequently passed. Irrigating ditches were frequently forded. Prices on all articles of commerce are high in this section and the store houses carry everything from a paper of pins to a coffin. The storekeeper usually is the undertaker and hotelkeeper, and on the side runs a saloon in which slot machines, faro, and card games are an important factor in figuring up the day's profit.

I met my first group of Indians Tuesday. They were in two wagons, and rode up while I was at dinner. A big six-footer drove each wagon, while a number of squaws occupied the rear seats. Inquiry revealed the fact that there is a large Indian reservation in the town of Blackfoot, a few miles north of Pocatello, from which the wandering braves and squaws roam at large over that section of Idaho. They are considered perfectly harmless, but are the greatest thieves to be found on earth, and the man stealing the most is regarded as the bravest Indian. We reached Pocatello Wednesday night. The run from McCammon was short but through a wild and mountainous region of the most picturesque description. Prospectors are at work on almost every mountain range, and some of them are reported to be "making good." Curious holes in the hillside, not much larger than badger or rabbit holes, show where gold seekers have dug in the ground in their frantic search for nature's treasures, while deserted villages, with many substantial houses, now the homes of small animals and snakes, mark the place where formerly men dug daily for gold. The rocks are mostly of a lava nature, and are very hard on pneumatic tires.

This entire section is watered and made fertile, that is, such farms as are fertile, by means of irrigation. Companies of farmers or ranchers are formed, and each man assessed a certain sum which he is allowed to work out with men and teams. In bringing these canals and ditches across the roads and trails, no attempt is made to bridge them, and, as a consequence, it is always a case of ford. The water is generally swift and the bottom uncertain, making it rather treacherous fording for Old Steady with its eight-inch clearance.

We pulled into Cottonwood tonight at 9:30, having made an even hundred miles across the desert. We had many misgivings when we left Blackfoot this morning, as we were informed that for forty miles we would meet neither man, beast nor water. We, however, passed two immigrant wagons in the first forty miles, scared up a herd of antelope, got two shots at a mountain lion, killed an eight-foot rattle-snake, and saw prairie chickens, sage hens, and jack-rabbits on every hand.

Before I take up our desert travels, I want to tell a little about the curious dress adopted by the women in the town of Moreland, a Mormon settlement, seven miles east of Blackfoot. As we pulled into the settlement we caught sight of a young woman of about twenty (at least Stanchfield so put her age, and he is an authority), attired in men's blue Jean overalls. We thought it some schoolgirl's prank and passed by, but at the next house we saw half a dozen women and they were likewise attired in men's overalls. It seems Moreland is a beet-sugar town and everyone works in the beet fields, especially the girls and women. Overalls have been found much more convenient in getting through barb wire fences and in getting down on the knees to weed the beet fields, so they have been adopted by the women of Moreland, and have been worn by them for years. Every woman we saw in that settlement was thus attired.

After leaving Moreland, we struck across the desert and saw no signs of cultivation until we struck Jim Murray's ranch, forty miles from Blackfoot, located at the foot of what is known as Big Butte. Here Jim lives with his wife and daughter, the nearest neighbor being some thirty-five miles away. The daughter, as fair a specimen of the western prairie girl as one would wish to meet, brought us out two glasses of rich creamy milk, while Mr. Murray offered us water for our machine, which we declined, as our tanks were still good for fifty miles.

This great desert, which extends from the Lost river at the north almost to the Snake river at the south, and from Blackfoot to Hailey, is pretty well stocked with wild horses, wild cattle, and in fact, wild animals of all kinds.

We were shown the tracks of a she bear and two cubs at a muddy crossing some two miles below Cottonwood tonight, and have been informed that the buttes and mountains in this section abound in bear of the silvertip species.

Cottonwood is the highest ranch in this section, as well as one of the most fertile. It is so surrounded by mountains that the winter temperature, on the coldest day last winter, was only eight degrees below zero. The altitude is 6,100 feet, and that of the mountains around it is about 7,200 feet. The ranch is unsurveyed, untaxed, and in addition to its rich farmland abounds with gold, silver, zinc, copper, and lead.

Old Steady has plowed along on sand, cinders, and through lava beds all day. We have been surrounded by huge craters of extinct volcanoes, and sometimes for miles the road would lie over solid lava rocks, almost as smooth as asphalt pavement. We had to keep our eyes wide open, however, as this solid rock roadway would be frequently split by huge fissures in the rock, any one of which would have wrecked Old Steady then and there.

Cottonwood, like most ranches hereabouts, is made up of about a dozen log buildings, the roofs of which are made of sticks, straw, and earth, perfectly tight in a summer's rain but slightly leaky during a winter's snow, when the warmth of the fire below has a tendency to keep the dirt roof soft and allow the snow to melt and leak through. The Drakes, like most of the western people, always keep the latchstring on the outside. Mrs. Drake prepared us an excellent supper upon our arrival, after which we swapped eastern tales for stories of the Wild West until bedtime.

Here at last! Stanchfield and I did not wait until we had arrived at the hotel to shake hands with each other, but went through this formality immediately upon passing a little sign on the railroad crossing reading "City Limits." The last day's run, fifty-five miles, was through the beautiful Willamette Valley, from Salem to Portland, and the roads were in very fair condition.

Leaving Cottonwood, Idaho, on Monday, June 17, we continued our journey through a desert of sage brush and lava rocks. Had dinner at Canyon Creek, a pretty little oasis, and a "right smart" dinner it was, to use the term generally adopted in the west as an expression of praise, and to further use the western expression, we paid "two bits" apiece for what we ate.

After some steady riding, we reached Boise City on Monday, and were tendered a reception by the local Board of Trade, and we were given the key to the city. Boise is a very pretty little city, situated in a valley and surrounded by cottonwood trees. The city itself is not visible until one has actually entered upon the streets, the groves of trees hiding all structures, save the tallest steeples. The streets are asphalt paved, and the city has a very businesslike and progressive appearance. Here we stopped at the Idanha hotel, one of the best we have found since leaving New York. There are a number of automobiles used here, although nearly everybody rides horseback, all using the big forty- to sixty-pound cowboy saddle with high back and pommel. The horses used are not the little broncos, about which so much has been said and written, but all are large-boned, and weight 1000 to 1300 pounds, the Kentucky thoroughbred having been imported and extensively used in breeding.

A large tonneau car, the vintage of 1902, is used as a stage for "Seeing Boise." The car is equipped with a canopy top, and makes regular trips through the city and adjacent country. Like most western cities, Boise has many saloons, most of which are open all night, and card games are in progress at all hours, yet the city is orderly and the police are seldom called upon to make arrests.

The ride from Boise to Ontario, Oregon, was most disagreeable. Mile after mile Old Steady's path was marked by clouds of fine alkali dust that completely enveloped us and made breathing difficult. Many ruralites, who endeavored to get a good view of their first automobile, were disappointed. After traveling seventeen miles, we were compelled to lose four hours waiting for a bridge-building gang to repair the bridge over Little Boise River, before we could cross and take the Riverside ferry over Snake River for Ontario, both rivers being too deep to ford. When we reached the ferry, Mr. McConnell, the ferryman, was busy with his farm work, and his wife ferried us across. The river was high and the current swift, so it was but a few minutes before we were safely landed on the Oregon shore. After paying "four bits" for the boat ride, and making a snapshot of the ferry-keeper and her craft, we rolled on toward Ontario, where we arrived in time to spend the night.

On Wednesday we covered the trail from Ontario to Johnson's ranch, about ten miles west of Vale Post Office. This route is used for all manner of freighting, emigrant wagons, stagecoaches, and mail carriers, and we were continually passing horse-drawn vehicles. The larger streams in that section are bridged, but the many irrigation ditches keep the driver busy.

We had hoped to reach the little town of Harney by Thursday night, June 22, but darkness overtook us with a deep and rocky canyon to cross, so we were forced to put up at George Buchanan's ranch, in Harney County. The next ranch below, which is owned by Mr. Buchanan's brother, is where Dr. Jackson stopped for the night on his trip across the continent two years ago. With the exception of Old Scout, this is the only automobile that has ever traversed this part of the country. When we rode up to the ranch, our host and hostess, like all western people we have met, ran out to the gate to welcome us, or possibly to ascertain the source of the strange nose, and we were soon provided with an excellent supper and beds in the loft. Before retiring, however, we listened to stories of the wild animals that abound in the neighborhood. The cougar is the latest and most dreaded animal yet introduced to our attention. In addition to the rattlesnake, we were warned of the scorpion, which abound in great numbers in the lava beds and rocks of this section.

After an early start Friday morning, we succeeded in reaching the stage station sixty-eight miles east of Primville, Crook County, in time for supper. We arrived at the station with the stage from the East, and that from the West pulled in an hour later. There were two beds at the station, and, as the stages brought but one passenger each, Stanchfield and I were able to secure one bed between us for the night, the two passengers "doubling up" in the other. Both beds were in the same room. We had intended to stop at Riley for dinner but the town was so small—one combination hotel, store, and post office—that we rode through the principal street and some eleven miles beyond before we knew it. It was probably just as well that we did, as we stopped at the ranch of W. B. Johnson, where our wants were well looked after, and we were served with a steaming hot dinner.

We found the Johnsons already had visitors, two Piute Indians, three squaws, and two papooses sitting on the back fence as we rode up. The Indians showed much surprise at our little car, the old one immediately concluding that it was the work of the "bad spirit," and would have nothing to do with it. I tried to get a photograph of him sitting in the machine, but he would not have it, and covered his face with his hands when I attempted to take a snapshot of him.

On Saturday we succeeded in making eighty-four miles, stopping at Hotel Poindexter, Primville, for the night. We left the stage station early, with the intention of covering at least 150 miles, but rain paid us another visit, and shower followed shower until the roads were almost bottomless. So heavy had they become early in the afternoon that the freighters were unable to draw their loads, and the big six- and eight-horse teams were unhitched and stabled for the remainder of the day.

After a hasty toilet and a hearty supper, we replenished our gasoline and oil supply, and, late as it was, posed for several local camera fiends, including two women photographers, who were out for the prizes offered by the Olds factory for photographs of the competing machines en route.

With an early start Sunday, we ran to within five miles of the summit of the Cascade mountain range. One hour out of Primville we sighted the three snow-capped peaks known as the Sisters, and said to be the highest points in the Cascade Range. We left Primville by way of the Valley road, and throughout the day we ran through pine and fir woods, for which Oregon is famous, and the entire trip was one continuous hill-climb, and the roads heavy with sand.

Cache Creek is the eastern end of the toll road, and a big gate with lock and key bars the way until toll is paid. The charges are: Eight-horse team, $4; six-horse team, $3; saddle horses, 50 cents; pack horses, 35 cents; loose horses, 15 cents; cattle, 10 cents, and sheep and hogs, 3 cents a head. There might have been some controversy as to the charge for our car, as the gate-keeper was puzzled. We had a 7-horse-power engine, but some of the freighters classed us as road-hogs, and as such we were entitled to passage at 3 cents a head. However, the manager of the Willamette Valley and Cascade Mountain toll road had arranged for this in advance by sending orders "No toll for Old Scout or Old Steady."

There was one little funny incident connected with our mountain running that will bear repeating. We had been advised to be sure and hitch a tree to the rear of our car in descending Seven-Mile Hill, as the third mountain in the Cascade Range is known, and we followed instructions to the best of our ability. When we had reached a point as high as we thought possible to attain, we stopped and looked around for a Christmas tree. We soon located one, but we had no ax. The nearest approach to this handy instrument was a cold chisel, and we cut our tree with this and a monkey wrench. Then, chaining it to our rear axle, we let things slide. That particular hill, while pretty steep, was only about a hundred feet long, and no sooner had we rounded the turn at the foot than we found a hill two hundred feet long to climb. Old Steady had resented the introduction of Santa Claus all along, and positively refused to haul Stanchfield, myself, and the Christmas tree to the top, so we walked and pulled the tree after us. It was a hard climb, but we were soon at the top. Then we piled in for what we thought would be the seven-mile coast we had heard of, but it was only another hundred-foot slide, and then we came to a three-hundred-foot climb. This time Old Steady refused to haul the tree to the top, even with both of us walking, so there was nothing to do but lift the muddy tree into the rig and let it ride, while we walked. Once more we thought we had reached the decline and piled in, with Santa Claus dragging, but again it was only a short coast, with a still steeper and higher hill to climb, so we cast our tree aside and went the rest of the way, including the seven-mile stretch, with only brakes and reverse. Everything went well until we were descending the sixth mountain range, when Old Steady commenced to skid. You who have experienced some skidding on smooth asphalt pavements have no idea of the sensation of a skid down a fifty per cent grade in the Cascade mountains, thirty miles from the nearest house. Down, down, we came, first the front wheels ahead, and then the rear. Finally the front wheel struck a moss-covered rock by the roadside and climbed over. The other front wheel, not to be left behind, followed suit, as did one rear wheel. When we first struck, both Stanchfield and myself were not only thrown out, but pitched bodily clear across the road into the bushes, followed by most of our trappings. The car, suspended by one rear wheel and the right step, which had caught in some bushes, hung over a 200-foot cliff, and Stanchfield and myself, rubbing the mud out of our eyes, sat on the side of the road, wondering why it did not go all the way over. A large prairie schooner, carrying a number of men and women, hove in sight about this time, and, between the lot of us, we were able to get it back in the road and continue our uncertain descent. All this time it had been raining hard, and we were soaked to the skin. My rubber coat was a mass of shreds, and Stanchfield's was almost as badly off. Our corduroy trousers were caked with mud, and our feet and legs were soaked. This is the manner in which we eventually arrived at Sweet Home, and I can tell you that no home meal ever tasted any better than that served up to the two half-starved, cold and wet automobilists.

The fifty-five-mile run from Salem to Portland was made in fairly good time. We kept our chains on both rear tires, and rode along at a fifteen-mile clip, stopping for luncheon at Aurora. Here we discovered a puncture, which necessitated the insertion of our last inner tube, but then, Portland was almost in sight. Harry Keats, of the Keats Automobile Company, Portland agents for the Olds, brought a number of friends out as far as Oregon City to meet us and escort us into Portland.

We found Old Scout, the machine that had defeated us, safely stored in the Keats garage. It plainly showed the hard knocks it had received en route. We also found the caps worn by Huss and Wigle on exhibition in a local hat store, labeled with the signatures of the two Detroiters. After purchasing a supply of clothing, we went to a Turkish bath for the night, the first Turkish bath I had indulged in since leaving New York.

We were recognized in the shoe store we patronized, and nothing would do but for us to exchange our old shoes for new, the old ones going into the window for exhibition. I am commencing to believe that possibly I do belong to the freak family, a belief strengthened by the numerous mailing cards sent me, usually containing in bright letters of scarlet, "It's great to be crazy and ride around in an automobile."

From Coast to Coast in an Automobile

One of the earliest cross-country motor excursions carried its own chronicler when writer M. C. Krarup accompanied E. T. Fetch and N. O. Allyn on their automotive voyage from San Francisco to New York in the summer of 1903. Loaded with their supplies and equipment aboard a twelve-horsepower 1903 Packard, Krarup and his companions encountered all of the obstacles inherent in such a venture, especially in the road-poor reaches of the Far West. Deploying not only his pen but another piece of rapidly evolving technology—the camera—Krarup illustrated his 1904 account of the trip (published in *World's Work* and reproduced in this volume) with photographs that depicted confrontations with four-legged westerners, desolate trails, and automotive mishaps (both theirs and those of other travelers). Krarup's photo of another motorist's "spill" in Colorado in particular highlighted the dangers that could await these pioneers.

Which all but barred the way by their curiosity.

A detour by an abandoned railroad grade strewn with rocks.

The Predicament of a party we met in the Canyon of the Grand in Colorado.

OLDSMOBILE

Promising that "all roads [are] alike to the Oldsmobile," this 1904 advertisement in *The Atlantic Monthly* asserted that the company's "pioneer runabout" could carry the motorist anywhere for any purpose under any conditions. Extending that promise to women as well as men, Oldsmobile made a pointed contrast in its illustrations between the limitations of the past and the possibilities of the present for travelers on American roadways. Ensconced in the end product of Oldsmobile's technological innovations, the modern travelers captured in this advertisement were clearly prepared for any motoring challenge.

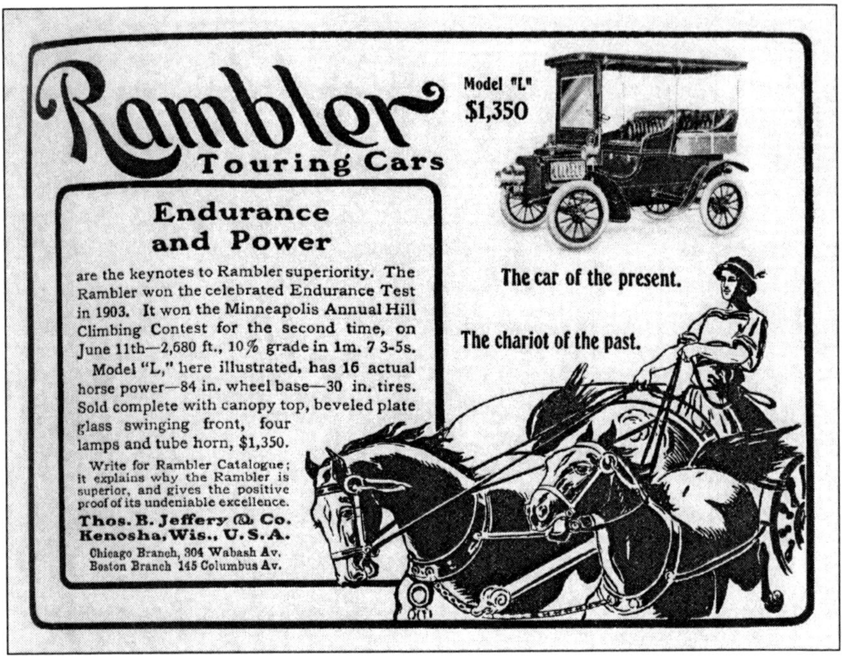

Rambler Touring Cars

As the prospect of employing the horseless carriage for recreational travel through the American countryside grew more common, manufacturers such as Rambler created models specifically intended for a motor-touring public. Carefully portrayed in advertisements such as this presentation in a 1904 issue of *The Atlantic Monthly*, these vehicles were often promoted with an emphasis on such virtues as power, reliability, and comfort. In this instance, Rambler not only offered those attributes but also highlighted such special features as its "canopy top" (since enclosed automobiles had not yet appeared) and a "side basket" (ditto for cars with enclosed trunks) to create a vehicle fit to carry even the most refined young ladies into the rustic settings that attracted the intrepid motorist.

"The 'Invasion of the West' is typical . . . by the Oldsmobile"

After two of Oldsmobile's seven-horsepower Runabouts successfully completed cross-country motor expeditions, they appeared at Portland, Oregon's 1905 Lewis and Clark Exposition, where the company also touted such products as its Model S "Palace Touring Car," which would guarantee the company's success across the United States and around the world. The Palace Touring Car, for example, overflowing with "style, speed, stability and *brains*" [emphasis in the original], would carry motorists to the very heart of the Wild West, where its grace and power would captivate America's original inhabitants, as seen in this advertisement's portrayal of the meeting of cultures.

"Air-cooling doesn't cool, eh?"

Automobile manufacturers in the early 1900s seized any opportunity to demonstrate the superiority of their product, the most audacious typically being a transcontinental motor excursion. Success in such an endeavor provided the sponsoring firm with notable bragging rights about its technological achievements, as exemplified in this 1907 advertisement from the H. H. Franklin Company. Promoting both the automobile itself and the account by L. L. Whitman of the 1906 journey that it published (reproduced in this volume), Franklin offered potential motorists a pairing of ultimate reliability and cross-country adventure.

Cluett Town and Country Shirts

With awareness of and interest in automobiles percolating through the newspapers and magazines of the early twentieth century, manufacturers of other products began relying upon the motor car to promote sales of their goods. In this 1908 advertisement, for example, Cluett, Peabody & Company (best known eventually for its "Arrow" line of men's wear) championed the stylishly up-to-date character of their "Town and Country" shirts through this implicit association with the youthful vitality of the motorist and the sleek appearance of his automobile.

"The Incomparable White"

As automobile manufacturers increasingly integrated the attractions of motor touring into their advertising efforts, their appeals became equally sophisticated. In profiling the unparalleled capabilities of the White steamer, for instance, this 1908 advertisement in *Sunset* assured the reader that it could surmount any obstacle on any road, ranging far beyond the realm of "improved highways." A "true" touring car, the manufacturer asserted, could take the traveler to the precincts of the "greatest natural beauty," even if it had to cross the most intractable terrain.

"The Call of the Open Road"

While many automobile manufacturers relentlessly sang the praises of their technological predominance in their advertising, other sales campaigns in the first decade of the twentieth century incorporated the alluring prospects of motor touring in their appeals. The siren song of "the call of the open road," for example, as seen in this 1909 Rambler advertisement underscored a theme that would constitute a pillar of automotive advertising throughout the twentieth century.

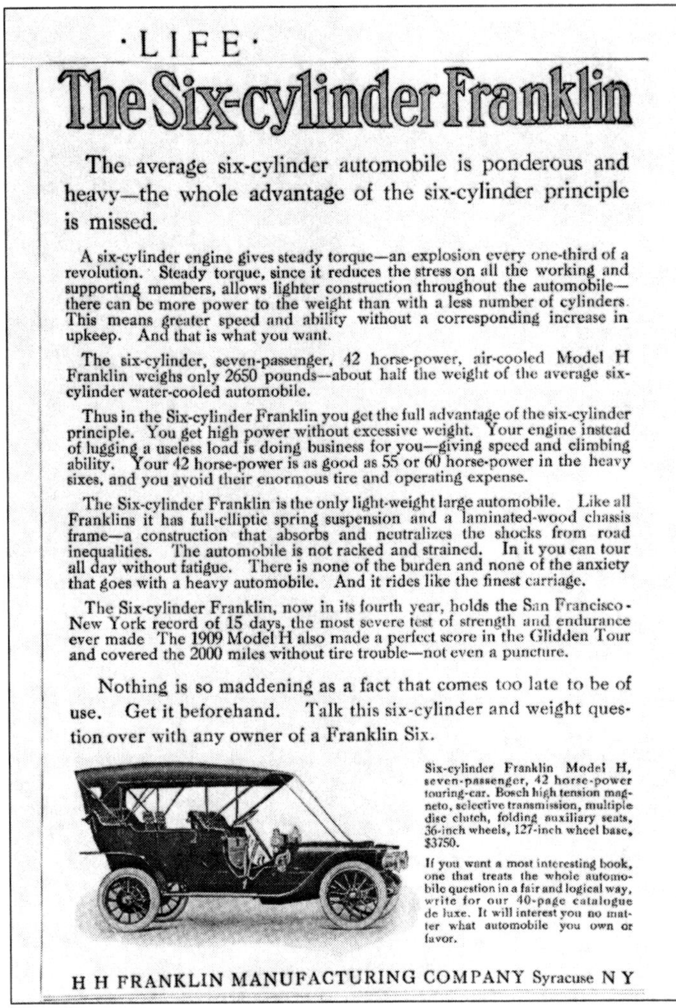

"The Six-Cylinder Franklin"

In a marketplace filled with competitors, early American automobile makers confronted many obstacles. Entrepreneurs such as the H. H. Franklin Manufacturing Company had to educate potential buyers about the nature of their product as well as convince them that the Franklin (or the Rambler or the Oldsmobile or the Pierce-Arrow) would be their most reliable, efficient, and effective choice. For this 1909 advertisement, the Franklin's creators emphasized a coolly factual presentation of its inherent technological superiority.

“A third person was added to the party in the shape of ‘Bud,’ a bulldog, who soon became an expert autoist and a pleasant companion.”

“CROSSING THE CONTINENT BY AUTOMOBILE”

BY 1906, ATTEMPTS TO MAKE A SUCCESSFUL CROSS-COUNTRY motor journey, although still quite uncommon, had nonetheless been attempted with sufficient frequency that the unnamed author of this *Scientific American* article could assert “there can be no question that the idea of a trans-continental trip was considered by motorists almost as soon as this sport began to assume its prominent position in America.” Beginning with the unsuccessful venture of Alexander Winton and Charles Shanks in 1901, this essay thereafter summarizes the endeavors undertaken to date (including several described elsewhere in this volume), concisely outlining:

- When the trips took place
- Which vehicles were used and who piloted them
- What routes were taken
- How the drives unfolded and what were the greatest obstacles encountered
- How long each expedition took to reach its destination

As these capsule histories make clear, each journey, whether pursued from west to east or east to west, found its greatest challenges in crossing the terrain of the Far West, a region still mostly bereft of good roads and reliable directions. Nonetheless, despite the variable circumstances met by these travelers, *Scientific American*'s commentator could still conclude with evident satisfaction that "the American light car has thus proved itself the stanchest [*sic*] and the most speedy of machines in a test such as has never been undertaken by European makers."

Crossing the Continent by Automobile

[*Scientific American* 94, no. 2 (January 13, 1906)]

THERE CAN BE NO QUESTION THAT THE IDEA OF A TRANS-continental automobile trip was considered by motorists almost as soon as this sport began to assume its prominent position in America. Apparently the first serious attempt which has been recorded was that made by Alexander Winton and Charles Shanks in a Winton car in 1901. This expedition ended unsuccessfully, for after the Sierras had been overcome with difficulty, the sands of the Great American Desert were found to present an insurmountable obstacle. It was not until 1903 that the continent was actually traversed from ocean to ocean in a motor car. The first successful machine was a Winton touring car carrying Dr. H. Nelson Jackson and Sewall K. Crocker, a professional chauffeur. In this year no less than three parties were able to perform the journey, the other two trips being made in a Packard car and an Oldsmobile runabout, respectively.

Dr. Jackson and Crocker left San Francisco on May 23, in a double-opposed-cylinder touring car of 20 horsepower. The route from San Francisco lay northward along the Sacramento to Redding at the upper end of the valley and thence into lower Oregon, striking boldly across that State and then along a course over the Rockies entirely off the line of all railroads and one that fairly bristled with difficulties. The most annoying troubles were often the minor ones, for not only were these very frequent, but they were of great diversity as well. At only one place did the travelers run out of gasoline, and on this occasion the unhappy Crocker walked 29 miles to procure a fresh supply. At one time they were without food for thirty-six hours and were indebted to a lone but friendly sheep herder for a generous meal. A block and tackle with which the travelers had provided themselves proved invaluable in rescuing the machine from sand, mud, or streams which had been "rushed" unsuccessfully. The steep, rough, and boulder-strewn grades were overcome one after the other, though the narrowness of the roads, or rather trails, necessitated the most careful driving. A very difficult portion of the journey was that between Redding and Pocatello, Idaho. At Caldwell, in that State, a third person was added to the party in the shape of "Bud," a bulldog, who soon became an expert autoist and a pleasant companion.

As was repeatedly found in later trips in the West, the deeply worn ruts of many of the roads gave almost as much trouble to the low-built cars as the sands. Frequent stallings in mountain streams were no unusual occurrences, but, on the whole, fairly good time was made in crossing the mountains, notwithstanding the loss of a set of ball-bearings from a front wheel with subsequent inefficient repairs by a wayside blacksmith. Travel through the "Bad Lands" was rough in the extreme, as the roads, almost impassable originally, had been rendered still worse by recent cloudbursts. The hardest climb was over Elk Mountain in Wyoming. The stretch through Laramie and Cheyenne, clear across the Great Plains to the Mississippi, was monotonous, but not very troublesome. From Omaha to Chicago, following the general line of the Chicago and Northwestern Railway, and thence through Cleveland, Buffalo, and Albany, to New York, the journeying was good, and was accomplished pleasantly and without much difficulty. So, on July 26, 1903, with the arrival at the great eastern metropolis, was completed the first automobile journey across the American continent, thus adding one more to the number of expeditions, beginning with the ox-wain and the mule-team, which started nearly a century ago.

Of the three transcontinental trips made in 1903, the journey of the 12-horsepower, single-cylinder Packard, with E. T. Fetch as driver and M. C. Krarup as observer, was the most direct and central between San Francisco and Denver, through California, Nevada, and Utah. The start was made on June 20, and the journey was completed on August 21, in a wild drive into New York City. The entire time on the road was 62 days, including a four-day stop at Denver for rest and necessary repairs. The car was of the regular stock type, and with two people aboard weighed nearly 3,000 pounds. Despite the severe strain to which the mechanism was constantly subjected, the interruptions due to breakdowns were trivial. The course, east of Denver, lay through Omaha, Chicago, Cleveland, Buffalo, and Albany.

Crossing the Sierras from Placerville was often exciting, particularly the descent from the summit of the divide to Lake Tahoe, about 8,000 feet below, where at one point the machine descended 800 feet in two miles, practically sliding that distance in 9½ minutes under brakes. The troublesome sand in Nevada was successfully combated by using two 24-foot strips of canvas to give traction in the worst places. The alkali marl and innumerable washes encountered in the 300-mile stretch across the Humboldt Valley taxed the endurance of the car and travelers to the utmost. Even more annoying were the ravines and gulches of the desert, and here further trouble was caused by the depth of the ruts, the higher middle portions of the road frequently lifting the wheels of the low-built car clear off the ground. The tough sage brush not only whipped off the canvas under the engine, and the paint from the car body, but completely wore away, as well, the tough wooden handle of a shovel strapped underneath. The steep sides of many ravines were climbed by "jumping" the car by fly-wheel momentum. The worst stretch of rocky, tortuous, and boulder-strewn road was encountered in Soldiers' Canyon, Utah.

The hardest portion of the trip was over when Denver was reached, though beyond that city barbed-wire cattle fences and irrigation ditches were often annoying. Through parts of Nebraska and Iowa the muddy condition of the roads made the travel almost amphibious, but through Illinois to Chicago, the conditions were excellent. From that city to New York, little trouble was found beyond occasional muddy stretches, and during this part of the trip a good daily average was maintained.

The third journey of the year, the remarkable trip in the little single-cylinder Oldsmobile, was made by L. L. Whitman and E. L. Hammond, who left San Francisco on July 6, bearing a letter from Mayor [Eugene] Schmitz of that city to Mayor [Seth] Low of New York. The machine was of the regular 5-horsepower runabout type, and carried, besides the occupants, only the most necessary articles. The road lay through Sacramento, Placerville, and Carson City to Reno, and was followed in a leisurely manner, no attempt at record time being made. Ogden, Utah, was reached after a hard struggle with the Great Desert of Nevada, which entailed considerable suffering from the alkali dust. During runs, which would last entire days, nothing was to be seen but sand and sage brush, but a two days' rest at Ogden thoroughly refreshed the travelers. On several occasions the trail of the Packard party was noticed in the desert sands.

The trip to Denver from Reno lasted eight days, following the line of the Union Pacific Railway through Wyoming. This portion of the route was extremely difficult and after passing through Webber Canyon the terrible roads, rocks, washes, and alternate adobe mud and sand gave a great deal of trouble. Some good roads were found over the Laramie plains, but otherwise it was almost necessary, at times, to make the road. The Rockies were crossed amid clouds and rain, and to Omaha the journey was enlivened by continuous rains and seas of mud. A nine-day wait at that city for better weather conditions proved to be of advantage, for with drier roads, the 600-mile run to Chicago was made in four days. The mud was still bad, however, and the season seems to have been one of exceptionally heavy rains. From Detroit to New York the conditions for travel were far better, and in one afternoon 125 miles were covered. The city and the Atlantic were reached on September 17, after days and weeks of untiring effort. The travelers were enthusiastic about the machine, which was found to have stood the grueling journey splendidly.

The transcontinental trip accomplished by L. L. Whitman and Clayton S. Carris, in a 10-horsepower Franklin car, in 1904, was remarkable in several ways, primarily as this was the first air-cooled car to perform this arduous journey, and as the entire time between start and finish was less than 33 days, cutting the previous record of 61 days nearly in half. The start was made from San Francisco on August 1, in a regular four-cylinder stock car, and on September 3 the wayfarers entered New York City, having made the excellent daily average of 155 miles, the highest day's run being 325 miles. The entire journey was performed without serious accident of any kind, and at the finish the machine barely showed even the slightest evidence of the numerous hard knocks and the unmerciful driving it had undergone. The most difficult portion of the trip, naturally, was that which included the crossing of the Sierras, the Rockies, and the deserts. The Sierras were crossed through Emigrant Gap, from Colfax to Reno, and here the roads were terrible. At one point a descent of 1,200 feet in one mile was accomplished. From Reno through Utah the roads were almost a negative quantity, and the deep sand, canyons, and gulleys gave the travelers a hard time of it. The performance of the air-cooled motor in the blazing heat of the desert was splendid, 600 miles of this Sahara being crossed in seven days. Through Wyoming the course followed the Northern Pacific Railroad and was difficult in the extreme. At one place, while running at full speed, the rear axle of the car struck a concealed sawed-off telegraph post, and this resulted in a dead stop, which precipitated the occupants of the car over the dashboard. Strangely enough, the only damage caused by this accident was a bent truss rod. Good roads were found across the Laramie plains, and the descent through the Rockies was safely concluded. Good weather permitted record speed to Omaha, and from there to the Atlantic the conditions were excellent, so that this portion of the trip was a mere pleasant jaunt.

An interesting tour was that of the two Oldsmobile runabouts from New York to the Lewis and Clark Exposition last summer, for not only was the journey made by a partly new transcontinental route, but the two machines were racing for a prize of $1,000 besides.

"Old Scout," driven by Dwight B. Huss and Milford Wigle, reached the goal first, June 21, followed just one week later by P. F. Megargel and Barton Stanchfield, in "Old Steady." The cars, which were of the ordinary runabout type, left New York May 8, and remained in company until Omaha was reached. Two weeks' rain had made the roads across Illinois, Iowa, and Nebraska almost impassable, and the cars were forced along through the mud under great difficulties. The distance from Omaha through Cheyenne to Laramie was safely accomplished, but the journey from there to Boise, Idaho, appears to have been more of an athletic contest than a road race, as to begin with the roads were usually conspicuous by their absence, or, if present, almost beyond description. Through Idaho and Oregon they encountered the best roads west of Chicago, though there was some thrilling traveling across the Cascades. The time of the winning car was 44 days, 40 days being the actual running time.

The first round trip from ocean to ocean and return ever attempted was that undertaken by Percy F. Megargel and David Fassett, who left New York in the 16-horsepower double-opposed cylinder Reo touring car "Mountaineer," on Saturday, August 19, 1905. The Atlantic-to-Pacific portion of the trip has been successfully concluded, and the travelers are now on the return journey from San Francisco.

From New York westward to Wyoming, the journeying was under excellent conditions, and 100 miles a day was easily covered. Crossing Wyoming the sand was often bad, especially in the Red Desert, and sand tires with which the "Mountaineer" was provided were very useful. The deep snow and terrific gales of the Rockies made the six days' travel over the mountains extremely dangerous, while at Bitter Creek a four days' delay was caused by an 8-foot rise of the water after heavy rain. Despite the hard going from Cheyenne, the party reached Portland safely on November 10. At the present writing, the tourists are nearing Albuquerque, New Mexico, on the southern return trip from San Francisco. This part of the trip has been far more thrilling and difficult than that to Portland.

Coming over the Cajon Pass in California, the travelers had a very narrow escape when the car, skidding on a sandy road, turned over completely and rolled down a steep embankment though strangely enough, without material damage to mechanism or passengers. The trip across the Great Desert was enlivened by a fierce sand storm. In the Arizona Mountains the snow was very troublesome, and near Flagstaff the travelers nearly perished in a terrible storm, being without food and gasoline for 36 hours. They were rescued by a search party seeking a lost ranchman, whose body was later found within a mile of the Reoites' camp.

The brief summary given above of cars which have crossed the continent would not be complete without mention of the trip made in 1904 by Mr. Charles J. Glidden in his English Napter. This machine ran to St. Louis in the tour to the Exposition, and thence to Minneapolis, Minnesota, where flanged wheels were placed upon it, and it completed the trip to the coast on the railroad track. For pleasure purposes this method of making the trip would seem to be ideal. But from a sporting and machine-racking point of view, the journey as accomplished by the six American cars was immeasurably superior. The record-holder, the air-cooled Franklin, is the only car fitted with a four-cylinder vertical motor, as well as the only air-cooled automobile that has ever made the trip. The other machines, also, are all of typical American construction, having horizontal single- and double-opposed-cylinder engines. Of the six successful cars, four are light runabouts, and three of these are of the same make. The American light car has thus proved itself the staunchest and most speedy of machines in a test such as has never been undertaken by European makers. Not only this, but the trip has also been made twice by motorcyclists—first in 1903 by George A. Wyman on a Yale-California machine, and second, last fall by W. C. Chadeayne on a Thomas Auto-Bi. The time of the former was 48½ days, and that of the latter 47 days, 11 hours, and 35 minutes.

"When you have read the story of our trip, you will say we did wisely to get official testimony that we were actually alive and had whole necks."

L. L. WHITMAN

EVEN AS EARLY AUTOMOBILES BEGAN TO POPULATE AMERICAN cities and towns, the alluring prospects of the publicity inherent in a successful transcontinental expedition kept attracting individuals and, more frequently, automobile manufacturers willing to pit cars and drivers against distance, landscapes, and, increasingly, time. By the summer of 1906, Packard, Oldsmobile, and Franklin had sponsored motor excursions that had completed the journey (including those described in this volume by Marcus Krarup and the Oldsmobile Company's *From Hell Gate to Portland*) and in doing so steadily reduced the time elapsed from beginning to end. Determined to set the most impressive record yet for such a trip, the Franklin Company that year launched one of its new Model H two-seater, six-cylinder, air-cooled touring cars from San Francisco to New York City. Crewed by five men who formed teams that would take alternating shifts behind the steering wheel or speeding ahead by train to the next rendezvous point, the Franklin would push ahead around the clock, in hopes of going coast to coast in ten days. To take on such a challenging goal, the Franklin Company recruited a set of drivers with considerable experience in long-distance driving for Franklin and other companies. Lester L. Whitman, for instance, had already made two transcontinental crossings for Oldsmobile and Franklin in 1903 and 1904, respectively, as well as various distance and endurance runs. (He also became the chronicler of this expedition.)

Starting from a devastated San Francisco only four months after the great earthquake of April 1906, Whitman and his companions had loaded their Franklin with four hundred pounds of equipment and spare parts, ranging from an axe, a shovel, block and tackle, and 150 feet of rope to extra tires, inner tubes, spark plugs, batteries, and an assortment of nuts, bolts, and "small parts." With the further addition of a large wooden storage box, a steamer trunk (for clothing), and a dash-mounted searchlight (for night driving), the Franklin had been thoroughly modified for a variety of contingencies. Keeping close to the transcontinental railroad line of the Union Pacific (and sometimes even traveling on it to avoid particularly recalcitrant terrain), the Franklin and its team also had access to bulkier spare parts, including running gear and wheels, which the company arranged to be shipped by train in case of dire emergencies. Although they encountered fairly few major problems on their dash east, the Franklin detachment endured sufficient hardships to ensure that it still could be called an adventure.

Following what had become a fairly familiar route through Nevada, Utah, Wyoming, Nebraska, and Iowa, the Franklin attacked rocky slopes, mud holes, washouts, thickets of sage brush, gullies, sand, dust, and dirt. Writing of the landscapes of the Great Basin, Whitman commented that "for six hundred miles of this country there is no real road. The early trail in these regions was made by the first adventurers driving where nature offered the least resistance [while] for a thousand miles the country is a destitute barren desert waste with no forests and few streams." By the time they had reached Wyoming, the preceding winter's heavy snows had left a legacy of unyielding mud and torrential streams that continued through Nebraska and tested the ingenuity of the various drivers in overcoming "floods, mud, sand, alkali, and gumbo" as well as the occasional mechanical failure (such as a broken rear axle outside of Laramie, Wyoming). Although their trip would be sidetracked for several days after a serious accident in eastern Ohio, Whitman and his colleagues set a remarkable record of fifteen days, two hours, and twelve minutes in their cross-country venture while continuing to foster an image of the Far West as a modern version of the Great American Desert.

Across America in a Franklin

By L. L. Whitman

[Philadelphia: H. H. Franklin Manufacturing Company, 1906]

Official and Encouraging

We started out with three kind letters given us respectively by Major-General A. W. Greeley to Major-General [James F.] Wade; President R. P. Schmerin of the Automobile Club of California to the President of the Automobile Club of America; and by Major Schmitz of San Francisco to Mayor [George B.] McClellan[, Jr.]and the citizens of New York, thanking them for New York's assistance to San Francisco in her recent calamity.

When you have read the story of our trip, you will say we did wisely to get official testimony that we were actually alive and had whole necks, when we started from San Francisco, August the second, Nineteen Six. Perhaps you'll think we need an official confirmation of the fact that we are still living.

What we went after

We were after a new transcontinental record.

The Franklin already held the record; but we wanted to cut it in halves and throw away about eighteen days which we had no use for. We also wanted to demonstrate what can be done with a motor-car that a sane man wants to do.

The outfit

Our car was a regular six-cylinder Franklin Stock Touring-car.

We took off the tonneau; substituted a large hamper; carried a steamer-trunk to hold clothing; an extra gasoline tank, two extra tires, five inner tubes, an extra set of batteries, extra brake-band, some spark-plugs, bag of tools; sack of bolts, nuts, and small parts; an axe, a shovel, pulley-block, two stout hickory poles, and 150 feet of rope—and thereby hangs the tale.

A bad Start

[Clayton S.] Carris, [Clayton B.] Harris, [Melvin S.] Bates, [James] Daley and Yours Motorfully undertook to do the honors; Bates and I taking the car for the first relay to Summit Station in the Sierras; Carris and Daley going on to there by train.

From the six-million dollar wreck that was once the San Francisco City Hall, we traveled through 2400 acres of pathetic waste, relieved by inspiring evidences that the New San Francisco will be greater than the old.

Rolling down Market Street at the start we met Mayor Schmitz, who shook hands with us and gave us "Good-bye and good luck"—which we certainly didn't strike at the start; for the Sacramento and San Joaquin rivers were all over the easy four- or five-hour road from Oakland to Sacramento; and instead of going this way we had to ferry all the way to Stockton—which put us ten hours to the bad at the very start.

From Stockton we skimmed through sixty miles of wheat fields to Sacramento in just two hours.

In the afternoon we climbed a hundred and fifty miles of mountain; through beautiful fruit-country, big pine forests, and twenty miles of rocky ledges; reaching Summit Station at the same time as the "Overland Limited," which made the hundred-mile run on smooth rails only two hours faster than the Franklin came up the 150 miles of crooked and rocky mountain road.

Dropping down the Sierras

Bates and I sought the solace which a dining-car grants; while Carris and Daley took the Franklin and plunged off down the 1200 feet drop in the first mile, toward Donner Lake.

They ran from 7:40 in the evening until 6 the next evening, except for the time that they were digging themselves out of the desert sand, salt marsh, or the hub-deep alkaline shore of Humboldt Lake.

In the Humboldt "Sink," as it is called, the hard top crust kept breaking through and letting them down into the quicksands; so that at one point they could only go seventeen miles in seven hours. Yet the motor did not overheat. No heavy car could have made any headway at all along this route.

They lost one canteen, and the other sprung a leak so that they were 10 hours on the burning sands of Humboldt Sink without a drop of water. And when they rolled into Lovelock they carried the most capacious thirst that ever was packed on a motor-car.

And there was I a'waiting at the trough—in a nearby restaurant.

The Franklin also was ready for twenty gallons of gasoline and altogether we had a brief but joyous tank-fest before piling into the machine—all four of us, and pulling out at 7 P.M. across the State of Nevada.

Later on we dropped this State behind; and we think of offering a liberal reward to the finder for leaving it just where it is.

There isn't a lake or river in the whole big State that has an outlet in summer. Every stream sinks into the sand or evaporates under the six months of cloudless sun. The sand burns your feet through leather shoes. On the railroad track you can cook an egg in the sun. Yet at night under the sparkling stars you need a blanket to keep warm.

The sun has the despicable early-rising habit; gets up red-eyed and ugly; looks you flat in the face, and says—"I'll make it hot for you today!"

Bumping the Bumps

From Mill City we bumped for thirty miles over the railway sleepers. If you want to know why, go out there and take a look at the situation—we took the easiest way.

About midnight we got off the track to get out of the way of two fast trains and went to bed on the sand until they had passed. Then we were on again, gone again, bump again, Finnegan—to Winnemucca, arriving at 2:30 A.M.

A roadless way

For six hundred miles of this country there is no real road. The early trail in these regions was made by the first adventurer driving where nature offered the least resistance; the next followed this track and so the trail was formed. But, when this became washed into deep ruts by heavy rains, instead of rebuilding the trail, another would be formed in similar fashion; and that in turn abandoned.

I have seen five sets of trails paralleling each other, all impassable but the last—and that was not a boulevard. Anything that a wagon-axle will slide over is considered good enough. Only our high ground-clearance made it possible for us to get along.

For a thousand miles the country is a destitute barren desert waste with no forests and few streams. Only burning sand, sagebrush, and dazzling alkali flats.

At Winnemucca Carris took the train for Elko; Daley took to bed in a hotel; the Franklin took gasoline and oil—dug up by an obliging freight-agent—and Harris and I took ourselves off through the night, reaching Golconda in the early streaks of dawn. This sounds very romantic; but it is certainly the Gol-condest hottest place on the map.

At Battle Mountain Bates met us with more gasoline and a guide to show us the next twenty-five miles of blind trail.

A large Beef Stake

Here we passed through a big 50 × 20 miles ranch—640,000 acres; 57,000 acres fenced in one field—said to be the largest fenced field in America—15,000 head of cattle and 5,000 horses roam here. I wonder what a woman with a red parasol does when she strikes that field—it must be fatiguing to go around.

We drove through acres of wild flowers ten feet high.

Ditches and Washouts

Reached Elko at 2:30 P.M. and gave the car up to Carris and Bates, who next showed up at Ogden, Utah, at 2 P.M., the following day, having passed clear around Salt Lake over some very bad roads. They encountered one big dry washout. And the heavy rains had left ditches from two to six feet deep. It took a great deal of time crossing these ditches at the best points. And at many places the machine was terribly racked.

This continuous severe punishment must have gradually weakened the rear driving-axle; for within twenty-four hours it suddenly gave way, from no apparent cause.

This held us up twenty-eight solid hours while we sent to Cheyenne for a new rear axle. When it came, we took about ten minutes putting it in.

Less than four days to Ogden

We reached Ogden in 3 days, 20 hours, and 30 minutes from San Francisco. The best former record was 10 days, made in a four-cylinder Franklin. The best time ever made in any other automobile was 16 days.

Harris and I sent her out of Ogden before sunrise and were up in Weber Canyon by sunset. We went up Devil's Slide, Devil's Gate, Echo Rock, through deep defiles and along rocky cliffs through a natural gateway in the mountains; through Evanston at 10 A.M.

and on until midnight when we reached an elevated plateau 7000 feet above the sea.

Here it was cold enough for rubber coats over the leather ones.

After a midnight luncheon we pushed on till stalled by a mud hole; pulled out with our blocks and nearby fence-posts; wandered and floundered through irrigating ditches of irritating frequency; spun through a fifty-acre oat field; rushed three nasty fords with water pouring into the engines; and made Granger at 9:30 A.M.

Carris and Bates stood on the far bank of the last ford like a couple of welcoming angels, gasoline in one hand and breakfast in the other.

"Water-cooling" with a Vengeance

They leaped into "the saddle" and disappeared in a cloud of dust, getting their next drink in four feet of water over the tops of the tires, in the middle of the "Big Muddy," an hour later.

Even Franklin engineering isn't at its best under water. The nearest team was at Green River twenty miles away; so after a little wireless "hellegraphy" which failed to "carry" the twenty miles, they got out their hickory sticks and pried their craft ashore inch by inch.

They had to draw the water out of the engine-base; bore a hole and let the water out of the battery-box; empty their shoes and wring their legs before proceeding. The engine started right away again as soon as it got its nose above water!

All the streams were higher this summer than usual on account of last winter's heavy snow-fall. And we were stuck or hampered by mud a good deal of the way.

An awful fix

Between Red Desert and Rawlins, Wyoming, we tried to cross the bed of a creek on a slippery clay bottom; but, although we put sagebrush down to make a track, our wheels would not take hold.

We went to a station two and one-half miles away for help; and about fifty men came and pulled us out.

But after getting out, there was only gasoline enough to run two and one-half miles. Then we bought some kerosene and ran seventeen miles on kerosene to Rawlins—which speaks volumes for the Franklin carburetor. I don't believe there's another carburetor that would run that distance on kerosene.

At Rawlins we got gasoline; left in an hour; ran to the Laramie River—which we forded; made Laramie at 2 A.M., and waited till daylight for more gasoline.

We reached Cheyenne at 11 A.M. the same day, August 9th. At Sherman we reached our highest elevation, 8000 feet.

We replaced a spring, one of whose leaves had slipped out; left Cheyenne at noon, and after traveling 24 miles, arrived at North Platte, Nebraska, 3 A.M. August 10th.

A HUNDRED MILES OF MUD

We put on our tire-chains here; and we needed them; for along the North Platte we found a hundred miles of mud. I do not mean a hundred miles deep, for after a good rain it is deeper than that, but a hundred miles long in one solid stretch. And at times the mud flew twenty feet high as we skated along.

Equal parts of corn, hog, and black mud are the recipe for this part of Nebraska after a rain. And they are all rich and fat. I wish I owned a Nebraska farm.

We waltzed and slid from "swung partners," all over this territory; occasionally landing in ditches and plunging into barb-wire fences.

You hear a lot about gentle Mother Earth and her kindness toward man; but when you've traveled a few thousand miles through floods, mud, sand, alkali, and gumbo, you come to think this maternal benevolence is altogether too strenuous and sticky; and that a good man-made road beats nature all to pieces.

At Kearney, dry roads appeared again, and we made the dust fly across three hundred miles of the finest farming land in the world.

We pulled the switch-plug at Omaha 12 midnight; having left North Platte at 4 A.M.—that's going some.

Held up

Over in Iowa the next day, just beyond Cedar Rapids Daley passed a farmer who immediately had a feeling that he wanted a new buggy-pole as his was a little cracked. He saw a cloud of dust, which looked good to him; so he telephoned down the line toward Chicago for the police to stop our outfit long enough to take up a collection.

Daley was stopped at the second town by three deputies with guns; and a hundred blood-thirsty natives demanding unconditional surrender.

The name of this town was Chelsea. And I'll never say again—"As dead as Chelsea."

The farmer declared that Daley smashed his buggy pole, although Daley never knew it; and has his doubts to this day.

But the farmer got a new pole; and Daley got eight hours—more time to the bad.

Arrived at Cedar Rapids Aug. 12th, 2 A.M., Chicago 5 P.M.

Chicago in less than eleven days

We came into Chicago in 10 days and 21 hours from San Francisco. The best previous record, made by Carris and myself in 1904, was 25 days. The next best, made in a water-cooled air, was 50 days.

Up to this point we had not touched a wrench to the engine except to change a few spark-plugs.

We put on new tires here solely for the purpose of beating the Chicago-to-New York record. They were not needed to finish the trip.

We tightened up the crank and connecting rod bolts a little; and Daley and Bates got away from Chicago at 10 P.M. August 12th. At daylight they were half way to Toledo.

Harris, Carris, and I met them there at noon the next day; and those two undertook to drive to Erie, Pennsylvania.

A BAD SPILL

They passed Cleveland twenty-four hours out of Chicago; and the old record began to look sick.

But pride goeth before a spill: About eleven o'clock at night nearly up to the Pennsylvania line, thirty-two miles west of Erie, while sailing along at almost forty miles an hour on a fine stretch of road, they swung around a curve too short to hold; missed an iron bridge by twenty feet; plunged down a steep bank into the creek; crashed into a stone abutment on the opposite bank—and the car stopped.

Harris and Carris, however, kept right on after the record. In order to have the proper "light and leading" toward New York, Harris took the searchlight with him—clutched to his breast—and Carris tried to carry away the steering-wheel; but thought better of it and left it bent up over the dash.

The guide on the steamer-trunk pointed the way over the tree-tops in a graceful arc for fifty feet or so, into a friendly mud-puddle.

He was the first to show up uninjured. Carris sprained his ankle and bumped the front of his intellect; Harris wrenched his knee. Otherwise they were all right.

It is certainly true that people born to be electrocuted will never be killed in a motor-car smash.

When 3,150 pounds of automobile running like a fast express jumps into a bank of rock there are apt to be some proceedings to report. Front-axle, springs, steering-post, lamp, and front mud-guards did not look exactly wealthy; but they were certainly better off.

The engine was in perfect running order. The wood-sills were all whole; except the tip of one, where the lamps bolt on; rear-axle all right, but one wheel had its spokes slightly sprung. The hamper hung out over one wheel, and the gasoline tank was aleak.

We towed the wreck back to Conneaut, Ohio, and took thirty-six hours getting machine and invalids patched up and on the road again.

Leaving Conneaut 11 P.M. August 15 we ran through Erie to Buffalo.

On the home stretch

Just out of Buffalo along about midnight of the 16th we suddenly passed a cop and surprised him so that he started to pinch himself to see if he was awake. But on second thoughts, he decided to pinch us. And took us back to make a fresh start about 1 P.M.

From Buffalo we flew on through Rochester, Syracuse, Utica, and Albany, and on down the river till we struck the end of Kingsbridge at Harlem, Aug. 17th 11:12 P.M. where the swarm of automobiles filling the road made us fear for a moment that we were held up again, till we realized that New York City begins at the bridge; and we had actually *arrived.*

Coming Under the Wire

Allowing for the difference in time, we made the trip from San Francisco to New York in 15 days, 2 hours, 12 minutes. We brought along with us the record from Buffalo to New York in 23 hours.

Then followed loud demoniac yells, red fire, a procession to Hotel Astor, fizz, bouquets—literal and figurative, a real bed and sweet oblivion.

The fifteen days of broken sleep were beginning to show and one of the boys was so foolish as to attempt a bath before retiring; the consequence was that he fell asleep in the bath-tub, soaked five hours, and when he woke up the water was cold and the sun shining in the window.

Some interesting lessons

Well, what did we do; and what did we find out after all?

We did pretty near all that a motorist *can* do, except get himself killed. And it wasn't our fault that we stopped at that.

We climbed, coasted, slid, drove and bumped 4000 miles twice as fast as it was ever done over the same route before.

Only eight automobiles ever crossed the American continent on their own wheels. Of the seven who tried for a speed record one crossed in 63 days; another in 61; another first crossed in 72 days and twice again in 44 days and 48 days; the four-cylinder Franklin in 33 days; and our six-cylinder Franklin in a little over 15 days.

Carving up the record

We were the only motorists who ever came within eleven days of touching our own precious record; and we beat it by eighteen days—crossed the United States in a month less than it was ever crossed in any motor-car but a Franklin.

We roasted, shivered, fasted, and thirsted most mightily. We plunged in, dug out, pushed along, came in under the wire, and chalked up some figures that beat the multiplication table. And that's a hard thing to do.

A Six-Cylinder Lesson

We knew that four-cylinders were good—smooth, swift and ready; and we found that six cylinders were even better for eating up the miles—with mountains, deserts, swamps and rivers all thrown into the reckoning.

Carrying 3,150 pounds we averaged 300 miles a day when traveling; and rain in many places at fifty miles an hour. We climbed three mountain ranges and reached an altitude of 8000 feet.

We made the run up the Sierra Nevada Mountains 7,260 feet almost in "Overland Limited" train time.

New Air-cooling Experience

We covered 600 miles going almost constantly through deep desert sand with the mercury at 120 degrees, at an average of eleven miles an hour. And most of the way not a drop of water was obtainable. What could a water-cooled engine have done?

We proved that Franklin air-cooling cools a big powerful engine as well as a small one; cools on a hundred-and-fifty mile climb or with the mercury at 120 as perfectly as in winter or on a level floor.

A Hard Bumping Trial

We traveled thirty miles over railroad ties with four passengers in four hours; which shows what human beings can stand in a resilient-frame car with four full-elliptic springs; and what such a car can stand without being damaged, or even stopping the motor.

A Severe Endurance Test

We demonstrated that high-grade light-weight construction gives a motor-car phenomenal endurance and resisting strength—more than would be possible with any other type of construction; more than we supposed was possible even in a Franklin.

Our wood-sills were substantially undamaged by that terrific smash near Conneaut. What would have happened to a pressed-steel sill? It would have been shivered to fragments.

If we had undertaken to arrange a special and infallible construction-test we could not have imagined a more trying and convincing climax than the various road conditions of this Franklin run capped by that frightful plunge.

The Reliability Question

What did we learn about motoring reliability?

"Comparisons are odious," according to the proverb, and I don't want to be odious. But I can't help drawing a few comparisons to put our experience on that score in its proper light:—

In the famous Glidden Tour the cars were two weeks on the road; traveled leisurely and covered only 1300 miles over civilized roads. Yet they had lots of trouble with axles and running-gear; although, according to the rules of the contest, they could repair at inspection stations and so make perfect scores.

In this Franklin transcontinental run only two hours' labor was required for adjustment during the entire trip.

Up to Chicago—during 3000 miles of the toughest going imaginable, we replaced three spark-plugs; repaired a leak in the gasoline tank; and repaired one front spring and one rear-axle drive-shaft. That was all the repairing we did until our accident near Conneaut.

Look at our big loss of time from causes that had no relation to the car—10 hours by floods; 12 by quicksands; 12 by the police; 32 by our only bad accident.

But making no allowance for accidents, ifs, or buts; after all is said and done, considered purely as a reliability demonstration, this run was certainly never equaled.

Economy

We used 263 gallons of gasoline; 1½ gallons of kerosene; 21 gallons of cylinder oil; 3 gallons of gear and transmission oil.

We used up four sets of batteries and four spark-plugs. One spring slipped and one was broken. We had two punctures; and only needed one set of tires as we changed tires at Chicago simply in trying to make an additional new record.

The *Motor World* truly says—"The performance was far more that of the car than of the driver, of which there were four." And *Motor Way* says that this run across the United States is "The most remarkable accomplishment in the history of American motor-touring." But to my mind it is even more.

When you consider the all-around nature of the test; its racking severity; what it shows about the fundamental principles of automobile design and construction and its great practical significance to the entire motoring fraternity—it seems to me that this six-cylinder Franklin performance makes the greatest of all motoring records. And we're all proud of our share in it.

L. L. Whitman

P.S.—We took this identical car after its 4100-mile run—back again 1000 miles to Chicago and then made the return run to New York in 56 hours, 58 minutes; clipping 1 hour and 45 minutes from the Chicago-to-New York record. 500 miles of the way we ran without any fan.

P.P.S.—What about Franklin air-cooling?

L. L. W.

“You can never feel quite certain about the tires.”

ARTHUR INKERSLEY

PROCLAIMING IN ITS FEBRUARY 1907 ISSUE THAT “FAST FLYing automobiles in pastime and trade” were “helping upbuild the far country of gold and sunshine,” *Sunset* magazine felt confident in asserting that “in the limitless West distance-killing motor cars have come to stay.” In keeping with its role at the time as a general-interest periodical dedicated to understanding the Far West, *Sunset* could gather writers such as *San Francisco Examiner* reporter Franklin Hichborn, English journalist Arthur Inkersley, author Allan Dunn, and others to comment at length on the many roles that the automobile now assumed all over the West. Ranging from descriptions of endurance runs like the celebrated Glidden Automobile Tours, sponsored by the American Automobile Association, to a portrayal of the crucial role of motor transport in the days immediately following the San Francisco earthquake and fire, these vignettes emphasized how well established the automobile was becoming in western settings. At the same time, these writings captured the automobile both at play (in Hichborn’s story about a motor excursion to the summit of Mount Hamilton) and at work (such as Allan Dunn’s account of a motor car’s journey along western railways to capture photographic images of the West for the Southern Pacific Railroad’s promotional purposes).

Although written from different perspectives about very different experiences, all of these articles highlighted the remarkable capacity of the automobile (still, of course, a machine in its comparative infancy) to endure extremely challenging physical conditions while greatly enhancing personal mobility for leisure travel and accomplishing the tasks once the province of other forms of motive power (such as the horse). Even at a point when the automobile's overall numbers remained relatively small (a total of only 140,000 cars were registered in the nation as a whole in 1907, for instance), it had clearly stirred up sufficient interest to attract the attention of the mass media of the day. The so-called "endurance races" (profiled in two of these articles), though intended to foster competition among various brands to establish new performance records, also highlighted what Arthur Inkersley described as the "wholesome, recreative part of automobiling"—the opportunity for motor touring. California, he continued, included "within its wide limits scenery of almost every kind," thus making the Golden State particularly alluring for such newfound recreation. With hundreds and then, in time, thousands of motorists in search of ways to employ their new vehicles, the outdoor world became increasingly linked to the evolution of this technology. Westerners perusing *Sunset* could find in it inspiration for the employment of the mechanical to pursue a fascination with the natural.

Motoring in the West

Fast flying automobiles, in pastime and trade, helping upbuild the far country of gold and sunshine

[By Arthur Inkersley, Franklin Hichborn, Allan Dunn, Wallace Everet, and others]

[*Sunset* 18, no. 4 (February 1907)]

In the limitless West distance-killing motor cars have come to stay. The country beyond the Rockies is the star field for automobile agencies. The fleeting touring car has usurped the place of the bronco and the prairie schooner. In California, this land of winter comfort, nearly every tourist runs his own machine, and thereby invites health in the out-of-doors. Here are a few stories of motor cars and their place in the West, today.

Midwinter Tour and Record Breaking

By Arthur Inkersley

During the early part of the present winter, before the heavy rain fell, and while the roads were in their dustiest and roughest condition, many attempts were made to cover the distance between San Francisco and Los Angeles in an automobile in the shortest possible time. Until recently the quickest motor-car passage between the two cities was made near the end of October 1905 by George Hensley in a fifteen horse-power White steamer, carrying four persons, over roads in a condition very unfavorable to fast travel. The record of twenty-one hours thirteen minutes, remained unbroken for more than a year, though repeated efforts were made to break it.

After four attempts, which were unsuccessful on account of the failure of the tires to withstand the rough usage to which they were subjected by the high rate of speed maintained over roads in almost the worst possible condition, a Franklin six-cylinder car, owned by Julius A. Landsberger, of Alameda, covered the five hundred miles between Los Angeles and San Francisco (going north) in twenty-one hours, three and one-half minutes. This beat the record by nine and one-half minutes, but the objections were raised that the Franklin car had traveled from south to north instead of from north to south, as the White car had done; and that it had carried only three persons for the last eighty miles of the journey, while the White had carried four all the way. Notwithstanding these criticisms, the driver, Tony Nichols, who was at the steering wheel of the Franklin for all but seven miles of the whole distance, received high commendations for his plucky, skillful work and was generally accepted as a record-breaker.

The Franklin record stood for a very short time only, a few days later Fernando Nelson's Columbia car, carrying four persons, covered the five hundred and four miles between San Francisco and Los Angeles in the surprising time of eighteen hours, thirteen minutes, beating the White record by exactly three hours and the Franklin record by three hours, less nine and one-half minutes. Hall and Himmelwright took turns in driving as far as San Luis Obispo, where their places were taken by Bert Saunders and Clarence Diehl. Fernando Nelson and R. McCord (a representative of the manufacturers of the "Diamond" tires with which the car was fitted) were in the car throughout the whole trip.

The motor car which made the record was not a specially constructed racing machine, nor was it by any means brand new from the factory. Mr. Nelson bought it just before the San Francisco disaster and it saw much hard service in the troublous days that followed. It did its full share of volunteer work in carrying those who were engaged in checking the conflagration, maintaining order in the streets, and rescuing the sick and injured. Afterwards it was driven on many long trips, and it made two or three strenuous journeys between San Francisco and Los Angeles before it accomplished its purpose and established a record that will be hard to beat. Since that memorable run, its engine was kept running for seven days and seven nights continuously in the Middleton garage and later was harnessed to a newspaper press.

All of which proves that the engine of the modern automobile is a really efficient and trustworthy piece of mechanism, combining strength, lightness, and high power in a remarkable degree. It also shows that the weak spot of the motor car is the tire: the engine of a good car, if well treated and operated by one who understands it, will accomplish a vast amount of work and withstand a great deal of rough travel. But you can never feel quite certain about the tires.

They may carry a car across the continent or they may break down in a run through Golden Gate Park. Of the five attempts that the Franklin car made before it beat the time established by the White, four came to an end through what is known among automobilists as tire trouble. On the fifth trip the Diamond tires withstood the strain. Fernando Nelson's car is fitted with Diamond wrapped tread tires. There was no puncture on the record run and the same tires brought the car back to San Francisco without damage.

The development of the rich mining districts of Nevada have been aided greatly by the automobile, which has "caught on" remarkably among the new millionaires of the sagebrush. Here is an example: a Pope-Toledo car was put into service on a Nevada stageline about eighty miles long and over exceedingly rough roads in the middle of May last year. The car made one round trip (one hundred and sixty miles) each day and ran continuously for four months, during which it covered from twenty-five thousand to thirty thousand miles. On nearly every trip, it was loaded to the limit of its capacity, carrying eight persons and at least five hundred pounds of baggage.

The manager of the automobile company that owns the car says: "Easterners can not realize what is meant by rough roads in the

West; it is really wonderful that cars can be built which will travel at high speed, carrying such loads as are piled upon them, over such roads as are found in the mining districts."

But, though there is always a fascination about record-breaking, especially in so exciting and nerve-thrilling a sport as automobiling, we all know that it is indefensible. A car out for a record breaks the state law governing the operation of motor vehicles every moment of its journey; it endangers the lives of its occupants and of people along the roads, and it accomplishes no really good purpose. For everyone who reads the daily papers knows quite well that any good motor car can keep up an average rate of thirty miles an hour over almost any road as long as gasoline, tires, and the endurance of its operators hold out.

The wholesome, recreative part of automobiling is touring. Few states of the Union offer opportunities for auto-touring so excellent as California, which comprises within its wide limits scenery of almost every kind—mountains whose summits are clad with perpetual snow; foothills and coast ranges of more modest elevation; fertile valleys where every product of the temperate zone and many semi-tropical growths flourish; prolific orchards that in spring-time are a marvel of beauty; rich gardens; teeming vineyards; streams where trout abound; rivers and lakes; sandy deserts; forests, woods, and sylvan glades.

The tour along the coast from San Francisco to Los Angeles, if taken at a reasonable pace and with due regard for normal rest and food, is a highly agreeable one. The first day out the motorist goes through San Jose and over the San Juan grade to Salinas, resting there for the night. Next day takes him through San Miguel, Paso Robles, and Templeton to San Luis Obispo; on the third day the Gaviota Pass is surmounted and Santa Barbara is reached. On the fourth day the traveler, having passed through Oxnard and Santa Paula, arrives at Los Angeles. This schedule gives a daily average of one hundred and twenty-five miles, which can be covered comfortably in eight hours at a rate of fifteen to sixteen miles an hour. This moderate but perfectly sufficient rate of speed does not conflict with the state law, reduces to a minimum the danger to horse-drawn vehicles and passing pedestrians, and renders it possible to get some idea of the country traversed. Of course, towards the close of the dry season, the roads are dusty, but during the spring and summer they are for the most part in good condition. Gasoline may be bought in all the towns, and in case of mishap, good repair shops are to be found at San Jose, Salinas, Paso Robles, San Luis Obispo, Ventura, Santa Paula and Los Angeles. Though the town officials are strict, the people along the route are generally friendly and do all in their power to make touring pleasant.

An interesting trip of a few days can be made to Ukiah. From Sausalito to Santa Rosa is an easy run for the first day; on the second fine roads lead to Healdsburg and thence through the vine yards of the Italian-Swiss Colony to Cloverdale. A mile beyond Cloverdale dinner may be obtained at McRay's and from this place it is a run of thirty-five miles along the banks of Russian River through the redwoods to Ukiah. On the return trip the motorist can follow the other bank of Russian River to Geyserville and thence to Calistoga. Besides being very picturesque, the road for nearly twenty-five miles is almost perfectly level and smooth. From Calistoga it is a pretty ride to St. Helena, whence the road runs alongside the electric railway to Napa. From Napa the motorist can proceed by way of Vallejo or Benicia. If the latter route is chosen, he will cross the Carquinez Straits in the ferry-boat to Port Costa and continue on to Oakland.

The tour to Byron Hot Springs by way of Oakland, San Leandro, and Haywards, is an excellent one. After leaving Haywards, the Dublin Pass or the Niles Cañon route may be taken to Livermore, the former being the shorter and prettier. After passing through Livermore, the autoist may cross the Livermore Pass to Altamont and Mountain House, the roads being unusually good and the grades easily surmountable by a powerful car. The return from

Byron may be made either by the same route or by way of Concord, Martinez, Port Costa, Pinole, Stege, and San Pablo to Oakland. The total distance is about one hundred and twenty-five miles and can be covered with ease and comfort by a daylight run.

Another fine one-day run is from San Francisco or Oakland to Del Monte by way of San Jose, San Juan, and Salinas. Though the climb up the San Juan grade is a stiff one, a good car has little difficulty in getting to the top. On the way up and from the summit, splendid views are obtained. The grade can be avoided by going around the base of the mountain, but while most of the road is fair, part of it is very rough. From San Francisco or Oakland to Santa Cruz, by way of San Jose, Los Gatos and past the Hotel de Redwood over the mountains to the seashore is another fine one-day run. The roads are for the most part good and the scenery is of varied beauty.

For a short morning or afternoon outing, it is hardly possible to find anywhere a more interesting run than from Market street, San Francisco, to the military reservation at the Presidio and along the heights overlooking Fort Point and the Golden Gate; thence to Golden Gate Park and out to Ocean Beach, returning by way of Ingleside. The roads in the reservation and Golden Gate Park are almost perfect, while the marine views are unsurpassable.

Several Californian automobilists use their motor cars on hunting trips. Among these may be mentioned W. W. van Arsdale, the well-known lumberman, who has made many runs through the redwood forests of Mendocino County; J. A. Marsh, president of the Mobile Carriage Company, who uses his Pierce-Arrow frequently on fishing and shooting excursions; and C. E. Maud, of Monterey, who, accompanied by Mrs. Maud, goes quail-shooting in a Franklin car.

While no one pretends that weather and roads are always good, even in the Golden State, an automobilist may tour from Humboldt County to San Diego, at ordinary altitudes, at any season of the year, without encountering anything worse than high winds, heavy rain (and for seven solid months he may experience not even a shower), some fog near the coast, dusty roads, steep grades, and (during the wet season) a swollen creek or a wash-out. This is nearly a complete catalogue of the ills that may befall him. By way of contrast, here is an account of an economy test that took place in the Berkshire Hills of Massachusetts in November last.

> That severe weather might be encountered on the run was known by the committee of the New York Motor Club when it selected November 14, 15 and 16, as the dates for its contest. The participants knew it too, and provided for it as far as possible by taking along enough coats, rugs and robes to brave an Arctic winter. But that heavy snow, progressing into a genuine blizzard, would be encountered, no one anticipated for a moment. Yet this is exactly what happened. Middle November broke all records by welcoming the contestants with a regulation mid-winter storm, with all its unpleasant concomitants—snow, wind, and extreme cold. The carrying out of the schedule became impossible, the arrival at havens of rest being the chief purpose. The storm became a blizzard on the afternoon of the 15th and raged unabated all that evening and early on the morning of the 16th. The howling wind drifted the snow wherever it got the chance and obliterated all vestiges of the road before night set in and made progress more difficult. From one to two feet on the undrifted level, the snow rose to six feet in places and through this, uphill and down dale, the indomitable motorists fought their way foot by foot, dogged, stubborn and unswerving as Fate. At a pace that was slower than a slow walk, they made their way mile after mile, surmounting obstacle after obstacle and rising to each occasion as it made demand upon them. Yet two women and more than a dozen men battled through it and managed in spite of all to get through in some sort of shape without casualties. Without food, almost without protection, exhausted physically by the work of shoving the cars through drifts, scarcely able to stand up, a few of the party hung together through sheer bull-dog pluck and arrived at their respective destinations without serious trouble.

And it was only a week earlier in this same month of November that Fernando Nelson's Columbia car was leaping along the coast road of California at a rate little short of thirty miles an hour for five hundred miles. After a stop of less than thirty minutes at Los Angeles, it was under way again on the return trip to San Francisco.

On the Top of Mt. Hamilton

Told by Franklin Hichborn

An automobile trip across the continent, around the world, up the Rockies or over the Sierra isn't worth a paragraph in the newspapers these days. But there was a time—strange as this generation may deem it—when no automobile had circled the globe, or even crossed the continent, or, for that matter, so much as climbed that little four-thousand-foot California hill, Mount Hamilton, down Santa Clara way. And—strange again—that time was only a half dozen years back. In those dark ages of automobiling, a venturesome soul in a moment of speculative enthusiasm bubbled over with a written article in which he predicted that the day would come when the automobile would be as common on the streets as a bicycle. The prediction was innocent enough, but the years of written demonstration of the impracticability of anything of the kind ever happening was not all good tempered; indeed some of it was ridiculously ill tempered. To the average man in the year 1900, the automobile was as much in the air as an airship is now—or perhaps it would be better to say as much as the airship is out of the air.

However, there were a whole lot of people in those distant days who saw in the automobile a joy forever—even the warmest of its advocates wouldn't admit it a thing of beauty—and backed their position with cash.

Among the most reckless of these enthusiasts was John Brisbane Walker, then proprietor of the *Cosmopolitan Magazine*. Mr. Walker went so far as to try to demonstrate at a cost of $1,700,000 that the steam automobile is a snare and a delusion. Few men have done more for the development of the automobile, and he did it gamely like a man, sold his magazine and paid the bills of it. But that is another story.

Walker's agent at San Jose in those days was Colonel Cotton. Colonel Cotton wasn't Colonel Sellers, but the two colonels resembled each other in many ways. Each was a decade ahead of his generation, each believed in himself and in his work, and each could talk the leg off a brass monkey. Cotton opened up at San Jose with a fine line of 1901 steam-propelled automobiles. One day somebody told the colonel that President David Starr Jordan, of Stanford University, accompanied by the present editor of SUNSET had managed to get to the top of Mount Hamilton in a gasoline single-seated run-about. This story rather staggered the Colonel, but he was game.

"If," he said, "any man can get up there in a gasoline run-about, I can go up in one of my double-seated steam machines with four men in it."

Cotton was politely but exasperatingly laughed at. Such a thing had never been done, therefore it was impossible. But the Colonel was game, every inch of the six-foot-six of him, and he made his bets like a man and got his machines ready. I use the plural, for there were two machines. Automobile accidents in those days were not uncommon, and the Colonel had more than a record at stake. If one machine broke down, he figured on the other holding out to the top. The Colonel was up to snuff. He also took along a photographer, A. P. Hill, of San Jose, to take pictures of the machines before the observatory—if they succeeded in getting there—a newspaperman to act as historian, a doctor—needless to say why—and three millionaires on whom he counted to buy machines. A game, thoughtful, prudent, and an ever business-like man was Colonel Cotton.

The start was made one bright morning in April 1901, from the Hotel Vendome at San Jose. One machine was guided by Colonel Cotton himself, the other by a man named Gammage. A quick run was made across the valley—at that season in its greatest glory of wild flowers, green grass, and billows of white and pink orchard trees—to the foothills. There were several delays caused by runaways—automobiles were great at horse scaring in those days—and one hold-up of a pretty girl on a horse whose frightened animal the gallant doctor insisted upon calming until the machines had passed. Incidentally, Hill took a picture of the doctor as a pretty girl saver. It was a fine picture. Everybody who witnessed his gallantry said that the doctor was a hero, and all who have seen the picture say he looks the part. Smith's Creek at the foot of Mount Hamilton was reached shortly before noon. Then the advantage of having millionaires along became apparent. Lunch was served with champagne as the beverage, and everything that was served was on a champagne basis. But Colonel Cotton didn't drink. Columbus never felt greater responsibility than did Cotton at that moment. The machines had done nobly that far—but they hadn't done any climbing worth mentioning

Before starting up the hill, the gasoline tanks had to be filled. For this purpose a five-gallon can of gasoline had been brought along safely tucked away under the seat. Cotton left the dining room to give a few extra, anxious touches to his machine as well as to fill the tank. He was soon followed by Photographer Hill, who had become greatly interested in the machines. Hill had dined heartily and wined well, but the sight that met his startled eyes when he neared Cotton fussing over the automobile, sobered him in an instant. Hill had been brought up to reverence and fear gasoline, and had never before encountered more than a quart of it at once in all his life. But he surprised Cotton in the act of dumping two whole gallons of it into the machine. When Cotton told him that on leaving San Jose five gallons was in the tank, and five under the seat, ten in all, and fire all around it, Hill was so affected that he had to sit down. He was a man of the world, he had had many startling surprises in his life, but nothing like the surprise he now experienced in the reflection that he had not been blown up.

"I don't believe you need five gallons to climb that hill."

"Perhaps not," replied Cotton carelessly, "but it's just as well to be on the safe side."

"You're right!" ejaculated Hill with several expletives. Now Mr. Hill is, under ordinary circumstances, not a profane man, and when he spoke so vehemently, Cotton turned and looked at him.

"I was only saying," said Hill, "that it's just as well to be on the safe side."

Twenty minutes later, the party was lined up on the hotel porch, all but Hill. "Where's Hill?" somebody asked.

"Oh," replied Gammage lazily, "he wanted to fill my gasoline tank, and I'm letting him."

As Gammage spoke, the crafty Hill was saying to himself, "It's always best to be on the safe side. If two gallons of gasoline won't carry us up that hill, we walk." To make assurance doubly sure he is alleged to have spilled upon the ground the extra three gallons that Cotton had left in the car. Later on in the afternoon he walked. So did Gammage. So did the two millionaire guests, up grade at that.

The start from Smith's Creek was made with a fine flourish, Cotton's machine leading, and Gammage's close behind. Up the hill they went, around precipices that are bad enough with a horse; with an untried automobile they were nerve-racking. The automobilist of these modern days who sweeps up the Mount Hamilton grade in a touring car, has no idea the number of levers and gauges and strings that Cotton had to keep track of. He had an oil gauge, a water gauge, and a gasoline gauge that he had to watch continually. There were as many tanks as gauges, each connected by a lever. There were speed levers, and stop levers, and a horn—quite a novelty in those days—and a mysterious something that he had to work with his foot, having no hands or fingers left for it. But he managed to keep his head, and not risk the necks of his passengers to any marked degree, until a rattlesnake in the middle of the road stirred his imagination.

The doctor wanted to get out and kill the reptile in the orthodox way with a stick. But this was too tame for Cotton. He'd kill that snake with his automobile. On one side the road was a drop of fifty feet; on the other, granite walls. Cotton's passengers looked at the drop, at the numerous levers and strings, and joined in an emphatic "Don't!" But Cotton did. Back and forth on that narrow road went the machine, missing the precipice by a half-inch one minute, grazing the granite walls the next. Every time the wheels passed over the snake, the snake was crushed down into the dust, to come up rattling with anger, but apparently unhurt. Cotton's passengers tried to reason with him, but to no purpose. The fool snake didn't have sense enough to crawl over the side of the road into safety, but contented itself with fighting the machine. The creature was quite as unreasonable as Cotton.

After a particularly narrow graze of the precipice, the Doctor insisted on getting out. The Colonel—with just a suspicion of impatience and annoyance—obligingly stopped the machine. The Doctor started to climb out over the side. But before he could reach the ground, the snake coiled and struck at him viciously.

The Doctor crawled back into the car. "Go on with your tomfoolery," he said emphatically, albeit resignedly. And the Colonel went right ahead.

For half an hour the performance went on, until, in a lucky moment, the reptile got the middle of its length across a stone. Cotton saw his advantage. Like a flash, the machine darted for the stone. The wheels on one side grazed the granite wall; on the other they hit that part of the snake across the stone squarely. I was going to say that the snake made its last kick, but it didn't. Snakes, whatever else they may be, are not kickers. It just wiggled. But three men of the four in that fool-driven automobile did kick, most strenuously. Life and limb had been risked that Colonel Cotton might kill a rattlesnake with an automobile. Just then the millionaire thought of the other machine which should have been close behind. It was not in sight.

"Where on earth is Gammage?" he asked.

Where, indeed! His machine was supposed to be five minutes behind them, and more than a half-hour had been taken up by the snake episode. Everybody looked at everybody else. There were a dozen points down the road where the machine could have gone over the grade to the rocks below. It was a tense moment. Without a word, Cotton started the dangerous backing of his machine down the hill. But before they had gone far, a faint, "Hey!" came from down the road. In a moment Gammage was with them. He was covered with perspiration, dust, and grime. In his hand was a gallon can. The indignation on his face was plainly visible through the grime that masked him.

"Say," he began in choking sobs, not waiting to get his breath, "what do you suppose that fool photographer did at Smith's Creek ?"

Nobody ventured reply.

"He didn't put any gasoline in the tank," yelled Gammage, his breath recovered by this time. "There wasn't more than a gallon in the tank. He threw the rest away! Threw it away! What do you think of that? He let me fuss with that machine for half an hour before he told me. The machine's stalled—if you can't give me a gallon of gasoline, it'll stay stalled. If you can spare a gallon, perhaps it will get me up the hill and they may have some at the observatory."

Here was a pretty kettle of fish, surely. For once that day, the Colonel lost his head. He blamed Gammage for not filling the tank himself, but wound up by giving a scant gallon of gasoline from his own diminishing supply.

Gammage started down the road and again the climb of the hill was begun. There were no more stops to kill rattlesnakes, time and gasoline were too precious, and besides there weren't any more rattlesnakes. About four o'clock, Cotton had the satisfaction of seeing his machine planted squarely at the door of the observatory, the first two-seated automobile that ever climbed the mountain.

But his triumph was by no means complete; there was no photographer to take the much-valued picture. That necessary individual was far down the hill with Gammage. Looking down the side of the mountain, Gammage's machine, a wee speck of an automobile, could be seen slowly climbing upward; Gammage was evidently husbanding his gasoline. Half an hour passed and it climbed closer and closer, until it disappeared around the last turn in the road, not three hundred yards from where Cotton and his companions stood. From the time it disappeared around the curve that machine should have been with them in two minutes. But it didn't come. Ten minutes passed, and four men of Cotton's party started down the road. At the turn, they found the machine—two hundred yards from the top—stalled. The last drop of gasoline was gone. Four grimy, disheveled, temper-lost men were trying to push it up the stretch which is almost level. As their companions neared—they stopped. Hill, the culprit, had been made to do the hardest work, and the dirtiest. He stood on the outskirts of the group, a sad object to look at. The perspiration had run down his face in streams and the dirt had settled on his beard until it stuck out straight and stiff like a mask. He had a wrench in his hand. He looked as though he had suffered much.

"Gasoline out," announced Gammage, acidly.

But fortunately that was a difficulty that could be remedied now, and in a twinkling the two machines were at the observatory door.

Hill took the picture, for no better natured man than he breathes. But as he passed the newspaperman, the only person present who had shown any sympathy for him, he said:

"I never rode in one of these things before in my life, and if the Lord will just let me get back to San Jose and civilization alive, I never will again!"

Cotton had intended that the trip should be given an interesting write-up in the *Cosmopolitan*. But sturdy John Brisbane Walker, through his secretary, announced that his steam automobile business was one thing and his magazine another. The magazine was not to be used to boom the automobiles. So the article never appeared; Hill's hard-earned photographs were not used. The trip was a successful one, but from an advertising standpoint there was "nothing doing," although all bets were paid.

Motoring Over the Overland Route

By Allan Dunn

Along the western rim of this, our continent, the rim which holds such a large proportion of our scenic grandeur, much of the latter is accessible only along the Trail of the Iron Horse. The climbing of the heights, the swoop from snow-covered solitudes, through forest, by lake, and over torrent, down to the flowering plains which man has captured, is chiefly the privilege of the traveler by rail; but there are rare occasions when railway motor cars, more or less official, go over the steel trail, giving their passengers the opportunities for sight-seeing that railway travelers enjoy, coupled with the delight of the out-of-doors.

From June to September of the past year, the writer, in varying company, motored, on the tracks of the Union Pacific, Oregon Short Line, and Southern Pacific companies, from Omaha to San Francisco, from San Francisco to Los Angeles and return, including trips along various branch lines, crossing the grassy plains of Nebraska, skimming Great Salt Lake over the wonderful trestles and fills of the Lucin Cut-off, through the cañons of Utah, by the trail of the Mormon caravans, the prairies of Wyoming, over the crest of the continent, through Nevada, through the snowsheds of the Lake Tahoe district, through the Bret Harte Country, a-down the Coast of California, where the Pacific surf breaks at the base of the railroad embankments, past the missions, past orange groves and fruit orchards, beneath stately oaks that shade natural parks carpeted with flowers, over mountain, hill, and dale, past pasture and prairie, ocean and river, cañon and valley, forest and field and farm; through lands where sojourned the Indian and his buffalo, the pioneer, the Spaniard. It is hard to imagine a more delightful itinerary; it would be difficult to duplicate as enjoyable a trip.

The car, still in active use, was put into commission for the replenishing of the thousands of valuable negatives belonging to the Southern Pacific library and destroyed in the great fire of April.

It is two-seated, comfortably cushioned with a top to keep off the sun. Rain and wind may be defied with canvas curtains. On such a perfect roadbed, not much power is needed to achieve speed and the one cylinder, eight horse-power engine was found sufficient and trustworthy. Five was usually the number carried, including the chauffeur, or engine man in railroad parlance, and the conductor or pilot, the latter supplied anew at each division and qualified to know the track with its spurs and switches by dark or by daylight. Similar cars are used on railroad systems for surveying and inspection work, while larger and more powerful cars are in use on suburban and other branch lines.

The car traveled as a train, either as a special, an extra or a section of some regular train. Stops were frequent for the photographers who, traveling this way, secured views of railroad scenery hitherto inaccessible or difficult to acquire. Regular train orders were issued to the conductor and in all respects the car moved as a regular train, meeting passengers and freights at sidings and being kept account of on the train sheets. As with other trains, telegraph stations could not be passed without the lowering of the semaphore or a clearance card. Safety thus assured, was made even more absolute by the possibility of, in a pinch, being able to lift the sixteen-hundred-pound weight off the track by handles provided at either end. This indeed was usually done at the end of each day's trip where there was no convenient spur track. The flange wheels were originally fitted with copper strips to achieve electric connections and throw the signals of the block system, but the oil of the ball bearings defeated this intention, save when the car was at rest and the strips were removed.

The length of daily trips depended on the number of pictures taken, and in this connection, the amount of the regular trains. Luxury accompanied the journey in the shape of a private car, sent ahead on a regular train and serving as a traveling hotel in many places where hotels are not. This was also fitted up for the development of photographic negatives. The record trip was from Monterey to Santa Barbara in twelve hours, a distance of two hundred and seventy-five miles. The record time, a spurt of fourteen miles in seventeen minutes, down grade, near Cheyenne and another of four miles in five minutes flat near Chatsworth Park, California.

The average speed on level track without a head wind was thirty-three miles an hour. The grades were accomplished without difficulty on the low speed, the chief enemy to progress proving the wind which often cut us down to ten miles an hour going.

The varying altitudes caused a close watch to be kept on the carburetor as every rise or fall of a thousand feet the engine showed a tendency to choke. At eight thousand feet, the mixture was decidedly weak in gasoline and the winds were highest and the grades steepest. But there were no stops. In five thousand miles, only three breakdowns occurred, once through poor gasoline; once because a screw dropped out of the crankcase and, the oil leaking out, a joint crystalized and the crank went out of commission; and once when a bearing froze and the car was run over an obliging culvert, stripped the engine, and ground down the shaft with emery.

The weight of the engine being on the front axle, there was no danger of the wheel flanges not taking the curves. A powerful foot brake was always effective and once, when an inquisitive cow appeared at a sudden curve, the brake and reverse in combination stopped the car dead from full speed within two feet. A regular police gong warned trackmen and alarmed at road crossings, though an improvement might be achieved here in using a whistle connected with the exhaust. A powerful carbide searchlight was all effective for night traveling.

A good deal of after-dark work was done, proving one of the most exciting pleasures of the trip. The big arc of the lamp's ray illuminating the landscape, the scurrying of prairie dogs or badgers across the track, the keen night air, fresh and sweet from mountain side or prairie, the thundering past of a limited express, ablaze from headlight to observation car, the wait on a siding for a delayed freight, coughing its way up the grade, the talks with the men of the railroad and the peep into their world and work, the explosion of torpedoes under the wheel or the burning of a torch spiked into a tie to warn of a train just ahead, the mysterious eyes of the road, red and green and white and blue; all combined to give a thrill to the night travel that made it an enjoyable anticipation and memory.

Of course there is one little joker in the enjoyment of such a trip. Railroad permission is needed, and cannot be secured unless the traveler is on official railway business.

The motor car proved a surprise party sometimes, as, for instance, when a heavy freight would be given meet orders for the car and the anxious gaze of the hog-head (*Anglice:* engineer) would see the little car revealed in the blaze of his headlight. "Gee, Bill," he would call to his fireman, "come and look at the toy wagon we got orders on."

Automobiles in the Sagebrush

By Clara E. Douglas

In 1905, there were two automobile companies in Goldfield, Nevada, but early last year the routes through that big gold-mining country were segregated, the Nevada Mobile Transit Company taking the southern field. This company uses Pope-Toledo, Columbia, Winton, and Rambler cars; also the Christman car. Of these last named, the company have two of sixty horse-power. Their Pope-Toledo machines are seventy horse-power. At Goldfield, the company has first-class repair shops.

Apart from public motor cars, the desert state sends innumerable private autos speeding from camp to camp. Goldfield has about fifty private owners; and Tonopah quite as many more. Record trips have been made from both camps, and some marvelous speed and climbing have been accomplished. A Stevens-Duryea car, driven by Renfro, came over the old Southern Pacific toll road, some six hundred and fifty miles, across the Sierra, without mishap or detention; and a Pope-Toledo car made fifty-one miles, over the old road between Tonopah and Manhattan in one hour and fifty minutes. A still more fascinating trip was that made by George A. Bartlett, a Tonopah attorney recently elected to Congress. He ran from Tonopah to Eureka, one hundred and fifty miles in eight hours and fifty-five minutes, in a Winton. Just how much of that time was consumed by a break-down in Pine Creek I do not know. The machine had to be pulled out by horses; so quite a little of the eight hours and fifty-five minutes must have escaped.

There are several other instances of record-breaking autos in this region. Without a car the modern prospector of means considers it not worthwhile to venture forth. A famous trip was that which was started from Goldfield by Messrs. Ish and Camp. They used a forty-horse-power Pope-Toledo, and visited parts of the desert never before touched by man. Their itinerary was from Goldfield by way of Tonopah to Manhattan; thence to Cloverdale, to Mina; and from Mina to Hot Springs, sixty miles, in a little less than three hours. They ran from Hot Springs to Fairview, to East Gate and returning by way of Austin another speed rate was registered—over eighty-five miles in three hours and twenty minutes. The entire trip, through heavy sands and in many instances over untraversed alkali waste, was made without mishap of any sort. What a contrast to the dreadful hardships of this trip for early-day prospectors!

The Overland Tour of the "Glidden Auto-Special"

A railway motor car officially designated as the "Glidden automobile special," pulled out of the La Salle street station, Chicago, on November 22, over the Rock Island road. Charles J. Glidden, of Boston, who in his machine, "A 3622" had already traveled, since 1898, a distance of thirty-four thousand, seven hundred and ninety-six miles through thirty-five countries in his chase for the world's mileage record, was the "engineer and fireman" of the "Special." He announced his intention to go over five thousand, three hundred and two miles of railroad tracks in the southwest before arriving at his destination, the City of Mexico, on New Year's day.

Mrs. Glidden, who is just as ambitious as her husband to make the "50,000 miles, in fifty countries, within ten years,"—the automobilist's goal—sat in the front end of the "Special" beside him. She really occupied a position corresponding to that of a fireman, and Mr. Glidden, with his hands on the steering wheel, remarked that she did have a good deal to do with "firing" him with zeal for the rail.

The air was sharp and there was no glass windbrake on the front of the car. Both wore fur-lined coats. Their schedule called for them to whiz over the prairies of Illinois sometimes at a thirty-mile clip and sometimes as fast as fifty miles an hour. Mrs. Glidden said: "The cold will lend snap to the fun." As the glass roof of the train shed sent back to the tracks the sounds of a "honk-honk" horn, at 8:45 A.M., they pulled out, waving good-bye to a small band of shivering railway officials and motor enthusiasts. "That will be pretty chilly sport for sport's sake," said he. "Especially if they run into one of those El Paso blizzards, but I sort of wish I were aboard."

The special was run under orders from the Rock Island's train dispatcher in the same way that any special of Pullman cars would be. The officials said that if John D. Rockefeller had a special train, it would have to run as a "second section" of some other train, under the operating rules.

It started out as "Second No. 29," following the regular train of that number, which is the California and Mexico express. Harry Fennimore, a Rock Island conductor, in the tonneau with Miss M. W. Barron, was more of a boss than Mr. Glidden, who is a retired telephone and telegraph magnate. Fennimore was the conductor of this strange special, as other train conductors on other divisions of the road became, later on. The car could not start until Fennimore had gone to the telegraph office and signed the following order received from the dispatcher:

"No. 29 will display signals Chicago to Rock Island for an automobile occupied by Charles J. Glidden and party. Second No. 29 will run forty minutes late, Joliet to Morris, one hour late Morris to Ottawa, one hour twenty minutes late Ottawa to La Salle, one hour thirty minutes late La Salle to Bureau, one hour fifty minutes late Bureau to Sheffield, two hours ten minutes late Sheffield to Geneseo and two hours thirty minutes late Geneseo to Rock Island."

The regular train preceding the special carried green flags on the engine. They were the signal for a second section. And on the back of the automobile Fennimore, acting as his own brakeman, stuck two green flags, the required markers for the tail-end of the special.

Telegraph instruments and pole climbers were stowed away in the bottom of the car. Mr. Glidden, who began life as a telegraph messenger, later became an operator and retains his knowledge of the code and his old-time skill at sending and receiving messages.

In case the car breaks down somewhere he will be prepared to climb a pole, attach his instruments to the wire and ask a dispatcher for a relief train. The steel-flanged wheels replacing the rubber-tired ones on the automobile, will be tapped by train inspectors' hammers at railway division points, just as those of regulation railway cars are inspected.

That the "Glidden Special" will be an object of considerable curiosity and speculation along its route, goes without saying.

Autos and the Great Fire

By Wallace Everet

A few men were standing on the stern of the ferry steamer *Oakland* the other evening going to Berkeley, the suburban college town across the bay from San Francisco; when an automobile boarded the ferry. It glided on over the apron of the steamer with a gentle whirr, stopped, and its occupants left it for the protection of the cabins. One of our party turned to me and said: "I am glad to see these trans-bay boats opened to those machines. In my mind there is nothing too good for them since the fire. Minus their efforts in those stirring three days of April last year, San Francisco would be a mass of ruins from the water front to the Cliff House."

These words, few as they are, sketch the feeling all San Francisco entertains for the motor car of these days of After Destruction, 1907.

It was some time near five-thirty on the morning of April 18th, that a small auto-car shot down Market street carrying two blue-coated fire officials. The dust was just clearing from the street and the people were commencing to notice the fact that fires were starting along the water front and elsewhere in the stricken city. This fire chief and his assistant were not out for a pleasure spin even though the morning was a beautiful one, as California April dawns normally are, but the officials were on serious business bent—were traveling at a rate of thirty miles an hour from the central fire station to the harbor district to superintend the movements of their men and engines. The clang of the silver bell at the side-seat warned the scurrying citizens that there was trouble brewing and the street was progressively cleared from Van Ness to the ferry depot at the foot of Market. The motor car, with numerous others, had started on a three-day, non-stop run which was harder than any other test in which motor vehicles had ever participated. There had been but a moment's carburetor's priming by way of preparation after the coolness of the night and then the race for life and property was on. No time for adjustments, as every moment was most valuable. The race was only for the swift and the prize was the greatest ever sought. It was a city's salvation.

In the year 1901, the automobile had commenced to attract the attention of the pleasure-loving people in the good old city by the Golden Gate, but the cars were small while the expense bills were inversely large. Dissatisfaction was rife amongst the pioneers with purchases few and far between being limited to wee runabouts with wire wheels propelled by steam. Runs then were confined to the Park trip, to the ocean side, and these were considered marvelous without a boiler burning out, a thermostat unsettled, or a pipe covering scorched. Drivers were timid and street crossing citizens rightfully even more nervous when the runabout approached.

These and less amusing events witnessed the birth of the automobile enthusiasm in San Francisco, and the subsequent years have seen its growth in favor and proportionate increase in disfavor. Those who owned enjoyed, while those who looked on at the gasoline festival cursed the impudence of those who operated, and the disgruntled ones later christened the motors "Those devil wagons." Much of the local prejudice was due solely to arrogant driving or gross carelessness on the part of owners or their hired operators with the attendant disregard of the rights of pedestrians or horse drivers whose animals were yet unaccustomed to the noises of the motors. Not a little of the antagonism was due to ignorance on the part of those who did not drive and who looked upon the introduction of the automobile just as they had upon the appearance of the bicycle. Human nature is the same the world over, and many who operated motor cars felt that, Monte Cristo-like, the world was theirs. The thoughtful and considerate owners of horseless carriages suffered for the commissions or omissions of their fellow operatives. Yet the world, with its advancing views, continued its onward march of progress. The motor-driven vehicle had come to stay.

Gradually, step by step, evolution by evolution, owner by owner, the period of advancement continued. The public commenced to drive about in the cars rentable from in front of hotels and cafés. Current prejudice was wearing itself away through happy frictional contact with the cause of the feeling. The motor was winning its way, slowly it is true but surely and, where tens of machines had been used in 1901, thousands were being operated at the commencement of 1906.

Still there existed a strong feeling against the machines, and many were the muttered epithets heard as one drove down crowded streets or caused a slight commotion amongst unaccustomed horses driven by even more nervous drivers. It meant years of education ahead before the motor car could win its spurs. It meant cycles of self-control on the part of owners and the exercise of patience with the bigoted narrowness of individuals both in city and country. The introduction of the bicycle was finding a parallel in the introduction of the motor car. The time was not yet when the operators of the self-propelled car could expect reasonable, fair-minded treatment from those who did not, could not, or would not own an automobile. Every accident was over-sketched in the press while the car was blamed for many troubles when over indulgence in intoxicants, either on the part of those affecting or affected drivers, might far better have been the basis of criticism. Then came the stirring moments of April 18th.

With a bound, the automobile was found to be the only vehicle that could answer the exacting requirements of that hour. Horses were powerless in their fright or too slow to cover the fast increasing bounds of the blazing district. Space was far too great and time was the essence of all contracts. When buildings were being totally destroyed, one to each minute, and crumbling walls were making streets impassable, it was absolutely necessary that yards should be forgotten in miles. The trial by fire had come, and the automobile driver with his car was making good in every place at every time.

There were firemen and fire chiefs who needed transportation; there were policemen and their captains who were sorely needed here and needed there; doctors were numerous but patients were legion; the army and the navy furnished their quota of supervising officers and they had to be carried from the Bay to Van Ness, from the Presidio to the Channel. Every second meant success if utilized and failure if wasted. Where were the horse-driven vehicles that could fill the pressing demands of the occasion? Never did breed of Arabia or Kentucky foal the thoroughbred that could answer the call of the hour. Flesh could not obey the summons, and the horses were sent to the Park for safe keeping. Gasoline was king. The petrol which starts blazes was now, in this modern manner, employed in the successful extinction of the encroaching flames. Without the motor cars, San Francisco would have been swept from off the map of metropolitan communities.

Motor cars of all sizes and ages were scurrying hither and thither in their work of mercy or patrol. Deadly dynamite was carefully transported from the docks to the outskirts of the burning districts upon the rubber tires of the cars. When fire forced the removal of the injured from the Mechanics Pavilion, the automobile alone could furnish the requisite dispatch and hundreds were saved when their salvation would have been absolutely impossible through the dependence upon horse-drawn ambulances. The ease and rapidity of the silent motor cars saved those lives as later was saved the entire resident portion of the city, beloved by many. Down the blazing streets, Middleton forced his fleeing Columbia; up the hills of the frantic business section, laden with officials, McBryde rushed his powerful Pope; here with a quick, hair-raising swerve came Watson carrying hundreds of pounds of deadly dynamite in his great red Toledo; Rosenfelt, with his Peerless, took his chances through the lane of flaming buildings; doctors in their Autocars and Franklins swept along on their errands of aid and mercy while Winton and Stoddard-Dayton, Reo and Ford, Cadillac and Maxwell, White and Locomobile, Napier and Renault, Pierce and Packard, Stevens and Thomas—each and every available car from the little Olds to the mighty Mercedes—labored for the common weal. The great need of cars was fuel, and no pains were spared to aid in the salvation work of the motor car. The Southern Pacific railroad officials opened wide the doors of the company's storehouses, and gasoline was poured into the tanks of the automobiles that were all-powerful and omnipresent in the hour of need. One big ferry steamer was pressed into service and brought a cargo from Oakland for free distribution to the motor-car men.

It was a truly glorious sight, this rush of the despised bauble of the wealthy, the vehicle which had been slurred and cursed, damned and deplored. Now that the hour had arrived, the black had been transformed into the snowy white swan; the motor car had come into its own. The populace now knew that that which had been built for pleasure had eased pain; that that which was supposed to have its only purpose in the killing of the lagging time of the Great Unoccupied had, in its elimination of the equation of hours, saved a city which was their own. No more will the car be cursed as it passes, for the memories of those hours of waste and travail when the automobile saved the day will never be effaced from the appreciation of those who saw and, seeing, understood. Let its fair name be well fostered and protected by those who operate it, for the future of the motor car is not now dependent upon itself but solely upon those who sit at steering gear and throttle.

"The Benzine Bus has done for the desert what the steamship did for ocean travel."

BARTON W. CURRIE

As Americans made the automobile an increasing part of their daily lives, they extended its utility to increasingly unexpected purposes. Even in the scorching deserts of southwestern Nevada, for example, entrepreneurs found a use for the motor car as passenger transportation around raw new boom towns such as Tonopah, Goldfield, Bullfrog, and Rhyolite. With thousands of gold seekers flooding into this once-empty region after 1901, motorized express companies took on a role once filled with horse-drawn stages. Enterprises such as the Bullfrog Express, described here by author Barton Currie, sprang up to fill a new niche. Relying upon the sun-baked, hard-packed landscape rather than engineered highways, these motor carriers pioneered trails from camp to camp, "annihilating distance, overcoming the hardships and tortures men and animals suffered in the earlier discoveries of the untimbered, unwatered treasure mountains." Prospectors, mining engineers, and speculators adopted the horseless carriage as well, ensuring that "in every camp for hundreds of miles . . . you will hear the clatter and rattle of motors day and night." Propelling many new participants in this "ceaseless treasure quest" across the countryside, these motor cars confronted bone-crushing, lung-choking terrain and sometimes terrifyingly unpredictable weather that could gyrate from pounding cloudbursts to "desert sunblaze with a furnace intensity." Clearly fascinated by the automobile's evolution into a "gasoline camel" in Nevada's deserts, Currie (an essayist who would write over the years for many magazines from *Harper's* to *Ladies Home Journal* and *Country Gentleman*) described the frantic races ignited by agents for investors "of great means" trying to outrun their competitors to grab the choicest claims in any new-born mining strike. With so many roles to play, it thus seems likely that these mining booms significantly influenced the upsurge in Nevada's automobile population from 10 in 1900 to 70 in 1905 and 460 in 1910, as noted by automotive historian James J. Flink.

The Gasoline Camel of the American Desert

By Barton W. Currie

[*Harper's Weekly* 51 (March 16, 1907)]

"I WISH TO HIRE A CAR FOR TWO OR THREE DAYS TO TAKE some friends to my Hedgehog claim. It is just across the Amargosa Desert. In some spots the sand is deep, and there is a 4000-foot elevation in twenty miles. Altogether, though, there is only thirty or forty miles of bad going in the hundred. I will need extra tanks of gasoline and water as we cut away from the main route. It would also be wise to carry surplus tires. What's the damage, pal?"

"One thousand dollars."

"Easy. You're on."

The Bullfrog express—a long rangy car, with big wheels and high clearance—had just brought in a little party of four from Goldfield, an even seventy-eight miles from garage to garage of the motor-stage company.

It was a burning day. The indoor thermometers scaled well above 100. Outside, dust that stung like lime-powder wove about in eddies and spiral clouds. The express had boomed down the trail, her Gabriel horn wheezing a nasal salute in a thick smother of alkali. The vermilion body of the car was coated a ghostly white. The faces of the passengers and driver seemed ingrained with chalk; under their goggles the whites of their eyes, cut by the dust, glistened like dull edges of flame. Jumping from the car, one of the party signaled the agent of the automobile station to follow into the Blonde Kid saloon. While sparkling drinks were gulped down thirstily, the above brief dialogue took place.

The bargain was made as casually as one would hire a hansom on Broadway. Yet this was in a corner of the world where, until a few years ago, the pale stars of heaven have looked down for ages upon neither man nor beast.

Then there had come the intrepid gold-hunters, with their mule-teams and water-bags; some to locate dykes of precious ore outcropping from mountain and desolate valley dip, others to lose their way and, wandering in narrow circles, drop by their exhausted animals and die beside them of the excruciating thirst of the desert that has made scores who were saved bubbling madmen.

Now the snorting automobile whirls along these arid wastes in the ceaseless treasure quest. The modern gold-seekers could not wait for railroads, and lost patience with the tedious stage route. So they have installed the Benzine Bus, as southern Nevada calls the big heavy-bodied touring-car. In every camp for hundreds of miles in the lower half of the third-largest State in the Union, you will hear the clatter and rattle of motors day and night. Should you go up in a balloon after the sun had gone deep to rest behind the California Sierras, you would see all over the ocean of desolation beneath flashing eyes of seeming invisible insects moving swiftly in many directions.

Hundreds of cars are employed in this way. They have conquered the barren gold-fields, annihilating distance, overcoming the hardships and tortures men and animals suffered in the earlier discoveries of the untimbered, unwatered treasure mountains. They are not the toys of leisure-loving millionaires down there; the hated juggernauts of over-peopled cities; the pests of the humble, conservative farmer—rather they are the new tools of conquest. Expensive tools, to be sure, but what is expense to the folk who are gripped by the lure of gold and spend lives and fortunes in the hunt with grim ferocity!

Experienced motor-drivers on the desert are better paid than many bank presidents in small communities. Gasoline is seventy-five cents a gallon, but water has often been sold to the desperately thirsty prospector for $30 a quart.

Who brought the first automobile into southern Nevada is a vigorously mooted question in the new camps. You will find claimants to this distinction in Tonopah, Goldfield, Bullfrog, Beatty, and Rhyolite. These towns (some of them have almost the population of cities) are strung along, north and south, for more than one hundred miles. Several score cars traverse the new motor trail that loops them together, with punctual regularity every day.

One of the original settlers of Tonopah told me last fall that a half dozen cars, as far as he had observed, arrived simultaneously. In his opinion they were brought to the new bonanza country by a San Francisco salesman, who was speculative enough to take the same chance with them he would with alarm-clocks. He sold them all in a day, and went back for another consignment. Then someone introduced the fad of motoring all the way from the Pacific coast to the desert, and many more machines arrived in this way.

The Benzine Bus has done for the desert what the steamship did for ocean travel. It has concentrated widely scattered mining centers that were formerly vague and distant from one another because of the difficulties, hardships, and perils of travel by stage and burro over the rugged sand wastes, through boulder-clogged ravines, and over platter-flat dry lakes, from which the summer sun seems reflected in shimmering waves of flame and white heat.

What was only a few years ago a day's journey is now only an hour's skim. Yes, and there are hundreds of miles of automobile speedways. Not of the metropolitan or boulevard sort, of course; and the method of construction has not attached any road builders to the country, though some of the wilderness thoroughfares are as fine as Roman roads.

For the most part they are made by the simple device of running a few cars over the most likely line of travel along the flats rimmed in by the unclad hills. Once pressed down in even ruts, the sand hardens to a granite durability. Generally the line of direction was established between the already well-settled camps by the early stage routes and burro trails. But the motor-car did not use the roads followed by the big wagons and trailers, freight-laden and hauled by teams of twenty and thirty mules. The more primitive vehicles sank deep into the sand, and the shuffling mules sifted drifts of dust to both sides.

For a fast-flying gasoline-driven car, such a trail was impossible. Therefore the harder sports and sunbaked mud lakes were selected, making the going sure and facile. The first batch of motors to appear began running between Tonopah, Goldfield, and Manhattan, and threading innumerable prospect trails all about the country circled by these camps. The successful wild-catters have their own cars, with which they flit about with parties their dazzling circulars have attracted from afar. One of these machines has been nicknamed the "Suckers' Steamer," and another "The Good-thing Carryall." These autos have been of immense value in selling "dead holes" and "barren drifts."

It is an impressive proceeding to be whisked away through the stifling silences of the desert in a high-power automobile, luxuriously disposed in leather cushions, smoking a gold-banded perfecto, and giving a ready ear to tales of golden marvels. More than one canny Easterner can look back with pain to a Nevada motoring journey, in which he was spun into a fine web of sham and had his fortune gobbled by a wild-catting spider.

Though the Tonopah and Goldfield Railroad runs one train a day between those two camps, the two dingy, sawed-off cars of the nine-cent-a-mile corporation carry few passengers. Hustling Nevada folk prefer paying $5 for the thirty-three-mile auto express, making the distance in a few minutes more than half an hour, and saving one hour and a half. Now it is possible to travel entirely by automobile from Tonopah to the new camp of Greenwater, making an intermediary run from Goldfield to Bullfrog.

The Bullfrog express from Goldfield makes the journey of almost eighty miles in a little more than three hours, if no tire trouble is encountered. There are water and gasoline stations all along the trail: also tiny road-houses that loom up like hermits' cabins in the waste. The distance from Bullfrog to Greenwater, California, just over the Nevada border, and fringing above the edges of Death Valley, is practically the same as from Goldfield to Bullfrog. The going, however, is far more difficult, as you must cross that grim ridge of purple hills known as Funeral Range.

Until you reach the borax works at Furnace Creek, an eye-delighting little oasis on the rim of Death Valley, you do not see a great thing—only sere and gray sage-brush and the crouching Joshua-tree, whose twisted branches resemble a cluster of Medusa's curls. On a moonlight night these stunned growths stand out on the plains like writhing ghosts, and cast long, wriggling shadows across the trail.

There are many stretches of sun-blistered sand-plats, where you will motor for miles without even a glimpse of a Joshua tree. In occasional sheltered spots you may find grease-wood and chamisal. On either side there will be an endless monotony of a stark and naked hillside. In the utter silence, the engine of the car becomes a mighty instrument of torture. Always, after a smooth run, sand-drifts roll up like oncoming billows. Then you have experience of what the desert can offer in the way of "Thank-you-marms." Having passed a rough sea of hummocks, limp and breathless, you shoot down grade onto a dry lake, flat and unyielding as asphalt, and not a whit dustier than the pavement of many cities. Here you may safely go on three speeds and see the wing of your speedometer jerk up to 60. On one of these dry lakes below Goldfield, the local motorists are planning an automobile meet for next spring, and hope to draw entries from all the gold camps for hundreds of miles about.

Rain is mighty scarce, and showers rare down there in the borderland of the Amargosa and Great American deserts, but they are as tremendous in their way as the mountains and wastes. They will wipe a splendidly beaten auto speedway out of existence in a few minutes. These showers came up with great suddenness. A mammoth black cloud will walk right across the sky and chain a black curtain from hill range to hill range. Then the sable canopy will break in great rents, releasing sheer walls of water. Wherever there is a gully or indentation on the mountainside, a river will shoot down with tossing waves. Like great mist-shrouded serpents, they will go twisting across the flat, gouging out the sand to a depth of from two to four feet, and rolling about rocks and boulders with a dull, rattling noise.

To be caught in one of these cloudbursts in an auto is vastly uncomfortable. You can think of no other shelter than crawling under the car, and there one of the made-in-a-moment rivers is apt to plunge after you, beat you with its water, and fill your lungs with its arsenic mud.

Once the sun comes out again, you are quickly dried, or rather scorched dry, for the moisture in the air will give the desert sunblaze a furnace intensity. Probably an hour afterwards, another car will come shooting along the trail and stumble into dry ruts and gullies where foaming torrents had been. Incidents of this sort raise havoc with tires. Often in the big camps you will see a lumbering machine clatter up the roadway with both front tires gone and the metal rims bent all out of circumference. It is far from joyous riding in a crippled motor through that wilderness, be it day or night. By day you have the consuming sunlight, and at night black palls of shadow that blot out all the world except a few blinking stars overhead.

The hills of this ungreened altitude are only beautiful when the rising or declining sun robes them in a purple that has the soft sheen of velvet. More often they are drab or tawny, looking like great calcined mounds; gloomy, and terrible in their aspect of external death.

Once, while crawling along in the Bullfrog express, with only one battery sparking feebly and a punctured tire flapping behind (the third that had blown up in twenty-five miles), a strange mirage sprang up before my eyes like a luminous curtain of steam across a distant mountain-top. A huge figure of unearthly and unnatural hideousness was crawling over the rocky shoulder of the hill, seemingly picking its way on a white ribbon of a mule trail that led off to an isolated mine fifty miles beyond. In shape the apparition was like some of the reconstructed monster of the Mesozoic family. It had many feet, a vast tail that whisked about amid clouds of dust. The head wobbled in an appalling red blotch, glistening with what I fancied were tongues of darting flame.

The terror of the strange mirage had just begun to strike in upon me when it suddenly vanished, and left the mountain again a blighted, forbidding monument of an age when worlds crashed together in volcanic labor. The driver of the car smiled sagely when I told him of the mirage. He said mine was a mild fancy. He had seen an entire range of hills peopled with hippogriffs, pterodactyls, hairy mammoths of gaudy color, and tangled clusters of snakes of prodigious size.

"It's this one-color scheme of hill and desert," he said, "and the glare of the sun. Some passengers, old-time gold hunters, told me that these mirages were actual photographs of chuckwallahs—huge desert lizards you find in the Death Valley region—and other crawling things. It's a trick of the atmosphere, they said, to slide these pictures across the sky from a hundred or more miles away. That may be, but I doubt if they would ever be magnified to such an extent. Other mirages—upside-down pictures of mule teams, automobiles, and the like—I've seen aplenty. Thirst-maddened prospectors perpetually see mirages of springs and water-holes. But none of these, as far as I can learn, are magnified to any great extent. Then, what should the little wriggling things be? Nix. It's either germs in your eye or the heat."

The southern Nevada automobile, with a modest grubstake, can still be seen trekking hill and plain as solitary as the Wandering Jew. His transit equipment is usually a team of mules or a tireless little burro.

A single fare in the Bullfrog express is $25, one dollar for every three miles. At Tonopah you can rent a car by the day for from $100 to $200, according to the capacity of the machine and the nature of the journey. From $50 to $100 extra is demanded when the trip is to be made over little-travelled trails, along which there is no water or gasoline. On the regularly travelled routes there are gasoline stations, and a telegraph wire that may be tapped whenever aid is required. Parties of prospectors often go out prepared for a week's stay in order that careful examinations may be made of remote properties and a deal closed without further tedious bickerings. Quite frequently a mine-operator will tell you how he paid for his new machine in a day, either in a race for a claim or in the sale of a prospect to which he, as agent for the owner, rushed his party across wastes and through mountain passes, beating out other agents who were negotiating the same sale.

Whenever a new hill range or valley dip is revealed as rich in treasure, there is furious activity in mining camps. Cars are overhauled and geared up to their best for an endurance run of perhaps one or two hundred miles. Accessories of comfort—hoods and other gear not emergently needed—are cast aside as flotsam and jetsam from a ship, whereupon the stripped machines charge out of the Big Diggings like racketing racers getting away from the line at the Vanderbilt Cup Race. Men like Charles M. Schwab, the Comstocks of Milwaukee, Senator [William] Clark, [F. Augustus] Heinze, and many other millionaires, who are investing heavily in Nevada mining operations, have their agents stationed at various points of vantage on the desert, ready at almost a moment's notice to mount their *benzene steeds* and get in the running for some new field where a big strike has been made. In this way the very best properties are secured under option by the men of great means.

When the Walker Reservation was opened in Nevada last October, a veritable phalanx of automobiles stood waiting on the line, their throbbing cylinders hammering in mighty chorus. At the signal of the government agent, there was a thrilling dash around the border of Walker Lake, which in some aspects resembled a chariot race, for there were several bad collisions.

There were many really "wooly" features to this race. Tires were punctured with rifle-balls. There was considerable bloodshed. Prospectors on ponies got into the running with the motorcars, and the mounted gold hunters were dead shots when it came to pinking a tire. The small force of Indian police was utterly helpless to preserve order, though they made a few arrests and headed off several crippled automobiles.

There was a great stir in southern Nevada over this Walker Reservation incident, and such a pother was made about the unfair advantage taken by the motoring prospectors that the government declared the opening off and set a later day, when a troop of United States cavalry will go down into the desert to see that there is no claim-jumping, squatting, and unnecessary bloodshed. The charge was made at the time that government engineers had located the richest claims and marked them so that confederates could dash into the reservation in fast automobiles and grab them.

“The effect of speedy motoring is that of drinking several cups of strong coffee.”

AUTOMOBILE CLUB OF AMERICA TRIP PLANNER

Among the profusion of early articles intended to engage the potential motorist, many of them took the prescriptive approach that typifies this concise guide to the practice of motor touring and camping. Beginning with such simple details as the availability of “touring baskets fitted with all the necessities for a picnic party,” Alfred Goodwin leads his readers through a thorough discussion of motor vacationing’s crucial characteristics, from what equipment would be required and costs would be incurred to what destinations would most fully reward the motorist and what steps would maximize the pleasure found in such trips.

A frequent contributor to *Country Life in America*, especially in profiling America’s recreational pastimes, Goodwin here brings to bear the expertise of other commentators about motor traveling such as Harry B. Haines and A. L. Westgard (both of whom are also represented in this series). Repeating an increasingly familiar argument made by auto enthusiasts, for example, Haines asserted that “with the auto one has the train speed and radius without the train discomfort and the vacation spent in touring will be the ideal vacation indeed.” Convenience and independence thus were woven into popular conceptions of the automobile, especially in its recreational capacity. Authors such as Goodwin— through forums such as the “Automobiles” column in *Country Life in America*—found opportunities to promote the advantages as well as the attractions of the motoring life. At the same time, by providing such methodical advice about what to take and where to go, Goodwin’s article (like many others published in this decade) remind us that motor vacations were far from effortless excursions and they still frequently required considerable investments of disposable income and leisure time. Moreover, such articles also emphasize that depictions of *process* were still essential for a neophyte motoring public.

The Automobile Vacation

By Alfred Henry Goodwin

[*Country Life in America* 12 (1907)]

It is possible now to buy touring baskets fitted with all the necessaries for a picnic party. Knives, forks, spoons, plates, cups, saucers, and even linen are all nicely arranged. A small ice-box skillfully hidden in the tonneau will keep drinkables cools, and one of the rubber robes will make a nice table-cloth.

"In preparing for a tour of summer vacation by motor," says Harry B. Haines, "one must first realize that a well-filled pocketbook and congenial companions, who will not fret or worry if any delays are met with en route, are essentials if a good time is to be enjoyed. Next prepare your schedule, which will, of course, depend greatly upon the character of country you are to tour through. In hilly or mountainous country from eighty to one hundred miles a day will be found a sufficient distance to traverse in comfort, while in level country where the roads are good, 175 or even 200 miles a day is not too far. It all depends, of course, on how fast or powerful a car one has and also on the luck met with in machinery and tires.

"Even if your car is geared to fifty miles an hour, that does not signify that you are going to be fifty miles away from your starting point at the end of each hour. If a touring machine, taking into consideration the vehicles met en route, the slowing down for turns, hills, etc., can cover twenty-five miles at the end of an hour, it has done most excellently. The general average hourly mileage in touring is from fifteen to twenty-two miles an hour. To cover even twenty miles at the end of an hour, one must needs have been running at the average rate of twenty-five miles an hour and to have been sprinting at thirty miles an hour somewhere along the route.

"The usual touring arrangement with a party of four is to have the two men in the front seats and the two women in the tonneau. With the new side entrance cars with cape tops, the dust nuisance as far as the people in the cars are concerned is obviated, but the women who dress in cravenette material will find that their clothes will brush up easily and look much better and cleaner at the end of the day's trip. An equipment for touring that is complete, if rather expensive, includes the following items:

One new casing in reserve.
Four new inner tubes.
Tire repair kit.
Tire irons for removing tire.
Tire pump.
Two screw jacks for raising rear or front wheels.
Two rawhide tire bandages to repair blown-out casings.
Nail pullers on rear wheels.
Extra valve for each tire.
French chalk for use in casing.
Bags for inner tubes to prevent their chafing.
Seat covers and lamp covers to protect car from dust and mud.
Goggles for all passengers.
Chain tire grips to prevent skidding on muddy roads.
Collapsible water and gasoline bucket.
Funnels with strainers for both water and gasoline.
A meter to test batteries.
Hydrometer to test gasoline.
Electric hand lamp to look around car at night.
Rear basket with concealed extra gasoline supply.
Luncheon basket.
Rain clothes for men and women.
Umbrellas, dusters, thin cravenettes which may be tucked away under the seats.

An emergency medical kit.
A dashboard clock.
Suitable road maps.
Extra oil supply.
Extra spark plugs.
Spare quick-wearing parts (these are different on every type of car).
Extra inlet and exhaust valves.
Extra chain links for chain-driven cars.
A complete tool kit.

"With this outfit the man who wants to take a summer vacation in his car will find himself well equipped for the trip and may start off feeling sure that he is going to reach his destination, safely and in good time. He can stop wherever the fancy strikes him and can enjoy the real beauty of the country as he could in no other way.

"The White Mountains, the Berkshires, New York State, New Jersey, Pennsylvania have hundreds of miles of improved roads that appeal to the automobile tourist and lead them to historic and interesting spots. Study up your route, know what is interesting and worth seeing, and look for it. With the auto, one has the train speed and radius without the train discomforts, and the vacation spent in touring will be the ideal vacation indeed."

Eugene Meyer, Jr., who puts in his summers motoring in Great Britain, said:

"It is a great help to be a member of an American automobile club. Go over with your ticket of membership, and with letters of introduction to the secretaries of two or three of the English automobile clubs, for instance.

"The secretary in London, let us say, will be the first man you meet. He will sit down with you and plan out routes for your trip, and give advice about roads and inns.

"When we arrived in Henley, just in time for the Regatta, the local club took charge of our machine, so that we could go out and have luncheon, and see the race. The courtesy of the foreign clubs is unfailing, and a great aid to the American tourist.

"Then here is another suggestion: Send your machine across the water three days ahead of you. I didn't do that last summer, however, but I sent it on the same boat by the Morris Express Company—the foreign branch of Adams. So perfect is the system, that at 8 P.M. of the day of the landing, the automobile was out of its crate, charged with gasoline and ready for action, with the numbers and everything prepared. Contrast that with the reception tendered you when you arrive home.

"My boat arrived on Thursday, and my machine was released for use only on Monday.

"Gasoline is obtainable all over the British Isles. In fact, I might say that gasoline distribution is becoming a great industry of Great Britain."

A. L. Westgard, who plots out five to ten trips a day for the members, one by one, of the Automobile Club of America, has planned the following vacation for readers of *Country Life in America.*—And first let it be said, get some sort of a route book so that you know in which direction you are going to tour. Such a book is "The Blue Book," giving maps, routes, hotels, garages, distances, and the other detailed information that lend definiteness to vacation plans.

Mr. Westgard said: "A capital three weeks' automobile tour can be taken from New York City up through New England. Strike through Connecticut to Springfield, Boston, then to Portsmouth, then to the White Mountains, where little side trips may be taken in every direction. Come back by the Connecticut Valley to Greenfield, to North Adams, to Pittsfield, Albany, Troy, Saratoga. From Saratoga turn toward New York by way of Poughkeepsie, Newburgh. From Newburgh run to Port Jervis. Take the Delaware River to the Delaware Water Gap, then home to New York City.

"This trip is as satisfactory as any eastern trip. There are no prohibitive hills. The roads are good. The scenery is fine. The hotels are excellent. There are good garage accommodations. Gasoline and general supplies are easily obtainable. Or, to state the matter in motor language—there is no stretch of thirty miles in the whole trip that leaves you out of reach of a garage and a hotel.

"In July and August ideal conditions prevail. The tourist will get away from the heat. And yet there are no high mountains to cross. The road goes by the valleys, to one side of the mountains. The speed he will be allowed to make is an average of twenty miles an hour in the open country districts. In the settled portions the speed will vary from four to ten miles an hour. The driver must use common sense in relation to the demands of the traffic.

"The cost will be $8 to $10 a day on the inside limit. The price of gasoline is twenty-five cents a gallon, almost everywhere. The time will come when the automobile association will be able to stretch out its strong arms of help and secure price reductions all along the route, in hotels, garages, and gasoline for members. Such aid is rendered to motor clubs' members on the Continent. In time we shall have the same admirable system. Meanwhile the bills of most hotels go up 200 per cent, as soon as they see the motor car. There is one price for the commercial traveler and ordinary citizen and another price for the owner of a motor car and his friends.

"Of course, there are methods of evading this in certain towns. You can put your machine in a garage and then go around to the hotel like a simple wayfarer. That will certainly help with the bill. But a good many men rather like to ride up to the hotel door.

"It is entirely possible to go camping with an automobile. Of course, Judge Dill does that in a fascinating way up in the forest country of Maine and Canada, but that is pioneering. And you have to be prepared to go for a stretch of 200 miles without replenishing. I know an auto party who took a light tent along and camped out in the White Mountains. They bought their supplies from the farmers. If people are willing to do their own work, they can do that sort of thing reasonably and successfully and happily.

"On an ordinary tour 120 to 140 miles a day will prove to be a good average. In starting out, don't drive too hard at first. The danger is to end up such a trip by getting over-exhilarated. The effect of speedy motoring is that of drinking several cups of strong coffee. The person ends up dizzy and tired unless the beginnings are gradual.

"For clothing you will certainly want clothing that will keep out moisture during the cool mountain evenings, and you will want wind-proof fabric—light rubber-silk."

"The speedometer will not cost much more than the fines a country justice may impose, to say nothing of the trouble and delay occasioned by arrest."

HARRY B. HAINES

EVEN AS AUTOMOBILE MANUFACTURERS MADE TRANSCONtinental motor trips a more familiar aspect of the automotive landscape, other motorists with less grandiose ambitions proliferated as well. To help them make the best possible use of the rapidly developing motor car, a robust prescriptive literature flourished. Incorporating the growing body of experience accumulated by drivers, manufacturers, and motor clubs, articles such as Harry Haines's in *Scientific American*, providing advice, education, and encouragement, continued what other writers such as Hrolf Wisby and Henry Sutphen had begun in earlier years. A New Jerseyan, Haines himself was the author of multiple articles about automobiles and motor travel and wrote first about what kinds of vehicles would make the best choice for auto touring. He then proceeded to comment at length about how the proper machine should be most effectively equipped and supplied. His various recommendations demonstrated that motor touring still required intensive preparations for many contingencies, from mechanical calamities to inclement weather. The prudent motorist would still carry a formidable array of materials, from extra tires and inner tubes, spark plugs, and valve springs to non-skid chains, assorted hand tools, a collapsible water bucket, and a flashlight.

Having enumerated such an imposing list, however, Haines could still urge his readers at the same time that "as in traveling by other means or when camping, the less paraphernalia one has to bother with, the greater is his ease of mind and subsequent enjoyment." By 1907, for example, Haines would argue, the automobile's "radius of action" had so expanded that camping was no longer a necessity even in long-distance travel, for motorists would rarely find themselves out of reach of accommodations as they rumbled across the countryside. Moreover, motoring tourists in a properly prepared automobile would escape the restrictions of time table and route that hampered railroad passengers. Instead, they could travel "all the roads of the country as [their] right of way [free from any] schedule other than that fixed by [their] own fancy and convenience." Independence, comfort, and practicality thus remained crucial characteristics of automobility, even as the nature of motor travel evolved.

How to Tour in an Automobile

By Harry B. Haines

[*Scientific American* 97, no. 19 (November 9, 1907)]

Ideas differ widely, of course, as to the most suitable type of car for touring. Many enthusiastic motorists who have toured thousands of miles prefer to drive in a light high-powered runabout of the style that has leaped into sudden popularity within a year.

A strictly limited amount of baggage can be stowed away on the rear deck in a leather waterproof bag or in a steamer trunk strapped on the deck, and a rubber poncho can be carried for protection against rain. With powerful headlights for night driving, and a good blanket for sleeping out at night, if necessary, one can drive for days through the roughest country in remote mountain regions. He will, however, enjoy a sort of selfish pleasure, for at most he can carry only one friend and a mechanic, as the car has only one regular double seat, which is supplemented by a folding rumble seat behind that offers nothing in the way of comfort on a hard day's jaunt. The majority of tourists prefer the regular touring car, with side entrance body, having comfortable seating accommodations for five or seven persons. In such a car, properly fitted out for the purpose, a whole family may travel for weeks almost as luxuriously as in a Pullman railroad car, regardless of weather.

The question of suitable equipment for touring is one that requires considerable thought. It is possible to spend many hundreds of dollars for all sorts of fittings. Some of these are almost indispensable to comfort and satisfaction on the road, while others only serve to encumber the machine unnecessarily. Although each device may really serve a useful purpose, it should be remembered that, as in traveling by other means or when camping, the less paraphernalia one has to bother with, the greater is his ease of mind and his consequent enjoyment. Too often we pack along on a trip or vacation a bothersome quantity of stuff, much of which is never used.

On the other hand, if we confine ourselves to the things that are really essential, we are likely to be surprised by the small amount of baggage that we have to take. Conceding that the automobile tourist desires simply to fit up his car with the attachments and devices that will add to the utility of the machine and to the comfort and safety of the passengers, there are certain things which it will be absolutely necessary for him to have. A comfortable Cape top and glass front are indispensable. In buying a Cape top, one should also get a waterproof protector, to be slipped over the top when it is thrown back. This will keep the dirt and dust out of the lining and prove a profitable investment. The machine should be fitted with a set of good shock absorbers, to protect the springs from breakage when traveling over rough country and also for the purpose of adding to the comfort of the occupants. A dashboard speedometer-odometer is another necessity when touring. Driving directions in many route books simply give the measured distances between prominent landmarks in sparsely settled country. For example, the book might read: "After passing large red farm house on left continue straight ahead a mile and a half and keep to right at fork in road." It will be seen that it is absolutely necessary to know when that mile and a half has passed, and the odometer is the only instrument that will accurately give this information.

The speedometer part of the combination is useful in view of the fact that speed ordinances and restrictions are becoming more severe every year, and when one is riding in an auto there is nothing more deceptive than speed. Even experienced men who have driven many thousands of miles are unable accurately to guess the speed at which a car is running, and five or ten miles an hour out of the way is no uncommon error. The speedometer will not cost much more than the fines a country justice may impose, to say nothing of the trouble and delay occasioned by arrest. Besides this, there is a great deal of truth in the statement, "It's nice to know how fast you go," and it is often fascinating to see the little needle on the instrument move up the scale as the car speeds steadily on under advanced spark and heavier charges of gas. When front and rear wheels are of different sizes, there should be one spare for each pair of tires. The new flat treads are recommended for the rear wheels, but not for the front, as they make steering rather difficult. Extra tires should be covered with waterproof and lightproof casings, as rubber deteriorates when exposed to light. It is advisable to carry at least two rear inner tubes and one front tube; when touring myself I invariably carry four rear tubes and two front tubes, having experienced as many as five punctures in a single day. Tire troubles are due to various causes, and it is well to be prepared for them. A pigskin repair cover will be found valuable in temporarily fixing a blown-out casing. In the event of a puncture, it is advisable to insert a new inner tube rather than to repair an old one, as it is almost impossible to make a satisfactory repair job on the road. Inner tubes for use in rear shoes should never be repaired with rubber patches cemented on. The heat caused by road friction melts these patches off. The only sure way is to have the tube vulcanized. Inner tubes should not be carried loose in a storage box, but should be put up in separate bags liberally sprinkled with French chalk, in order that they may not become chafed and so be rendered unfit for use.

An experienced tourist is not ready to start until the car is equipped with a full set of tools, extra valves, valve springs, spark plugs, and such small moving parts of the engine as are likely to wear quickly or break easily. Of course, this list will differ with each make of car. In machines that are chain driven, extra links of chain are carried in the toolbox. A jack, tire tools, and full tire repair kit are, of course, essential. In mountain touring it is necessary to have non-skid chains, which must be used when coming down long hills slippery with mud after a heavy rain. The car, unless equipped with these, may skid and become unmanageable. In the early days rope was tied around the rear wheels to give them traction, but the newer and more serviceable tire chains or non-skid treads have taken its place and made driving on slippery asphalt or "greasy" country roads much safer. Protection of the car and its occupants from mud and water has been looked after mostly by the manufacturer before the car left the factory. Cape tops and folding glass fronts do much to keep the car dry and comfortable in rainy weather. The machinery is also protected from mud and water by metal casings. It is advisable, however, to have mackintosh covers for the lamps when touring, so as to avoid the need of continual cleaning and polishing, and if the magneto is under the bonnet where rain may possibly reach the connections, they should be protected with a rubber arrangement suitable for that purpose. Many manufacturers neglect to furnish this, and as a consequence their cars have been stalled in wet weather by water getting into the magneto and short-circuiting it. The greatest care should be taken to keep water away from all the electrical parts of the machine.

It is possible, of course, to make a tent part of the equipment, but this will scarcely be used unless the party intends to camp out for the night. The automobile of to-day has such a wide radius of action by reason of its high speed that this is seldom necessary, as it is nearly always possible to reach a town or large city by night. It is best to have the car equipped with good headlights and a reliable generator or gas tank, as it sometimes becomes necessary to do night riding in a strange country. Even with good lamps it is never safe to drive faster than twenty miles an hour at night on roads with which one is not familiar, as danger can arise in an instant. The machine should always be kept under perfect control; half of the accidents that occur are due to careless driving.

Among the miscellaneous items that are needed and which come in very handy are a collapsible gasoline bucket with chamois strainer, collapsible water bucket, ammeter and voltmeter for testing the batteries, small electric flashlight to examine the car at night in the event of accident, and a dash clock.

Most cars of today have plenty of carrying and storage room. The extra tires are usually strapped to the running board with special holders. Inner tubes may be stored in the space under the rear seats. Extra boxes on the running board will provide a place for carrying tools, while a metal trunk rack fitted with leather auto trunks that are dustproof and waterproof, will serve for baggage.

The modern touring car, properly equipped, is capable of railroad speed and will take a party safely across country, uphill and down, in rain or shine, with more pleasure than can be derived from any other method of transportation. The man who owns his automobile has his private car as luxurious as a Pullman, with all the roads of the country as his right of way and no schedule other than that fixed by his own fancy and convenience.

The writer has always found it preferable to lay out the route intended to be followed. He has also found it a convenient practice to have a leather case made with a celluloid front in which the road directions can be placed. The map or directions can be read through the celluloid, which, however, protects them in case of rain. The easiest way to get along when asking road directions of natives in various towns is to know the name of the next following town and then ask the best road to it, if the road book directions are not explicit. For instance, before starting on a trip I generally take a map of the country through which I am going to travel and ascertain the various small towns through which I have to pass. These are listed, and as I proceed I inquire the way from one to another. This method has been found satisfactory, for when one asks the road directions to the larger cities, which may be ten, twenty, or more miles apart, it is difficult to find anyone who can direct you properly, but any boy or girl can tell you the best road to the next town, which will probably be from three to give miles away.

Having selected a route that you wish to travel, it is well to make out a time schedule and try to follow it, making due allowance in advance for delays *en route* and for the time that will be spent in viewing the scenery and points of interest.

You may have a 50-horse-power car, capable of a mile a minute speed, but if you are going to use the car for touring and expect to get any pleasure out of the tour, it would be better to have the machine geared down to forty miles an hour, so that it will have additional hill-climbing power. It is not the car that can go fastest on the level that can cover the greatest distance in a day, but rather the machine that is consistent in its performance and keeps "plugging" along, uphill and down, hour in and hour out, and always drawing steadily toward its destination. The tourist who really wants to see the country through which he is passing and to enjoy a sensible ride rather than a mad dash against time would do well to plan his schedule on the basis of covering twenty miles an hour—or less, if he does not have a high-powered car. This would be slow on the smooth, level roads, but where the country is rolling, an average of twenty miles an hour is a good one, and to maintain it, the car will be going at twenty-five and even thirty miles at many places. Besides, twenty miles is the legal limit in most States. Connecticut's new law, however, abolishes the speed limit but makes arrest possible for reckless driving if one travels over twenty-five miles an hour.

It is safe to presume that every motorist seeks to get as much pleasure and comfort out of touring as possible. The States of New York, New Jersey, Pennsylvania, Connecticut, Rhode Island, Massachusetts, Vermont, New Hampshire, and Maine offer not only the most beautiful and varied scenery but the finest of roads. One particularly beautiful route which I have had the pleasure of taking leads from New York City up along the west side of the Hudson River to Newburg and Pine Hill, New York, and then to Binghamton, Bath, and Buffalo, whence last year's Glidden Tour route may be followed to Rochester, Syracuse, Utica, Albany, Saratoga, and

Lake Champlain, New York; Three Rivers, Montreal, and Quebec, Canada; Jackman, Maine; Rangeley Lakes, and then to Bretton Wood, in the famous White Mountains of New Hampshire. The roads, with the exception of some stretches in Canada, are good. The return journey may be made by the way of Concord, New Hampshire; Boston, Worcester, and Springfield, Massachusetts; then to Lenox in the Berkshire Hills, down through the beautiful Housatonic Valley, across to Poughkeepsie, and down along the east shore of the Hudson River to New York. This route can be considerably shortened and many bad roads avoided by following directly up the west side of the river from Newburg through Kingston, Albany, Schenectady, Saratoga, Glens Falls, Ticonderoga, and Plattsburg to Montreal.

Taking a trip like this, which is one of the most attractive in point of scenic grandeur in the eastern United States, the itinerary can be laid out so that each day's run can be made easily and comfortably, allowing time for a noonday stop for luncheon, and confining the riding to daylight. The shorter trip could be made with ease in from two to three weeks, allowing plenty of opportunity to jog along easily, rest each Sunday, and enjoy the tour without hurry or bustle.

"With a supply of gasoline to last for a run of two or three days, it is possible to break away from all civilization and spend a long period in complete retirement."

GEORGE ETHELBERT WALSH

ALTHOUGH MANY AMERICANS IN 1908 NO DOUBT WOULD have agreed with author George E. Walsh's characterization of owning a motor car as an expensive "luxury," Walsh wasted no time in making the case that the automobile could still play a part in ensuring vacation pleasure for a great many people. Arguing that "few are so restricted in their vacation expenses that they cannot make arrangements to go touring for a few weeks," he urged his readers to abandon the dubious virtues of "summer hotel or boarding house" in favor of a motorized holiday whose ultimate purpose could be "pleasure and recreation . . . not time and space annihilation." For a comparatively meager sum (at least to Walsh's budget) of twenty-five dollars per week, aspiring vacationists could rent "a good touring car" that would provide "'starting out' space" while driving and facilitate "loitering here where the country is inviting, camping there where conditions for a few days of rest are ideal."

Like all promoters of auto touring, Walsh stressed the importance of hauling along a wide selection of necessary equipment, from tent, cots, and blankets to cookware, an ice chest, and pure water. Unlike so many other writers, however, Walsh dispenses with such details quickly and focused upon the joys of being surrounded by all of nature's treasures, observing that the motor tourist is "independent of towns and cities and all the rush and turmoil of strenuous business life." Even in discussing the importance of selecting a "good route" for the excursion, Walsh avoided the customary detailed discussion of maps and directions in favor of waxing poetic about eschewing a "cut-and-dried itinerary."

A novelist and later the author of children's books such as *Bumper the White Rabbit* (1917), Walsh seems to have had a compelling affinity for what he described as "those little ideal spots where the spirit is soothed into restful harmony with nature." Reiterating that "it is a heart-free, care-free trip . . . one is planning," Walsh left his readers to ponder the prospects of outdoor delights made accessible by technology that represented an apogee of the Industrial Age.

Vacation by Motor Car

By George Ethelbert Walsh

[*The Independent* 64 (April 16, 1908)]

Not everyone can afford the luxury of owning a motor car, but few are so restricted in their vacation expenses that they cannot make arrangements to go touring for a few weeks instead of spending the same amount of time at a summer hotel or boarding house, where the physical test and mental change are somewhat doubtful in quantity and quality. A good touring car can be hired today by the week or month for not much more than one would pay for carfare to some distant vacation point—say, from $25 a week to $75 per month, a good average rental. Such a car is capable of carrying six or seven, but it is better to limit the vacation party to two or three, reserving the extra seats for baggage and "stretching out" space. Anything but cramped, crowded space for a vacation tour! It is pleasure and recreation that one is seeking, and not time and space annihilation. The object is not to get to any particular point in a given time, but to make every mile a pleasure, loitering here where the country is inviting, camping there where conditions for a few days of rest are ideal, and scurrying along in another region where nature has not been kind to the scenery.

With the touring car in commission, the next essential is a sleeping tent and hammocks or folding beds. For an investment of $15, such equipment can be secured for two persons, and they can be rolled up and tucked away in the back part of the car so that they will be little in the way. Simple cooking utensils, such as one would use for camping in a tent, should be added to the permanent equipment of the traveling camp. Warm blankets, a change of clothing, and a storage box for simple culinary articles will complete the outfit.

The touring car is in reality a moving camp. One can ride through almost any part of the country and explore new regions. In the heat of the day or at night the camp can be pitched at some suitable place. Today it is pitched in some grassy field or meadow, where the flowers spread around their bloom in abundance; tomorrow it is in some woods or grove where the cool wind lulls one to sleep and idleness; and the next day the rest is taken by some lake or stream where fishing can be enjoyed to the heart's content. One is independent of town and cities and all the rush and turmoil of strenuous business life. With a supply of gasoline to last for a run of two or three days, it is possible to break away from all civilization and spend a long period in complete retirement. With sufficient dry groceries carried for such a trip, one can then depend upon the fresh fish caught in the streams or upon the products of the lonely farmhouses for the little delicacies of diet.

The ice chest which goes with most touring cars is a very convenient arrangement for keeping articles of a perishable nature in good condition. Drinking water can be carried in sufficient quantities to make one independent of any doubtful stream or spring by the wayside. Indeed, the drinking water supply is always one of the serious problems that vacationists have to face. It hardly pays to drink from contaminated sources of water supply and find, when too late, that all the benefits of the vacation are neutralized by an attack of typhoid. When sure of your water it is better to stock up an adequate supply and not run any risk.

If one enjoys camping, what better method of enjoying it than in a moving camp? Suppose a heavy downpour of rain floods your camp? There is the touring car, with its waterproof sides and tops. If drawn together properly, one can sleep inside comfortably while the rain is forming great puddles outside, or, in an emergency, the car can travel on to some farmhouse or country hotel, where lodgings can be had for the night. There are many hot, dusty days when it is pleasanter to rest in the cool shade of the trees than to go motoring. Then the movable camp becomes a resting place where all the cares and worries of life are banished. No matter whether moving swiftly across country or camping by the wayside, the life is all out of doors, and that is the main end in view. A vacation in hot, stuffy rooms is not a restful experience. Even though the rooms are occupied only at night, the experience is not desirable and the hygienic results somewhat doubtful.

In a two weeks' vacation in a touring car one can cover only a few hundred miles or travel six or seven hundred. It all depends upon the pleasure of the motorists.

The selection of a good route for traveling is the final point for preparation. A cut and dried itinerary is not desirable. In a general way a route must be selected and some attention paid to the roads. One can't plow through woods that have no trails or across meadows filled with quagmires, but on the other hand no one takes a vacation of this nature with the idea of following well-traveled roads. His object is to get away from the railway line, away from the trolleys, and if possible, away from the dusty highway. In some simple, rustic wagon trail or on some back lane which leads to nowhere, he is most apt to pick up those little ideal spots where the spirit is soothed into restful harmony with nature. What if the lane or trail leads to nowhere, and sooner or later you must return on the same track? There is the joy of exploring, of finding out for yourself what no guide book attempts to explain.

From almost any town or city the roads lead off in all directions to the country beyond, and any one of these will do for the beginning of the trip. Then when the city is left behind and the country ahead beckons, the journey should be made from day to day as the spirit dictates. Let the preparation for each day's itinerary suffice. The care for the morrow should be left for the new dawn. It is a heart-free, care-free trip that one is planning.

Last summer two men took such a trip, covering in three weeks five hundred miles. They made side trips into every imaginable out-of-the-way place. They discovered sections of the country never explored by the summer tourist; they fished in old brooks and hidden ponds which reminded them of their boyhood days, and sojourned with rustics whose simple life let in a flood of new light upon their souls. They returned to the city strong, healthy and brown, and their total expenditures were a trifle less than a hundred dollars. That was a cheap trip to them in many ways. It took them into the open air for a good part of a month, taught them how to cook and shift for themselves, and made them realize some of the independence and resourcefulness of the primitive man.

But an appendix should be added to all this; a list of "don'ts" which may save some imitator from unpleasant experiences.

Don't forget that a car running every day needs oil and gasoline—and plenty of each.

Don't take a grumbler along for a companion; better take a deaf and dumb friend than a fault-finder.

Don't forget an extra allowance for paying fines, but better yet, don't forget the speed laws.

Don't leave your dirty, soiled suit behind, for that may come in handy when exploring the dusty road under the car for a loose nut or bolt.

Don't overload your car with unnecessary equipment; a few simple things are better than a Saratoga trunk of useless stuff.

Don't subscribe for a daily paper or leave your telephone address behind to friends; you might miss connections in your flight across country.

"Can you wonder we came near to loving that loyal car?"

FLORENCE M. TRINKLE

WHILE FEW IN NUMBERS, EVEN AMONG THAT SMALL SUBSET of Americans who were automotively engaged, those individuals who had undertaken the transcontinental trek after 1900 still exerted a considerable impact upon the nascent pursuit of motor touring. Well before the end of the decade, individuals or manufacturer-sponsored teams had demonstrated the viability of lightly powered runabouts as well as heavy-duty touring cars for cross-country excursions, and they also confirmed the ability of cars drawn from stock production runs to surmount the challenges of western geographies and reinforced the essential need of programs to build good roads all over the nation. In 1908 at least two separate parties reached yet another milestone: a husband and wife, Fred A. and Florence M. Trinkle, took a Brush runabout from Denver to San Francisco, and businessman Jacob Murdock made the journey from Pasadena to New York City with his wife, three children, and a mechanic in a Packard touring car. Having established their place in the motor car from the time of its earliest appearance first as a passenger and then as a driver (albeit in the latter instance very slowly and in the face of vociferous and unrelenting opposition), American women before 1908 had not yet taken part in the successful pioneering journeys across the continent. In this document, however, Mrs. Trinkle described the odyssey that she and her husband followed across the Far West in that year.

As had been the case with many prior cross-country voyages, the Trinkles traveled at the behest of a manufacturer, in their case of the Brush Runabout, one of several concerns that made up the United States Motor Company. In 1907 Fred Trinkle became the Denver representative of the Brush Runabout after accumulating several years of experience as a salesman and mechanic with various auto makers, and in 1908 he took part in Brush's attempts to promote its product, a single-cylinder, two-seat automobile with wooden frames and axles and a top speed of about thirty miles per hour, a car built for reliability, durability, and affordability.

By the time Trinkle agreed to the Denver–San Francisco run depicted here by his wife, he had already driven one factory model from Detroit to Denver and then on to the summit of Pike's Peak, part of a major Brush campaign that summer. In hopes apparently of further maximizing favorable publicity, Brush then asked Trinkle to drive a Runabout on to San Francisco, have it shipped to Detroit and then drive it to New York City for that winter's automotive trade show. With his wife's offer to act as his observer on the westbound voyage, Trinkle accepted the offer, and the couple set out from the Mile-High City at the end of September.

Treating their journey as a challenging expedition, just as their transcontinental predecessors had done, led the Trinkles to load up with everything from extra gasoline to chocolate and raisins (the latter items to fill out their emergency rations at the suggestion of an "Alaskan miner"). Listing such now-familiar items as spare tires, rope, a block and tackle, an axe, and a wide assortment of waterproofed clothing, Mrs. Trinkle demonstrated that she and her husband strove to prepare for all manner of potential crises. Of particular note would be their decision to accept that, with no room for camping equipment, they would be "forced to run the risk of finding accommodations along the way as best we could." Bearing north initially into Wyoming and then west across southern Wyoming, northern Utah, and the deserts of central Nevada, the Trinkles concluded their journey by entering the Golden State near Big Pine in the Independence Valley, crossing into the Central Valley and then motoring on to San Francisco. In describing their travels, Florence Trinkle's account emphasized that a transcontinental journey still demanded unremitting toil in coping with nonexistent roads, recalcitrant landscapes, and unpredictable weather. It reminded readers that the lack of accurate and detailed maps and directions represented a critical obstacle for any motorist traversing the West. And it pointed out that the motorist and the motor car still depended upon the built environment of the railroad, whether following the right of way as a marker across otherwise trackless terrain, relying upon railway freight services to deliver crucial replacements for broken parts, or (especially in the case of the Trinkles) seeking shelter and sustenance with the inhabitants of section houses along the transcontinental line. Whatever their ultimate hopes for unfettered independence, early motorists often found themselves still linked to the route of the iron horse.

Coast to Coast in a Brush Runabout 1908

By Florence M. Trinkle

[Los Angeles: Floyd Clymer, 1952]

Pikes Peak or Bust . . . in a Brush

I don't suppose my husband and I could possibly make clear to modern motorists the intense affection we developed for a piece of machinery—our little Brush Runabout. But at the end of our ordeal (it was 1908) we parted with the car as if it had been a favorite child.

It would be difficult for the drivers of today's luxurious cars on our modern highways to visualize the adverse conditions that faced the horseless carriage when it was first coming into use after the turn of the century. Naturally, these early automobiles were primitive affairs and few drivers knew much about their mechanical parts. Repair and service stations were few and far between—especially where we went—and mechanics still were groping in the darkness, for the most part. There were no highway signs anywhere; in many states, particularly in the West, roads were almost impassable for a low-built vehicle, and it was taken for granted that on a trip of any length there would be many streams to ford.

In 1908 there was no transcontinental automobile highway. The Lincoln Highway was not started until 1913 and wasn't finished for more than a decade. It filled a great want, linking the East with the West and making it possible for travelers to locate towns and cities by calculating exact distances. This was especially valuable in sparsely populated areas. Previously, only the hardiest motorists ventured any distance from home base, and a cross-country pleasure trip was out of the question. A few factories sent cars on long trips for advertising purposes, but the danger and trouble they encountered made the ventures questionable.

In rural districts the populace usually was antagonistic to the automobile because it frightened horses and accidents resulted. Often, upon the approach of a horse, the motorist would stop his car and stand in front of it until the animal could be maneuvered past the evil-smelling contraption.

Once a motorist approached a Michigan farmer driving a spirited team, and seeing the fright of the horses and the women passengers in the buggy, he stopped his car, alighted and gallantly offered to lead the prancing horses past the machine. The farmer said: "Never mind the horses, young man, I can take care of them. You just hold the women."

If the unwary motorist stopped at a farmhouse to ask directions, the farmer invariably would direct him through some mud hole or over some steep hill to be sure the car got stuck. Then in the evening at the corner store the farmer would brag to his cronies how he had sent that "buzz wagon" down the wrong road, and all would be merriment.

After the first world war this nation became road-conscious, spending immense sums on new highways until improved roads with numerous signs and signals extended in every direction. Eventually the motorist was catered to in every state with such innovations as service stations, hot dog stands and motor clubs.

My husband, Fred A. Trinkle, began driving and repairing automobiles in Denver, Colorado, as early as 1900, and in 1907 he became agent for the Brush automobile for the state of Colorado. The car was designed by Alonzo P. Brush and built in Detroit by the Briscoe Manufacturing Co. The Brush Runabout was a two-seated, one-cylinder, double side chain-driven car with a coil-type spring under each corner, acetylene headlights and Prest-O-Lite tank, with no top, windshield, or doors. It was a very sturdy car and could go anywhere there was a road. The chain-drive on each side gave it great climbing power although it was not fast. But that was not a serious deficiency because there weren't many good roads on which to speed in those days, and drivers were not speed-crazy.

To advertise the Brush in 1908, Frank Briscoe decided to send five factory models to different destinations, and asked Fred to come to Detroit and drive one to Kansas City, as he was the only Brush salesman familiar with the West.

At a banquet the evening before the start, each of the drivers was called on for a speech. When Fred's turn came, he told the crowd he could not make speeches, but he could drive a Brush Runabout and that, when he reached Kansas City, he would ask permission to drive on to Denver, climbing Pike's Peak on the way. After the applause had subsided, all forgot about the boast except Fred and Briscoe.

The five cars started the next morning, each driver accompanied by an observer who kept track of the credentials on the trip. Arrangements already had been made by the factory in cities along the routes for pictures to be taken when the cars arrived, and newspaper stories along the way were to provide more advertisement for the cars. Fred's itinerary took him through Michigan and Ohio to Cincinnati, west through Indiana and Illinois to St. Louis. Towns in these states were close enough together so he and his companion always could find accommodations, but finally the observer objected to not getting a bath every night and returned to Detroit. The factory sent another observer for the trip from St. Louis to Kansas City.

Throughout Missouri, Fred could get little information about roads or directions. For instance, people living ten miles from Bowling Green had no idea where it was. The roads were so bad he drove much of the time in low gear with the wheels in a solid mass of mud. It was a hard grind across the state, but luckily time and speed had no bearing on the final summing-up of the trip.

The factory required a telegram every night giving the car's location, also a daily written account signed both by driver and observer, to be mailed each night to the factory. Fred won first place among the five cars at the end of the run, later receiving a silver cup and ebony pedestal. The points which won him the decision were prompt and full reports, high gasoline and oil mileage and fewest repairs.

His only replacement was a 10-cent commutator spring which he installed himself.

In Kansas City he received instructions from Briscoe to continue to Denver with the Brush, look over the possibilities of a Pike's Peak climb and report if it would be feasible. Fred soon found bad roads all through Kansas, and driving was strenuous work. Beyond Dodge City, he stopped to speed up his engine in the heavy mud and in starting, the chain jumped off the sprocket teeth. This had happened before, as the chains and corresponding teeth had become worn in the steady drag through the mud. He tried to flip the chain on while the engine was running, his usual custom, but in a moment of carelessness he caught his hand between the chain and the teeth of the sprocket, stalling the engine and trapping him as completely as though he were in a bear trap. He couldn't move to reach the gear-shift lever.

There was little travel on the road and he was forced to remain in a crouched position for some time. Finally he hailed a tramp walking on the railroad and, after much persuasion, got him to leave the tracks and come to the car. He directed him how to turn off the ignition, put the car in reverse gear, then crank the engine, thus turning the sprocket and chain backward and releasing his hand. He reflected later that he might have been caught for hours; as it was, the flesh on his hand was cut through to the bone. Fortunately he had a box of salve in the car, and the tramp helped dress and wrap his injured hand.

Fred carried the tramp with him to the next town and took him to a restaurant for a meal, but as soon as they had finished eating the tramp made a bee-line for a freight train—and oblivion, as far as Fred was concerned.

At Lakin, Kansas, he stopped with cousins for a few days, meanwhile selling two cars to be delivered later.

When he reached Colorado Springs, he found good weather and no snow on Pike's Peak, so he telephoned a photographer friend in Denver and told him to meet him at the Springs next morning with his large camera, and ride up with him. Then he removed the running boards and fenders and had a sprag made to drag behind the car so as to hold it on steep grades if necessary when he stopped to speed up the engine.

The old road had been abandoned for years, a cog road and burro trail having taken its place, and the present boulevard was not built until eight or nine years later.

From Colorado Springs, at an altitude of about 7,000 feet, Fred and his photographer drove to Manitou where they bought a hand ax, a shovel, and about 200 feet of rope. Then they drove to Cascade, where they had an early lunch. Here they were directed to follow the canyon road a mile and a half, where they could see a dim road turning to the left, and a small wooden bridge across a creek; there they turned immediately and started a stiff climb on a shelf road dug on the side of the mountain and ending directly over Cascade.

When this route was pointed out to them, they looked up a thousand feet or more to a line on the mountain side which was their road. This seemed to be the crucial part of the climb as it was so steep most cars could not get gasoline to their carburetors and so became stalled. Up to this time no one had heard of vacuum tanks or fuel pumps, and automobiles obtained their gasoline supply by gravity only. This did not bother the Brush Runabout because it was equipped with the only known diaphragm fuel pump which brought the fuel from the tank under the floor boards to a fuel cup on top of the engine. With that arrangement, the motor could be kept running even if the car were standing on end, which accounted for the Brush's ability to get over steep places.

At the top, before getting out of sight of Cascade, Fred backed the car into the bank and the two got out to stretch their muscles. Looking below, they saw a large crowd gathered in the street, each person seemingly only an inch tall, watching them climb the steep shelf on the mountain side. They took off their hats and waved and the crowd answered by waving hats, handkerchiefs, aprons, or anything that was handy.

Starting the car, they went down grade before resuming the climb. Rocks, boulders, fallen trees, and other debris blocked the road and had to be cleared away, while washouts were numerous. At the Halfway House, there was a mountain stream with very steep sides. It had once been bridged just below timberline. The two men carried poles from a nearby corral, lashed them together in pairs with their rope, buried the ends in the earth to make them firm, and drove over them as if they were a bridge.

Nearing the top, they came to the famous "W" where the road travels left for half a mile, then doubles back on a hairpin curve to the point where it started but about 200 feet higher, then back on another hairpin curve, completing the "W." The camera man, tall and heavy, climbed from road to road taking pictures of the car on the "W." They climbed completely around the mountain, coming to the top from the opposite side of the "W." It was a 23-mile climb and had taken all day. Often during the trip both men sat with one foot outside the car so as to be ready to jump to safety if they saw the little car tottering on the edge of the narrow, crumbling road.

That night I received a wire from the Pike's Peak telegraph station, highest in the world, that Fred was safe at the top and would come down next day. To Briscoe in Detroit he wired,

PIKE'S PEAK CLIMB POSSIBLE FOR WE ARE AT THE SUMMIT.

The two men stayed all night on the top at the Summit House, 14,147 feet above sea level. Next day they found the descent much more difficult and dangerous than the climb, for it meant holding back around boulders and other obstructions on narrow, rough, curving trails. On the way down, the bottom of the gasoline tank hit a rock and broke off the drain plug, but they grabbed a gallon can they had in the car for carrying water and saved enough of the gasoline so that by using a squirt gun, they were able to feed enough fuel into the gas line to keep the engine running until they reached Cascade, where they bought a gallon more and this took them to Colorado Springs.

The gas tank had to be soldered, besides replacing the fenders and running boards, before they could start for Denver that night. While working in the garage, another car backed up in front of Fred and began shooting the exhaust in his face. He quit work, went over to the owner, and asked him to move the car, as the fumes were very annoying. The man answered that if he didn't like it, he could move his own car. There was no room to move back, so after a few words—tired from his climb and anxious to get home that night—Fred lost his temper and hit the man on the chin with his fist. The other shook his head and said, "Did you mean that?" Fred replied, "Yes, I did," and soon the two were a rolling heap on the floor. The cameraman had to separate them. The man then moved his car and before Fred left, he came back and apologized to him.

As soon as the Runabout was in commission that night, they started for Denver, two very tired men anxious to get home. I was wakened by a noise to see a man standing in the bedroom door about four o'clock in the morning. I thought it was a burglar with a brown mask over his face, with eyes looking like two burned holes in it, but Fred's grin relieved me of my fears and a bath brought out the original man.

Sometime later a nicely dressed man came into Fred's sales room, introduced himself and said, "You remember me, don't you?" It was the man he had clipped on the chin in the Colorado Springs garage. After a chat, he gave Fred a ticket to the Denver Athletic Club for a certain night, making him promise to go to the fights there. When Fred did, he found that the man was a prizefighter in the principal bout of the evening. I thought this was a very clever way to let Fred discover his occupation; then and there, Fred decided to be more careful about starting a fight with any other athletic stranger who might not be the gentleman this man was.

Many cars had tried to climb Pike's Peak, but a Locomobile Steamer was the first. The second was a 70-horsepower Stearns. The Brush Runabout was the third and went every foot of the way under its own power.

Westward Pioneers—A Brush and the Trinkles

Everyone at the Detroit factory was jubilant over the climb, and we thought the trip was completed when Fred settled down to his garage work and selling cars.

However, in a few days Briscoe wrote to Fred, asking if he would outfit the car in Denver, drive it to the Pacific Coast, then meet it in Detroit and drive it to New York City in time for the winter motor show. He said he would send a man from the factory to go as observer if he had no one in Denver to go with him. It appalled us at first to think of driving such a little car over the long, uninhabited distances we knew existed throughout some of the *western* states. We never would have entertained the idea if Fred hadn't been such a good automobile mechanic. We had been to California by train several times over different roads and knew something of what to expect, traveling over the mountain ranges and passes so late in the season.

My parents came from New York State to Michigan as early settlers before I was born, and Fred and his mother came West in a covered wagon to Colorado when he was a small boy, so I guess there must be pioneer blood in our veins; the "call of the road" won.

So Fred accepted Briscoe's proposition and persuaded me to go along as observer, wiring Briscoe to that effect. The answer was,

PERFECTLY ACCEPTABLE. COMPLIMENTS TO PLUCKY MRS. TRINKLE.

The factory wired us $500 to outfit and start, with more to be sent when and where we ordered. We were told to spare no expense and to send tires, gasoline, and spare parts ahead for use wherever we thought best. Briscoe never had been West, but he knew that few cars *ever* had crossed the continent and that we would not have a pleasure trip, to say the least. Since I had previously lived in Nevada and California, it seemed like a homecoming for me, or I might have taken the trip more seriously.

Our first thought was about equipping our car, because as long as we could keep it moving, we would be safe. The next thing was to make sure we would keep warm and comfortable ourselves so we could endure the hardships we were bound to encounter for several weeks along the way. We had to use our own judgment in selecting what to take, as no one we knew ever had made this sort of trip.

The little car already had done strenuous work, so Fred went over it carefully to see that every part was sound, meanwhile selecting the necessary extra parts. The Brush's most serious fault was that it didn't hold enough gasoline for long distances in places where gas stations were few and far between. Fred had an extra gas tank built under the seat and in all we could carry 16 gallons. As the trip progressed, we took on extra gas every time we had the chance, so as to never run short of the precious fuel.

He built a box on the back of the car which would carry oil, ax, tools, tires, rope, block and tackle, suitcases, spare parts, and the like. Then he put endless interliners in each tire so we could wear the tire through to them, then take them out and put them into new tires. Once we cut one tire badly on a rock, exposing the interliner and making a tire change necessary, but the other three went all the way to San Francisco with Denver air in them.

There was no room for a camping outfit, and we were forced to run the risk of finding accommodations along the way as best we could, though we carried an emergency hamper containing bacon, skillet, canned meat, crackers, coffee, chocolate, raisins, matches, medicines, and other items.

We had been told by an Alaskan miner that chocolate and raisins make a substantial diet and will sustain life for days. We added chewing gum, which quenches thirst if water is unfit or absent, and we thought we could keep from starving for quite a time if the car broke down far from help or we got lost. We knew there were no road signs of any kind along the way, so we carried a compass and railroad maps.

Back of our feet in the car were a shovel and an umbrella, ready for quick use. We dressed in serviceable, warm clothing, gauntlet gloves, and high, waterproof boots. At the very last, I added a silk face mask and goggles to my wardrobe. We each had a rubber coat that slipped over the head to protect us from rain, snow, and cold. We each carried a suitcase with one full change of clothes, knowing we could buy more on the way. We divided our money in case of emergency, and both of us had a revolver.

What directions we could get were very vague but we expected to get information on the way from old stage drivers, teamsters, and livery stable men. We knew that at this time of year we must avoid the Sierra Nevada mountains through Reno and Truckee, Nevada, and Donner Lake, California, where the whole Donner party had perished in the early days in snow so deep that the tops of trees showed in the spring where the party had peeled off bark to eat in a desperate endeavor to keep alive.

Friends told us later that they never expected to see us alive again, but they were wise enough not to fill us with forebodings. Fortunately, both of us had optimistic dispositions and did not anticipate trouble before we came to it.

To send his nightly telegram to the factory, Fred carried an identification card ordering all Western Union offices to accept messages, to be sent collect. I took shorthand notes each day and sent letters to the factory when I could find time to use a writing pad and pencil. Maps were hung in a window at the factory and at all dealers' stores and little cardboard cars were moved along our route each time they heard from us. People passing the showroom windows would stop each day to see how far we had gone.

We did not try to make fast time, because safety was our first thought. Fred went over the car carefully each morning before starting.

We left Denver September 28, 1908, stopping at the office of the *Denver Post* for a picture, then passed through Fort Collins on the way to Tie Siding, Wyoming; where we came to the Union Pacific Railroad. We followed it for days, near or far, according to the way the wagon road ran. At Tie Siding we got a late dinner and after much shifting about of sleeping children, we were given a bed.

We passed through Laramie before noon the next day and about 2 P.M. we stopped at a section house on the railroad and asked the only visible occupant, a woman, if she would serve us lunch. She prepared a meal and seemed glad to talk to us, being especially eloquent about her children, saying among other things that they had not been tardy or absent at school in the past year. I had seen no other building for miles so I asked where the schoolhouse was located and she naively replied, “Upstairs. We hire the teacher and the three children are the whole school.” I gasped in astonishment at the wonderful record she thought they had made.

As night approached and we had ridden many miles without seeing any sign of habitation, black clouds were gathering. We decided to try another section house on the railroad for food and lodging for the night, as we had no idea how far it was to the next town, Medicine Bow, but we knew there was a river which we did not care to ford after dark in such a small car. We found a Japanese man who looked at us in such a surly way, only grunting at our questions, that Fred said, “Let’s get out of here,” and we hurried out over the railroad track, feeling safer in the dark and storm. To cross the railroad we had to open and shut a wire gate on each side of the tracks. We couldn’t see far beyond our dim headlights in the darkness and rain, and the feeling of loneliness was great. Finally we saw a tiny light to our right in the distance and Fred told me not to lose sight of it.

We ran into a high road center and embedded the flywheel in the earth, but we managed to back out and soon were headed toward the light which shown from a rancher's window. It was about nine at night. A barbed wire fence halted us before we could reach the house. As I sat under the dripping umbrella, Fred walked along the fence until he came to an entrance near the house. A man opened the door, and very definitely refused to let us spend the night there, but after some urgent pleading on Fred's part he relented and told him how to drive the car into the yard.

I went into the house and sat down behind a warm stove, very meek, cold, and hungry while the men were putting the car under shelter. The rancher's wife was there, and when Fred came inside, he asked me, "Did you tell this lady we haven't had any supper?" I smiled and said, "No, I didn't." She got busy at once and soon we were enjoying an excellent meal.

We never hurried the next morning after we had driven late the night before, so after breakfast we chatted about our trip and I enthused over the distant views, pure air, and delicious odor of the sagebrush after the rain. Then our hostess said, "I'll tell you now why we didn't want to keep you overnight. We have had so many easterners coming here late at night who were rude and disagreeable, cussing the roads, the climate, the people and everything in the state that we said we would never take in another traveler, but you are different and like it here." I had, unknowingly, won them over by my appreciation of some of the beauties of their locality. The couple ended by wanting us to stay a few days and go antelope hunting with them. It was with real regret that we could not accept their invitation, for they were fine people and we never have forgotten their hospitality during the storm in the first stages of our trip.

Within a mile after starting again, we forded the river where we might have had trouble after dark, and came to Medicine Bow. We had trouble through this section with the high road centers. The roads were sixty inches wide while our car was fifty-six inches, the regulation width, and the ruts were worn deep by wagon wheels so our flywheel did not always clear the ground beneath.

We were constantly worried that we would be stranded if our flywheel broke; we had no other with us. This was a desolate country and somehow very depressing, with clouds presaging a storm. This feeling was intensified as we passed the deserted town of Carbon, where open doors swung in the wind and paneless windows stared at us. In one window we saw the head of a horse, and in another we caught the partially hidden face of a man. We were glad to leave the desolate ruins and climb to higher hills, although we still sensed trouble around us.

The eeriness of the day was climaxed at Hanna, where we ate lunch, by the pervading gloom of the villagers. Upon inquiring what was wrong, we were told that a second mine disaster had occurred within the last few days and bodies still were being brought up out of the shaft. We were glad to move on, even if it might be to trouble of our own ahead.

In mid-afternoon, the snow came down so thick and fast that I was kept busy clearing it from the top of the umbrella, which was being bogged down by the snow's weight. The roads, such as they were, were beginning to disappear under the blanket of snow and we had to crawl along, fearful of damaging the car on some hidden rock. Then we saw a section house, about dusk.

We stopped, determined to go no farther in the storm. We covered the car, took our suitcases and robes, and walked a half mile through the snow, ditches and sagebrush to Edison, as it was marked on the railroad map. A light flashed in a window—a beacon in the stormy night, reassuring evidence of habitation. At our knock, a smiling Japanese section boss opened the door and ushered us in.

Although he was alone, everything was spic and span. His wife was coming from Kansas City the following week, and he had everything shining. He served us a meal, even making hot biscuits, which we enjoyed greatly after our cold day. He built an extra fire in the front room of the good-sized house so we could dry our clothes, but he had no bed for us. We had to sleep on the floor in our clothes, but our host brought out some new wool blankets to soften the floor. In the morning, Fred remarked that there were a lot of wrinkles in the Trinkles.

But the storm was over, the sun was shining, and we were happy although a little sore from the effects of our hard bed. We ate breakfast, took pictures, bid the friendly Japanese goodbye after settling our bill, and waded back with our belongings to the car. It was shrouded in snow and canvas, just as we had left it. We uncovered it and started off.

The sun had melted the snow, making the road so slippery we slid off several times, stalling often in the six miles to Walcott. We had to dig out the flywheel each time, shoveling earth and packing it under the wheels to raise the car and free the flywheel. We finally reached the town for lunch, wondering how far we could go that day over such roads. We were often in mud so thick that it clung to our boots so we could hardly walk.

We had plenty of money, but what good did it do under these circumstances? If our car had been larger and heavier we never would have got through without a tow car, something which was unknown in those days anyway. But we never quite despaired as our sturdy little car kept chugging along.

That afternoon's journey was slow and monotonous. After dark we crossed the North Platte River on a bridge that careened so much I was afraid we might slide off into the stream; then we progressed along a muddy road on the sloping bank of the river to Fort Steele, a big, barren building. It was a relic of the old Indian fighting days, but we found that food and shelter were the most important things after a hard day's work.

We reached Rawlins at noon the next day and had lunch in a quite pretentious hotel. Sandy roads slowed us up in the afternoon and we had to stop at Daley's, a big sheep ranch, for the night. We were made welcome by six young men who showed every possible courtesy. One young man was very anxious about a bad ditch we would have to cross the next morning. He offered to take a team of horses and pull us through, but Fred said the car was going every foot of the way under its own power. I believe they felt sorry for us because our car was so small, not realizing the Brush could get through places impossible for a larger automobile.

We got stuck, just as the young man feared, and our shovel work could not extricate us, so out came the block and tackle. Hitched to the root of a big sagebrush, it slowly inched us up and over the bank of a deep, slippery ditch. This delay cost us an hour or more.

After four or five miles Fred turned to me and asked if I had put the shovel back in the car and my heart sank when we found we had laid it down behind a sage brush and forgotten it in the confusion of starting. Every mile was gained with so much effort that we couldn't possibly think of going back for the shovel, because we could buy one at the next town if we were lucky enough not to need one before we got there; but here, again, we were to find that money did not avail us.

It was always my duty, while Fred attended to the car, to scout around and gather up all our tools after we had stopped to work on the side of the road in Wyoming—and that was very often—so I felt the loss of the shovel was all my fault.

We reached Wamsutter that night without needing a shovel, and we were confident we could buy a new one there. But we couldn't, for love or money. The Union Pacific Railroad owned everything in sight, and no one dared sell any of the road's equipment. We were pretty blue, because a shovel was an absolute necessity to us every day along the road. Nothing which had happened to us so far balked us so much as the loss of the shovel. Now we had nothing with which to dig ourselves out of high road centers and fill in bad places.

Just before we started the next morning, a man among the crowd around the car quietly told Fred that about a mile down the road he would see a railroad switch with a broom and shovel standing by it. Then he winked. We drove slowly with our eyes glued on that track, found the switch with its broom and shovel, quickly added the shovel to our outfit and were ready for any emergency once more. Now it was my concern that the handle, stamped U. P. R. R., was kept hidden back of my feet when we came to a town on this railroad, where keen eyes might see it and know it did not belong to us. This shovel saved us later in many places.

We fought bad roads all day through the Bitter Creek country where we were warned not to drink the water or put it in the radiator because it contained so much alkali. The good water was brought in on tank cars, from which we filled our radiator. At night we found the road impassable because of mud and water, and I thought we were stuck there for the night. Fred and "Road Louse 2," as a facetious friend had dubbed our car, left the road and went bouncing on its coil springs over sagebrush and around rocks, while I held my breath and gripped the side of the seat in my endeavor to stay with them. We went over a hill and down, landing at a section house occupied by Austrians who spoke or understood very little English. We surprised them as much as if we had come down in an airplane.

The woman asked how we got through the mud and where were our children, but my explanations seemed unsatisfactory to her. They gave us the best food they had, but we could scarcely eat it and I sat with my head in my hand, very tired and nauseated by the smell of the food.

Fred brought in our two canvases and put them on the bed for sheets—the woman had given up her bed to us, sleeping in the bunkhouse with the workmen. In the morning we left her well paid, but as soon as possible we threw away the thick coffee and hunk of bread she was determined we were to take for lunch.

After leaving this place we had to use the shovel three times in the first mile, and put in a strenuous time over lonely country roads, reaching Rock Springs for the night. There we found a new hotel with steam heat, but we shocked the proprietor by asking him for a room with bath, and found there was no such thing in the building.

Fred took time here to have the metal posts that supported the coil springs lengthened two and a half inches, so as to raise the rim of the flywheel above the front axle. The body was raised and the steering gear changed, and when we started again we just missed going off the end of a bridge, but Fred soon adjusted himself to the change and all went well.

After good food and a restful night at Rock Springs, we were quite ourselves again as we started another day's work. We ate lunch at Green River and continued, slowly covering ground in this barren land. About sundown we came to a river which high-wheeled wagons and long-legged horses could ford, and Fred was sure he could drive the car through it, but it was pretty wide with rapids and I walked over the railroad bridge, while he and the little car plunged into the water. The motor stopped in midstream.

Fred got out in water above his knees and cranked the car over and over but it would not start, so he called to me that he would walk back a half mile to a construction camp we had passed, and get a man and team to pull the car out of the river.

I sat on the further bank, cold, discouraged and hungry, looking at the river and hearing it gurgling around our few belongings in the car. It was nearly dark when a team appeared with a man riding one of the horses, and Fred waded into the water again, fastened the team to the car and it was soon on dry ground. Fortunately the water had not reached our luggage. It was a frosty night, so Fred had to open his suitcase and get into dry clothes before we could proceed.

The engine started at the first turn of the crank and we wound our way in the dark over a road hemmed in by sagebrush, and after three miles came to a camp at Marston. The chug-chug of our motor brought out the whole section gang to see what was coming, and they gave us a noisy welcome. A double track was being laid and the block signal system was being installed on this division of the railroad, which accounted for the construction camps which were such a help to us.

The camp cook took us into his box-car kitchen and served us a most appetizing meal, including parker house rolls. The signal maintainer, a Scotchman, took us to his house, made a fire to dry Fred's clothes, and gave us his bed for the night. He was the only person on our whole trip who would not take any money. All he wanted was a postcard from us when we reached San Francisco, probably thinking we would never reach such a place. We always carried plenty of fruit to supplement our scanty meals, and we gave him some. He said it was a great treat. Later, when we reached San Francisco, we sent him a picture of the St. Francis Hotel, where we stayed.

Next morning, after a few miles we ran into that same river to ford again, but good fortune was still with us; there was another construction camp and gang. Fred went over to where they were working and bargained for a man and team which towed the car through the water, the man sitting in the car as proud as a king while he drove the horses. I walked over the railroad bridge again.

After the man was paid and given a cigar, he beamed all over and said, "I'll go back and tell the boys I've had an automobile ride." It was an eventful day for him, making extra money, getting a good cigar and having his first automobile ride even if the car didn't run under its own power. Being on the right side of the stream to suit us, we enjoyed a good laugh as he and his team waded back through the water.

Fred put in the batteries he had taken off the running boards to keep them dry, and at the first turn of the crank the motor was chugging, ready to go. We neared Granger, Wyoming, at noon, but could not go into the village because there was no bridge across the river. We were told we would find one eight miles up the river if we followed the Oregon Short Line Railroad. This we did, stopping on the rustic bridge for lunch from our hamper, as no one was at home at a ranch where we had hoped to get a meal. There was hardly a sign of a road on the other side so we decided not to go back to Granger for our main road, but to go across the prairie toward train smoke we could see at times in the distance, keeping on the high ridges where it was smoother for the car. There was more or less uncertainty in this, but it was necessary at times that we should decide many problems by ourselves, so we took the risk. After an hour or so we came to a road; we followed it and it turned out to be the right one.

We saw no building or person all afternoon. Late in the day, when everything was going nicely, we came to a small, innocent-looking brook but the track had been cut down so deep by high-wheeled wagons that we dared not try to ford it. We walked up and down the stream, searching for a place we could cross safely. Finally we selected a spot with a sandy landing on the opposite side, though the steep bank must be cut down before we could drive into the road.

Feeling quite confident, we forded the stream and stopped the car on the sand while Fred leveled the high bank in front of us with the shovel, as I sat near and watched. When we went back to the car we found that the rear wheels and axle had sunk in quicksand and the car was resting on the body, perfectly helpless, and no help near for miles.

We were utterly dismayed at the sight. When we fully comprehended the plight in which we found ourselves, we got busy. Fred unpacked the jack while I brought a flat stone from the stream on which to place the jack after he had dug out sand to make a place for it. I brought more stones and he packed them and dry earth he had dug from the bank under the wheels, rocking the car back and forth to pack the base solidly. We worked frantically more than two hours. Finally we started the engine and both of us pushed the car to solid ground and into the road.

We were wet with perspiration, so we put on warm wraps, never stopping for a morsel of food, and started on our way without knowing how far it was to a place we could stay overnight. What it would have meant to us to see just one road sign pointing some place!

There was a fair road with a telegraph line to follow, and a full moon overhead. Many times we thought we saw a light but it faded away before our eyes, leaving us bewildered and uncertain. About eleven o'clock, Fred stopped the car and asked me if I saw anything or if there was an optical illusion. It looked like an iron bridge a little to one side of the road, but it appeared so fairy-like in the moonlight that we doubted our eyes, so we stopped the car and walked over to see if it was a real bridge or a mirage. It was real.

We left the road and drove over the magic bridge, eventually coming to the little town of Carter, where we got a room at what seemed like a hotel. It was so late we didn't dare ask for a meal, so we lunched from our hamper and dropped into bed worn out.

Difficulty Going In the Mountains of Utah

Next day, on our way to Evanston, we stopped to choose between two roads. Fred thought we should take the one that went down into a gulch or river bottom, while I urged that we keep to higher ground, because if we made the descent, sometime we would have to come back to a higher level. We sat there pondering for a while, for we could not afford to take the wrong road, when, looking behind us, we saw a man on horseback coming up the gulch. We ran back and hailed him before he could get out of sight. He saw us, stopped, waited for us to reach him, and told us to keep to the higher road. All day long it seemed that a miracle had happened just when we were in our worst straits.

We had an easy trip to Evanston that day, near the edge of Wyoming. We had been ten days crossing this state that motorists now cross in a day. We found good accommodations at Evanston, but when we asked for a room with bath, we were told the bathroom was packed full of stored goods and could not be used. We got a good laugh out of that.

Next morning, as we climbed a long grade to the top of the

Wasatch Mountains, a dozen or more cowboys on their ponies surrounded us, lighting cigarettes, laughing, fixing saddles, in front and then behind us until we began to get nervous, wondering what they were trying to do. Just before we reached the top of the hill, one of them reined in his pony, faced us and said, "I guess you won't need us to pull you up this hill."

"We never would have gotten this far if we did," Fred answered.

We decided they thought our car would get stuck in the deep sand on the steep grade and they would have some fun pulling us out, but the car had crawled along slowly and steadily, spoiling their fun.

As we started down Weber Canyon, Utah, we saw a tiny stream of water which, by the time we left the canyon that night, had become a roaring stream of water, rushing out to the valley between towering cliffs. Weber Canyon was beautiful in its immensity and autumn coloring, but a sucking, sighing wind made us fearful, and we hurried down the narrow roads past Mormon towns in the valleys, and out by the side of the noisy river, reaching Ogden late that night.

We carried signs on the Brush—"This car climbed Pike's Peak"—"From Detroit to San Francisco," and the like. Before we could remove our wraps at the hotel, reporters besieged us for information concerning our trip. We also received a call from a couple in the city who owned a Brush Runabout, and they used all kinds of persuasion to get us to stay a few days and visit a beautiful canyon with them, but Weber Canyon had quenched our desire for more canyons at that time and we were bent on moving as fast as possible. However, we did appreciate this courtesy in a strange city.

We found a bathroom in this hotel at Ogden, but could use it only by paying extra. We stayed in Ogden half a day, sending and receiving mail. Then we were on our way to Promontory in the afternoon through a fitful wind and under threatening skies. A single Mormon family lived there, but they kept travelers. We stayed with them two days during a rain, meanwhile hearing much about the bad roads ahead of us around the edge of Salt Lake. We were told we would have to drive on the railroad tracks to get through, but we thought this was a bit exaggerated. We were glad for the chance of a rest at Promontory, which gave us a chance to catch up on our correspondence.

We heard there were three feet of snow in Weber Canyon, which we had just come through, and were most thankful we had wasted no time on the way.

A golden spike was driven in the railroad at Promontory May 10, 1869, to celebrate the connecting of the Union Pacific and the Central Pacific railroads, thus completing the first transcontinental railroad in the United States. The spike had been removed, but a large signpost gave the date of the event and we were shown where the spike had been.

Soon after leaving Promontory, we got into such bad gumbo mud we were glad to back out, after much trouble, and drive on the railroad track as we had been told we would have to do. There were three trains a week on this road to hold the right of way (the main line had been built across Salt Lake). Since this was not a train day, we drove over the road bed and ties, stopping often, as the bumping from tie to tie set our car bouncing on the coil springs, endangering the flywheel. Once two wheels slipped off the tie-ends into the mud and the car hung on the inside of the rail by the other two wheels, at an angle of thirty degrees. We worked with old ties and sticks to raise the wheels from the mud, finally getting them on the ties again. We drove all day in a fog, never stopping for lunch, and made all of 17 miles.

Toward evening a section boss met us and ordered us off the track, under penalty of arrest. We were tired, wet, and discouraged. I looked down at him from my side of the car and said, "I guess being arrested wouldn't stop us any longer than that mud would." He smiled and said he guessed it wouldn't, but for us to get off as soon as possible, for the dirt road was better now. Fred told him we would be only too glad to get off, because the bouncing over the ties was getting the best of us. In a short time we found a crossing and drove onto a road which was none too good. When we came to a box car, a woman greeted us and, realizing this was a last desperate chance for a night's lodging, I asked her if she would keep us overnight and she agreed.

We never thought of those three cars on the siding as the home of the section boss, so when he came home from work there, we were, warming and drying ourselves at the stove. They were a charming couple and we all had an enjoyable evening. We were a little crowded for sleeping quarters but the next morning they urged us to stay over and go duck hunting on Salt Lake, which was in full view of their box-car home. However, we could not tarry for amusement.

Luck had favored us here, for a train had left the three cars the night before, and the cars would be moved the next day. These people refused to take any money for entertaining us, as others had done, but Fred always left some money on the table. They were wonderful to us and to find food and shelter, far from any habitation, on a cold night was a blessing, and we were only too glad to pay for it.

My face mask came into good use around Salt Lake, for the air was filled with gnats in the mornings, but Fred thought it was ugly, so I removed it whenever we passed through towns.

Our next stop was Kelton, 17 miles away, but we found low ground with mud and water all the way. Travel was slow, with the car very erratic in starting and stopping. Fred couldn't find the reason although he fussed over the car, hunting for the trouble in every conceivable part until he was worn out tramping around the car in the mud.

We never had had any mechanical trouble with the Brush, and its actions were a puzzle. Late in the afternoon the car took another rest. Fred dutifully alighted and began another search. Suddenly he announced he had found the trouble. My spirits rose at once; all I had been able to do all day was sit and worry when the car stopped and enthuse when it mysteriously started again. The trouble was a simple thing, but it had made the day tragic for us. The insulation was worn through on a wire under the machine, short circuiting the engine when the bare wire happened to touch the metal frame. Locating it was the difficult part, but a little tape remedied it and the car was itself again, fairly spurning the worst mud of the day with its wheels and bringing us to Kelton and a railroad for a Sunday night cold lunch, though we persuaded the waitress to augment it with some hot soup. There was a smug crowd of clerks, teachers, and the like at one table, with not a thought beyond food. They sat there in their Sunday best as we entered dressed in our soiled traveling clothes. They looked at us as though we were something the cat had dragged in. That didn't bother us in the least because we had completed another lap on our journey, with food and shelter for the night, and our trusty car waiting to go at the turn of the crank.

We had hoped to make Lucin the next day, but heavy sand held us back through a barren land—the only human being we saw that day was a man driving a flock of sheep. We camped by the roadside for lunch from our hamper, frying bacon and making coffee. That night we stopped at a sheep ranch, the owner coming in late at night with the flock of sheep we had seen on the road. We spent a good night there, little thinking what was to be ahead of us before we slept again.

From here we found many dry ditches, one so deep that we considered building it up from the bottom but that would mean we would have to go through soft earth, so we decided to try it as it was. I walked ahead, afraid to watch the car go down into the ditch, but as I heard the continuous chugging of the motor, I looked around in time to see it slowly crawling up and over the edge after an attempt no big car ever could have made successfully. Can you wonder we came near to loving that loyal car?

We reached Lucin, at the west end of the railroad across Salt Lake, for a late lunch. In a small restaurant with uninviting food, the waitress warned me several times, in a very low voice, about a high, pointed rock in the middle of the road and hidden by weeds, that had proved most disastrous to a local automobile party the week before. I thanked her silently many times afterward for her warning, though I paid little attention to it at the moment.

After lunch a well-dressed man gave us directions, pointing up a hill. It was long and steep and we climbed it slowly. I noticed a crowd watched us from below near the restaurant, but I thought nothing of it at the time because so many people were surprised to see the car climb steep grades.

After driving for a couple of hours, Fred stopped the car, got out his compass and map, consulted them and said, “We should leave Salt Lake at Lucin, but here it is on our left, with a mountain range on our right. We must turn around and go back to Lucin.”

We couldn’t understand where we had gone wrong, although we had commented on an increasing steepness and roughness of the track. We had come down hills so steep that when we went back I walked behind the car carrying a rock to block a rear wheel when Fred stopped to speed up the engine on these hills, so that if the brake didn’t hold, the car wouldn’t start rolling backward. When the car started, I would pick up the rock and follow to be ready when he stopped again, and so on, to the top of the hill, when I would drop the rock and get into the car.

When we got back to a sheep herder’s wagon that we had seen in the foothills earlier in the afternoon, Fred walked through the flock of sheep to the wagon where the herder had just lit a candle. He said we should have stayed in the valley and must go back to Lucin to get on the right road. We were pretty discouraged, and to add to our troubles, the car came to a stop a few miles further on. Upon investigation, we found that a pin was lost out of the propeller shaft and, since we had no other and could not find this one in the dark, we were obliged to camp there for the night, though it was cold and snowing. There was dry wood all around us, so we built a fire for light as well as warmth, pushed the car up into a tall juniper tree after cutting off some branches, spaded up the sand and put some canvas on it for a bed, using the car cushions for pillows, and hung up some more canvas on the side of the car and tree to keep off the wind. We ate a little lunch from our hamper and our chewing gum came into good use, as we had no water except that which we drained from the radiator for fear of freezing. That was not fit to drink, so we carefully conserved it for the next day.

We were carrying a five-gallon milk can to use in Nevada, but had no need to fill it yet, as water was not scarce along the railroad. Fred put me to bed first, clothed in all my warm things including cap, gloves, and boots. He covered me with robes and shoveled sand on the canvas over my feet to keep out the cold wind, and put the umbrella over my head to keep off the snow. I fell asleep almost at once and when I awoke, Fred was sitting by the fire. It was four o'clock and he said he dared not go to sleep because the wind blew the sparks everywhere, and he had been busy all night extinguishing sparks around me and the car, some sparks even catching in the resinous twigs above us.

I made him take my place for a few hours and I sat down to watch the fire. When it got light enough to see, I went back to search for our lost propeller shaft key, a piece of steel a quarter inch square and four inches long. I found it some way back where the car had come to a stop, and it was imbedded in the sand where we had stepped on it while searching in the dark.

So I had good news for Fred when he awoke. After breakfast he put the car into commission and made the only tire change on the trip. We were just ready to start when a covered wagon appeared carrying three young men going prospecting. They stopped to find out what we were doing there and after hearing our story, one of them said that evidently the man at Lucin didn't believe our car could climb the hill and we would have to come back, when he would have the laugh on us and then put us on the right road in the valley. The young man said there was nothing, not even water, for more than a hundred miles the way we were going, and that probably we would have lost our lives.

One of the men knew of an old road around the foot of the mountain and took Fred to show him where he could get on to it. Our car pushed its way between shrubs and overhanging trees until we came in view of the valley and down to the road. We were thankful for help in time of need.

Then I remembered the warning the waitress had given me the day before about the rock in the middle of the road, so we saw it in time although it was nearly hidden in the weeds, and gave it a wide leeway, saving ourselves a bad crack-up that probably would have ended our trip right there.

We were sorry we didn't again meet the man who had given us the wrong directions. I often have wondered what he and his friends thought as they saw us climb the hill and go out of sight down that barren, uninhabited, waterless valley in a little car with no camping outfit, no sign of any food, and probably not any quantity of gasoline. He had put our lives in jeopardy just to be funny, had missed his laugh, and might have let us ride to our deaths. It was only Fred's careful study of maps and the lay of the land, with his keen sense of direction, that saved us in time.

Reaching Tacoma, Nevada, for lunch, we found a family hotel and had a chance to wash away the traces of our night's camping and enjoy a real meal. We left the town, never thinking we were to return there two more times, the last visit taking several days.

A man pointed down a road but it took us through a marshy field and we could find no way through, so we came back to Tacoma late in the afternoon for further directions, and the man said we should have turned but he had not told us, and there were no signs of any kind. It was late, but Montello was only seven miles away and we decided to continue that evening because we had lost so much time the day before, so we left Tacoma the second time.

About halfway to Montello the car came to a stop. One look under the hood was all that was needed. Three teeth were broken out of the timing gear. That meant three things: First, to get a team to tow the car into Montello, for we were determined to keep advancing; second, to get a new gear from the factory; and third, a long wait, perhaps making us get to the Coast too late, although we still were on the main railroad and that was in our favor in getting the gear from the factory. So much had happened in the last twenty-four hours, and now to have our cheerful little car silent and still was tough luck.

I had to stay alone with the car while Fred walked to Montello for a team, if such a thing existed there. It was almost dusk, but I preferred no light on the car to call attention to me as I curled up on the seat with my revolver tucked under the robes. He started down the road for help. Evidently the little car was not going every foot of the way on its own power, even if we had good roads now. Indian campfires gleamed in the distance, coyotes yelped and answered each other from all sides, and the railroad might produce a tramp.

These were not happy surroundings after dark. The hours passed slowly and the night was dark, and it seemed the car and I were deserted out there on the prairie among the sagebrush, when about ten o'clock I heard a harness chain rattle in the distance and knew help was on the way. A great relief came over me, although I don't think I had been in any danger. There was only one team in the town. When Fred located the driver, he was eating dinner and refused to stir until the horses were fed too. Fred could only sit and wait patiently until the man was in the mood to start, then he walked the horses all the way to the car.

Hospitality Shortens a Long Wait

Montello was a small place, the end of a division on the Union Pacific. Its hotel had recently burned down and the crude rooming house which took its place was so open and cold the water froze in the water pitcher every night. The Japanese restaurant proved so unsatisfactory we could not eat there. Fred spent the forenoon sending to the factory for a new gear and trying to get the car under shelter, but there was no place for it and we had to leave it outside, trusting to the honor of the inhabitants.

While scouting around, Fred found that the railroad company had a dining car there to serve meals to the train crews as they came in from their division runs, so he made arrangements for us to have our meals there.

Among his discoveries, he found that there was one piano in the town, and the owner and his daughter invited us to their home for the evening for some music. We went, but the piano was so out of tune it could not be used. A tuner from Ogden, across Salt Lake, would cost forty dollars, and since the girl did not play anyway, they had done nothing about it. The middle C was down a tone, and others nearly as bad. The owner loved music, and we sat there rather dejected when Fred, a resourceful chap, suggested we tune the piano with his monkey wrench. I was used to tuning a violin. I objected at first to what seemed like a ridiculous idea, but the man was delighted and urged so insistently that I finally relented. The front of the piano was off in no time, and I warned Fred to turn the pegs that held the wires very carefully as I plucked the strings. I was fearful of a wire breaking, but after the third tuning the pegs held and the instrument sounded fine. The man was delighted, and brought in a box of candy from his store, and we played and sang what could be remembered, there being no sheet music.

Not enjoying our cold room and remembering the comfortable family hotel in Tacoma, we decided to go back there and keep warm while we were waiting for the gear. The express agent promised to send us word as soon as the gear arrived, so we packed our suitcases, took the noon train, and arrived at Tacoma the third time. There we had regular meals, a room with a stove, and plenty of fuel.

There was a copper mine in the mountains back of the hotel which gave this place considerable patronage and kept it in existence. We enjoyed the quiet and rest we had there, and were better fitted when we left to continue our trip. One day an Indian woman who was cleaning windows got up the courage to ask, "Where you come? Where you go?" I could not make her understand, and after a long look from her beady eyes she merely snorted, "humph!" The Chinese cook was very happy this same day, laughing when he saw me, saying, "We have chicken on the fence tonight."

I had no idea what he meant, so I just smiled. In the evening people began arriving and putting children to bed until I began wondering if each mother ever would find her own child. No one introduced me as I sat and watched the crowd until a white-haired old man with a violin under his arm appeared in the doorway, peered about the crowd, and asked if the lady who had played the piano in the afternoon was there. I asked if he meant me, and his face lit up as he asked if I would try and accompany him on the piano. Here was another piano no one knew how to play!

My father had played the violin and for years I had accompanied him on the piano, so it was a real pleasure for me. The old man's face was serenely happy as I followed him in some of the same pieces I had played with my father, but this man put in his own improvisations and kept perfect time. Presently some men rolled the piano into the empty dining room, and I discovered a crowd had gathered there for a dance, and from then on the old violinist and I were busy while feet kept time to our music, the piano having taken the place of the usual mouth harp. Between dances the old man told me had been a prospector for years, and that someday he would find a gold mine and become rich. His daughter and grand-daughter were dancing on the floor, but the miner's hope of gold still lived in his heart and anticipation showed in his eyes.

I found out what the Chinese cook meant in his remarks about chicken; it was served, not on the fence, but on the table, and was accompanied by other good things to eat. Everyone made us feel at home. After the grown-ups had eaten, the table was reset and every child was awakened and brought out to eat, then put back to bed. After the meal, the tables were removed and the dancing began again. Later a stranger offered to take my place. I gladly relinquished it and went to bed. I do not know how long the party lasted, but some of the people were there for breakfast when we came down in the morning.

On the ninth day of our wait, word came from the express man that the gear had arrived, so we went back to Montello after lunch. In two hours Fred had the gear in, the engine timed, baggage packed, and we waved good-bye to our friends. We stayed that night in Cobre, Nevada.

We left the main railroad there to avoid possible snow at the California border, spending an uneventful day through a sparsely settled section of Nevada. On our way we saw steam coming from the earth in a circle, perhaps a mile in circumference, which caused much speculation on our part. We reached Cherry Creek that night and Ely about two o'clock the next day. There we went directly to the post office where we expected mail, and while Fred was inside a well-dressed man wearing a wide rimmed, black hat examined the car and its signs, then came up to me and asked if we were going on that day and if we knew the route. I told him we were going to the restaurant first, then get our directions and go some distance, if possible. He introduced himself as the guide for the famous Thomas Flyer car which had gone through that section a few months previously, while competing in the New York-to-Paris road race. He said he would be glad to go with us to the restaurant and give us full directions while we were having our meal. I thanked him and said we would be pleased if he would do so.

When he joined us at our table, we felt acquainted at once, since he knew drivers and automotive friends of ours. He gave us much valuable information besides drawing a crude sketch of our roads and the ones we must avoid on the way to Tonopah, a distance of 250 miles with no place to get gasoline on the way.

There were two ranch houses where we could stay overnight, and he advised us to carry all the gasoline possible when we left Ely. We greatly appreciated his help and in consequence we took extra precautions, laying in food and fruit, looking over the car to see that everything was in good condition, filling the tanks with gas and carrying on each running board a five-gallon tin can of gasoline for use when needed. In all, we carried 26 gallons.

We left Ely about three in the afternoon, expecting to reach Barnes's ranch that night or have to camp out, as there was no habitation along the way. We could reach out and touch snow in many places along the eight miles to the top of Murry's Canyon. The truss rod on one side broke as we were climbing, allowing the rear axle to move forward, thus loosening the chain, which came off the sprocket teeth.

Fred cut a small tree the right length and size with his hatchet, notched it to fit where the truss rod should go, drove it into place to hold the axle firmly, and we were on our way again. He had to repeat this procedure several times, finally carrying several pieces with him as they kept splitting. We reached the Barnes ranch long after dark.

A man cooked us a meal there. Many Indians were around the place. Our principal thought was to get an early start the next day, but Fred took time to go to the woodpile, where he found a piece of broken doubletree of hard, tough wood from which he shaped a substitute for the broken truss rod. It lasted more than 200 miles across a desolate section of Nevada. Perhaps Mr. Briscoe had been right to call him resourceful.

We came as near to catastrophe this day as any time on our trip. It was uneven country with some steep hills, and on one I walked behind the car carrying a rock to block a rear wheel when necessary. The roads often followed creek or river bottoms on the climb to the summit, where the mountains usually broadened out before the descent on the other side. But on this one, the descent began as soon as we reached the top, and on a curve we had to avoid a bad rock that towered in the center of the road.

The brakes were slow in taking hold and we were headed for the rock when Fred, with a supreme effort, brought the brakes into concerted action with the steering gear, missing the rock by only a few inches.

There was utter silence between us as we started down the steep road in Currant Creek, and when we dared look at each other, we saw that each was white as a sheet. We passed one house on our way down into a level valley which had a hazy mountain range on the farther side. That day we saw only one man, and he was raking rocks out of the road. He seemed quite out of place, but we decided he had come from a mine in the hills. We stopped to ask him directions and, as we were eating fruit for lunch, we gave him an apple. He asked more questions than we did, but he told us to keep straight down the valley until we came to a road that turned directly toward the mountain, fifty miles across the valley, and that by going across this valley we could come to Twin Springs ranch, where we could stay for the night.

There was no sign of civilization for miles, and the area wasn't a nice place in which to break down or run out of gas. I doubt if we would have found the proper road if this man hadn't been working on the road on this particular day, and so was fortunately in a position to direct us.

It was sunny weather and we had good natural roads. We kept putting the miles behind us and kept nearing the hazy mountain until we were around the foot of it and in another valley. It was ten o'clock at night when we came to some haystacks and buildings which we could hardly tell apart in the dark. Fred's knock was answered by a voice saying they didn't keep people overnight. After some argument, Fred threatened to sleep in the haystack if they didn't let us in. When the man discovered there was a woman outside, he came to the door partly dressed, with a candle in his hand, and agreed to get us a meal and let us stay overnight, but he said there was no bed for us. We found he was only the cook—a surly old Englishman. The others at the ranch were away, driving cattle to Tonopah. He must have seen how tired we were, for after a substantial meal he said he didn't think anyone would be back that night and that we could have the extra bed. There wasn't a white sheet on it, but everything was clean and of good material, for which we were thankful. Soon we were fast asleep.

When we appeared in the morning, the cook was getting breakfast, and asked Fred to go outside with him and bring in the meat. Fred returned with a grin on his face and a hind-quarter of beef on his shoulder. He carefully laid the meat on a table and the cook cut off immense steaks for our breakfast, which we ate ravenously in preparation for a long day's ride to Tonopah. When he found I had lived in Smoky Valley, Nevada, and visited the A. B. Millett family, who were old friends of his, he changed from a cross cook to a genial host, telling us about the hot springs we would pass on the road that day, showing us the twin springs from which the ranch got its name, and giving us directions so that we had no trouble all day. We brought some of the outside world into his life for a short time, and I don't believe he ever forgot us, besides being paid well for his extra work.

After fifteen miles we came to the hot springs steaming out of the ground and rocks. There is always an uncanny feeling about an earthquake or steam coming out of the ground. We stopped, and Fred took off his shoes and stockings and waded around in the water as I took pictures. Indians came here from miles around for hot bath treatments, running the water from pool to pool as they wanted different temperatures.

We passed through a rolling section of the state, coming down into a level valley that led us straight across to staked mining claims, probably located during the mining boom, but looking like monuments now. Soon we were in the town of Tonopah, mostly a one-street village. We found a room with a promised bath, but at ten o'clock at night we were informed that the water could not be heated. We had become accustomed to excuses like this when we asked for a bath, so we were not surprised or disappointed.

Fred found a garage in Tonopah and the proprietor allowed him to use the machinery to repair the broken truss rod. We stayed here half a day, picking up mail and meanwhile changing our plans. From here we had expected to go south through Goldfield, Stovepipe, and Skidoo, but we were warned we would find sand on the edge of Death Valley, below sea level, where we would have to be towed ten miles by a team at the cost of $40.

Because of the extremely low level, which affects me seriously, Fred began to make inquiries in Tonopah, seeking another route into the southern part of California, and was told there was a horse-and-cart trail used by a power line rider, going west. He consulted the power line officials about taking this road and they said a rider with a horse and cart went over this road three times a week, weather permitting. They telephoned and found there was no snow on the passes and fair weather was predicted, so we decided to go that way, avoiding the deep sand below sea level and saving the towing bill.

We went straight west over uneven country, crossing a dry borax lake where the 98 percent–pure substance was shoveled up and shipped for commercial use. There was no one living on the way, and the trail was hardly visible at times. In one place we could find no track over a bank and hunted for a suitable place to make the plunge over the edge. Then Fred made me walk ahead to avoid the worry of having another person in the car while he steered it down. He hoped the sand at the bottom would assist him in slowing and stopping, which it did, so we were able to continue on our way intact. Such risks had be taken, for there was no help near for miles—and no turning back—consequently we went through some anxious moments at times, and our nerves got a little frazzled.

That night we came to Silver Peak, a famous mining camp of early days, with hot springs and bath houses, but it was dark when we arrived and we did not discover them until morning when we were ready to leave. Around here, the ground was strewn with black rock, very much like soft coal or slag, which looked to us as if it had come from a volcano, but we had no idea we were near the truth. When I went outside in the morning, the first thing I saw was an extinct, gray-sided volcano looming high above the green mountains not far from the town. It looked like a big cup and was so old and menacing in a beautiful world it had not been able to destroy, that it fascinated me, and as we left in the morning I couldn't take my eyes from it until it was behind us, and then I was sorry to leave it.

Before leaving, our host took me out and showed me a rocky knoll that he said in early mining days would be covered with rattlesnakes that came out to sun themselves, and the glitter of their bodies could be seen a long distance as the sun shone on them. One miner began shooting them and saving their rattles, until he was able to send a peck of them to Tiffany's in New York.

This morning, word came that William Howard Taft had been elected President, this being the day after the 1908 election. We went through an uninteresting, sagebrush-covered land, reaching California at Oasis, a ranch house and store with nothing near it for miles. Two young men were eating lunch but curtly refused to serve us a meal, not even a cup of tea for me. Upon inquiring the price of gasoline, one man said shortly, "Gasoline is a dollar a gallon. How much do you want?" Fred quietly replied, "None. We have plenty."

When they came out of the store and saw our automobile with its signs, they woke up and began asking questions, but we got in the car as they declared that no auto had ever been over the road, and that no auto could get through. We paid no attention to them and drove away as they stared in astonishment. They watched us out of sight, probably expecting us back before evening. We went through sandy valleys and over summits until at dusk we found ourselves climbing between towering bluffs with stars peeping at us through the opening at the top. On the broad summit other roads converged on ours, and soon after we started the descent, we were flagged to a stop by a man with a red lantern. He demanded seventy-five cents toll, which we gladly paid.

He said the road down the mountain was good but narrow and steep, and that we would find good accommodations in the valley. We took it slowly, because it seemed the rocks reared their bulk to oppose us in the dark, but as we came to them, there always was a good road around them, though I found myself bracing my feet for a bump that never came. We realized that this passage was never meant for an automobile and that more than once the Brush Runabout had rushed in where a long-wheelbase car would have feared to tread. We reached a railroad at Big Pine in Independence Valley, where much later all the traffic went that way, the road having been built through and the man who had made his living towing autos through the sand at the edge of Death Valley had moved away, there being no business. Years later we learned that the Brush was the first car to go from Tonopah, Nevada, to Big Pine, California, on that road.

Sunny California—The End in the West

We were now east of Mount Whitney, the highest point in the country, and we must go a hundred miles south to find a lower mountain to cross. We had level roads and warm weather and enjoyed our ride through Independence Valley where workers on the mountainsides were constructing a $49,000,000 aqueduct to carry water to Los Angeles. We had a little experience with deep sand in this valley at the edge of the Mojave Desert, getting into a spot where our wheels went round and round without moving the car. We could have deflated our tires and pumped them up by hand, but we thought it easier to get out our two canvases, spread them on the sand, and run the car on them, then carry one ahead, spreading it in front of the car and driving onto it, and so on.

Some Indians hooted and jeered at us, getting a great kick out of seeing us work, but we laughed with them because we were making slow but sure progress and would soon be gone. We were two days in this valley, turning west at Coyote Park to go over a low range of mountains.

The odor of fried bacon led us to three loads of hay, with the wagon drivers camped by the roadside. They were on their way to the aqueduct workers with their teams, as trucks were rarely thought of then. The men aroused from their beds in the hay and waved us a greeting, evidently surprised to see the little car scampering across the hills in the dusk. This was a weird evening, passing tall cactus plants, yucca plants, and Joshua trees in the moonlight, coming down into a mountain-enclosed valley where cattle were so frightened at us we slowed to a snail's pace so they would not injure themselves, running away in panic. We found an exit where a river flowed out into another valley, and came to Onyx, which consisted of a store and post office with a southern California ranch house.

The family was not at home but a Chinaman cooked us a late meal, breaking out every few minutes with a chuckling laugh. He was quite confused when he couldn't find the key to our room, so we just pushed the dresser across the door and forgot about it.

We met the family in the morning. They were curious about us and the car, and four bright-eyed little boys and their timid mother had their first automobile ride before we started. We thought it would be a good advertisement for the car, but the four pairs of brown eyes were sad when we left; it was just the plaything they wanted.

We were told to follow the river road and we would have no trouble. We assumed we had a delightful day ahead of us along the river, but we found ourselves going over mountain tops on narrow shelf roads with hairpin curves and so far above the river that a horse on the river bank looked no larger than a dog. In one place, we turned a bend in the road and came face to face with an old white horse, a cart and driver. The horse hunched down and rolled his eyes in terror, but never moved, leaving that to us, as he was wise to the ways of narrow roads and knew safety lay on the inner side, no matter how scared he might be. We backed up some distance until an inner curve widened enough to let the horse past. His eyes were filled with fear as he passed, keeping strictly in the center of the road and taking no chances with the outer side. I had sympathy for the horse, as I was nervous also after riding all day on the outside, looking down on treetops.

When we stopped to rest, I lay down on the ground to relax and recover my poise. We did not even stop for lunch, as the skies were dark with clouds and we didn't want to be caught in rain on narrow, slippery roads where we might go over the edge and get hung up in a tree. At last we realized we had been going downgrade all day. About dusk we came into open country and long after dark we reached Kern, a town of oil wells and derricks near Bakersfield, California. Here we found a hotel and a much-sought-after bath after our strenuous riverside ride.

We turned north next day, heading for San Francisco, and felt, after fighting bad roads so long, that we had nothing to do all day. There still were no road signs, but the region was so well settled we had no trouble in finding our way or getting food and lodging.

Our shovel was forgotten and the umbrella was worn out from the wear it received back of our heels. Flowers were in bloom—especially oleanders—and when we came to the grape and wine districts, we stopped at a winery and climbed a long ladder to look into one of the immense vats of claret, which looked like a lake of ink. The owner gave us a sample, running it out of a hose to rinse the glass before filling it, as one would water. It was a common sight to see a wagon and hay rack full of grapes.

Near Dos Palos, where we were delayed one evening by a stoppage in our gas line, we saw a beautiful sight. The honking of wild geese attracted our attention, and we saw flock after flock coming through the air like black clouds, alighting to feed in the marshes nearby, then rising and going on while others came to take their place.

We went through Fresno, San Jose, past Stanford University, and soon the breeze from the Pacific Ocean brought the salt odor of the water as we rode along "El Camino Real," the old Spanish road used by the padres, Spaniards and Indians long before California was part of the United States. It is bordered by tall eucalyptus trees, with small mission bells at intervals.

We entered San Francisco by the peninsula, going to a post office where we found word for us to meet a Mr. Harris, the Brush sales manager, at the St. Francis Hotel. He had not arrived, so we registered and spent the afternoon buying new clothes. The first thing I bought was a fragrant bunch of violets, such as grow in California only.

Next day we drove the dirty, dingy car to Golden Gate Park on our way to the ocean, but a policeman stopped us at the entrance and said no autos with signs were allowed in the park. Fred told him how far we had come, how long it had taken, and all we wanted now was to get to the edge of the water and wet the wheels of the car in the Pacific ocean, then it was to be shipped to Detroit, where he would met it and finish the trip by driving it to New York City in time for the midwinter automobile show.

Getting past the brusque-appearing policeman was easy compared to getting past some of the mud we had along the way. He smiled indulgently at our earnestness, and said to go and come by the South Drive, and it would be all right. Having overcome the last obstacle, we drove through the lovely park, past the site of historic Cliff House and Seal Rocks, and down to the ocean, where a wave gently came up, wet the wheels of the travel-stained car, and slowly receded.

This was the end in the west, and there was no way to show how dear the little grey car had become to us after carrying us across so many miles and through so many dangers. The chug of its one-cylinder engine had been the sweetest music in our ears during our month-long trip. I could only put my hand on the hood and choke back the tears.

The car was shipped back to Detroit by express so as to be ready to finish its journey to New York City, and Fred was to follow it to Detroit.

We looked up old friends and scenes. Meanwhile, Mr. Harris and a new car arrived by train. After a few days he decided to go to Los Angeles to look over the automobile situation. He went by train while we and the new car went by ship—a delightful and unexpected pleasure. We disembarked at San Pedro, the car being swung down from the upper deck. Then we bought gasoline and drove to Los Angeles, twenty miles away. Business took us to Pasadena several times, and we enjoyed driving beneath the palms and through orange groves, where the trees were heavily laden with fruit, not quite ripe but of a beautiful color, always with a few bunches of waxy blossoms.

We spent Thanksgiving in Los Angeles, and Fred sold the new car to Fred Ingersoll, a mail carrier in Pasadena who had written the factory. He was one of the first mail carriers to use an automobile in his deliveries, and eventually drove the car enough miles to have circled the earth several times.

The night after the sale and delivery of the car, we were in a Pullman returning to Denver. We spent a day in Salt Lake City and reached home December 1, having been gone a little over two months.

On December 20 Fred left Detroit with the old car to complete the trip across the continent, with Harvey Lincoln, a factory man, as observer. They went through Toledo, Cleveland, Buffalo, and to Little Falls, New York, where they were stopped by a blizzard.

Next morning they started in the snow but found the roads drifted badly and had to return there. After a day's delay they were directed over a high road through timber where the snow drifts were not so bad. At night they came back to the regular route and managed to get through after much shoveling.

From Albany they went down the side of the Hudson River, but on a steep hill the car coasted to a stop. They found the timing gear had lost some teeth again. It was similar to the accident we had had in Nevada. Fred, fearing much trouble, had the foresight to add an extra timing gear to his parts at Detroit before starting. They simply pushed the car to the sunny side of a barn and made the change in zero weather. After an hour and a half the new gear was in place, the engine timed, and they were on their way.

The car reached New York City December 30. Fred drove over Brooklyn Bridge, through Brooklyn to Coney Island, dipped the wheels of the Brush in the Atlantic Ocean, and was in time for the automobile show which opened January 1, 1909. The insignificant, shabby automobile had reached its goal. It stood in the huge hall with its signs, much-used shovel, and all the dirt and mud it had accumulated on its long trip, among its more aristocratic companions in Grand Central Palace. With its driver, it attracted a great deal of attention.

After returning home, Fred received a communication from the Bureau of Tours of the American Automobile Association, with a map marking his route, and informing him they had a record in his name as the Seventeenth Transcontinental Automobile Trip.

This was a happy climax and far beyond our expectations, because we had thought of the trip only as an advertising stunt for the Brush factory and the Brush Runabout.

"In his beautiful new motor he spins out into the country and . . . is not only learning to be an excellent mechanic, but a nature-lover, with a broader, sweeter personality, an enlarged horizon and a saner view of life."

WILLIAM F. DIX

BEFORE MOTOR-MINDED AMERICANS CHOSE TO EMPLOY THE automobile for leisure as well as labor, of course, they had to be as convinced of its utility for the former purpose as for the latter. Essays such as William Frederick Dix's commentary about automobiles and recreation, therefore, had to demonstrate that the motor car would not only make the trip to the office, factory, or market more efficient but that it would allow the "man of affairs" to become a "country gentleman . . . with a freshened mind and a new zest in life [as he becomes not only] an excellent mechanic, but a nature-lover, with a broader, sweeter personality, an enlarged horizon and a saner view of life." The enhanced mobility represented by the automobile would lead inevitably to a notably enhanced quality of life as it released more and more Americans from their imprisonment in exhausting, overcrowded cities. Thus, in Dix's vision of a motorizing America, the automobile would become both an actual and a metaphorical vehicle for relocating increasing numbers of its populace into living spaces that would be in balance with a restorative nature.

Writing about the opportunities that "motor enthusiasts" in the Northeast were already seizing through which they could immerse themselves in green spaces, Dix (a native New Jerseyan, novelist and former editor of *Town and Country* magazine) described developments that would have been quite familiar to a resident of that region. In doing so, he also highlighted an increasingly common theme for many authors and intellectuals at the turn of the twentieth century. With a mounting vehemence, these commentators denigrated urban settings and encouraged a flight to the countryside for year-round living as well as the recreational motoring that is reflected in this volume. As Dix himself noted, "surely the time is coming when the roadside taverns and country inns will be revived . . . when travelers, instead of being herded together, will travel lightly, swiftly, and noiselessly from place to place in its own vehicle [and] a perfectly constructed, swift-winged motor will [be] carrying rich and poor alike into a better understanding of nature and teaching them the pure and refreshing beauties of the country." Thus, unlike earlier American writers who frequently expressed their skepticism about such technological advances, Dix and others like him actually sought to bring the machine *into* the garden, for the automobile could help blaze a trail to a better civilization.

The Automobile as a Vacation Agent

BY WILLIAM F. DIX

[*The Independent* 56 (June 2, 1909)]

TWENTY YEARS AGO THE AVERAGE CITY BUSINESSMAN worked steadily throughout the year, with almost no recreations, except for one midsummer trip into the country or to the sea. For eleven months he was immured in the city, an absolute stranger to the beauties of the changing season, to the spring burgeon upon the hills which lay beyond his horizon, or to the autumn brilliance of the countryside. When midsummer came he tore himself from his work and, with tired eyes and brain, strove, usually in vain, to come into sympathetic touch with nature. For one transient period he struggled to break the methodical, work-a-day habits enchaining him and, completely reversing his daily routine, strove to be athletic, to find pleasure and rest in those recreations which had grown, through disuse, foreign to his nature. Thus, just as he was perhaps commencing to adapt himself to the new conditions, he returned to town and forgot everything outside of it for another year.

One has only to remember this to realize how vastly the times have changed. Today the busy city man is also a sportsman, a lover of nature, with greater energy for his business, because his body is healthy and active through constant exercise in the open air, and because his brain is the clearer, more buoyant, and vigorous in consequence. Instead of shutting himself in the city from one midsummer to the next, he either owns a country place near town, where his family spends six months of the year and where he raises fancy poultry or cattle or fine horses, or he is a member of a country club and runs out there once or twice a week for a game of golf. The city businessman nowadays is studying model farming or the breeding of dogs, he hunts, drives or motors, and is keenly alive to the beauties of the country as they are revealed to him throughout the year.

What has brought about this marvelous and splendid change? First, the influence of foreign travel and the observation of English and continental customs; second, the bicycle, the vogue of which swept the land and afforded countless thousands of city dwellers a cheap and quick method of faring forth into the country; third, golf, which caused the building of country clubs in the neighborhood of every town and city in the land, and which lured men to the enjoyment of vigorous, physical exercise under the pleasantest of circumstances; and, fourth, and in some ways, most important of all, the automobile.

Through these agencies the city man learned several lessons. He learned that all work and no play not only makes Jack a dull boy, but does not accomplish the best of work. He learned that, with the development of the stenographer, typewriter, and telephone system, his work grew more and more nervous and concentrated, because much less time was spent by him over mechanical details. He was accomplishing, so far as results went, an eight-hour day's work in a morning, and that consequently he had to have exercise and recreation or else break down. He learned that frequent and short holidays kept him in far better trim, both for his work and for his play, than taking the latter in one solid, indigestible chunk at rare intervals. He learned that a model dairy was as fascinating a problem as a Wall Street deal, and that a morning ride form his country home to the station on his way to town was quite as enjoyable as preparing a brief for his largest client. He learned that he looked surprisingly well in shooting or golf clothes, even at forty or fifty. And he took a sudden interest in how the English country gentlemen dressed.

When he reached this promising state of mind the automobile arrived.

And, behold, today the American man of affairs who is also a country gentleman! In his beautiful new motor he spins out into the country and, with a freshened mind and a new zest in life, he is not only learning to be an excellent mechanic, but a nature-lover, with a broader, sweeter personality, an enlarged horizon and a saner view of life. The automobile is not only one of the greatest of vacation agencies, but a power in our civilization, because it creates a wider, richer world for the owner. And nowadays his name is legion.

Such men as Mr. Foxhall Keene, Mr. William K. Vanderbilt, Jr., Col. John Jacob Astor and Mr. George J. Gould have done much for the motor in this country. The first two have gone in chiefly for racing, and, being thorough and all-round sportsmen, have helped place motor racing on a very high plane. The races at Ormond Beach, Florida, last winter, for instance, brought together a distinguished crowd of motor enthusiasts, and added much information to the subject of high speed cars, both as to their construction and their management. The latter two gentlemen have not taken as much interest in motor racing as in motoring for family and general country use. Each has a perfectly equipped garage on his country place, and is a constant experimenter in the latest models. The Automobile Club is officered by men of the highest distinction, and such members as Mr. James B. Dill, the corporation lawyer, who motored from his home in East Orange, N.J., to his summer camp at the Rangeley Lakes of Maine last summer; Mr. James L. Breese and Mr. Harry Payne Whitney attest the practical interest which men or larger wealth and responsibilities take in the subject.

Mr. Winthrop Scarritt, the President of the Automobile Association of America, has written that the value of the automobile as an educator is incalculable. Boys of today whose minds have been considered not sufficiently developed for the digestion of abstruse problems readily learn to work out horse-powers from cylinder diameters and crank throws and to explain the difference between steam engines, electric, and gasoline motors. Imagine, for instance, the possibilities of a generation of Americans, with their natural aptitudes for inventions, having a thorough knowledge of mechanics, which, in the application, will help to make life's burdens less irksome and pleasures more intense. The motor teaches mechanics under the guide of a pleasurable recreation. It has come to us as a luxury, but it is past the stage of being merely a fad and has emerged into one of the necessities of life.

The time is not far distant when the inevitable slump in price will come, and it then will become the vehicle, not only of the few, but of the many, bringing with it a relief from city life, from congested street car and railway travel, and opening up the country for modest homes, to which city workers may daily escape.

Already as a vacation agent it opens up the countryside to the city dweller, and it is fascinating to picture its future, to imagine the creation of thousands of miles of smooth and well graded highways, born of its influence, piercing the country, over which sweep endless processions of light, graceful and inexpensive vehicles, bearing men and women to and from their homes and places of business. Imagine our city business streets free from horses, clean, and dustless, and great national highways stretching from ocean to ocean and from North to South, bringing isolated villages in touch with the larger life of the world! Imagine a healthier race of workingmen, toiling in cheerful and sanitary factories, with mechanical skill and trade-craft developed to the highest, as the machinery grows more delicate and perfect, who, in the late afternoon, glide away in their own comfortable vehicles to their little farms or homes in the country or by the sea twenty or thirty miles distant! They will be healthier, happier, more intelligent, and self-respecting citizens because of the change to live among the meadows and flowers of the country instead of in crowded city streets.

It is not difficult while in this strain to imagine a complete revolution in railway travel. Mr. W. H. Hayden, the railroad expert, predicts that the time will come when, by means of automobiles, railway companies will collect their passengers from their homes, just as they collect their freight, and that from each station innumerable automobile services will extend into the country on all sides, opening it up to city dwellers. Possibly this comparatively clumsy railway train and the trolley car, restricted as they are to the rail system, will be supplanted by methods of transportation accompanied by less dirt and noise and marked by more deftness and responsiveness to the hand of man, by engines that would be under such perfect control that rails will be unnecessary. Instead of cumbersome, gigantic railway trains departing at infrequent intervals, there will be innumerable smaller vehicles for two or more passengers each, running constantly.

In other words, may there not be a reversal to the picturesqueness of the old stagecoach days without the attendant discomforts and slowness of those historic vehicles? Surely the time is coming when the roadside taverns and country inns will be revived to enjoy a new period of prosperity, when travelers, instead of being herded together, will travel lightly, swiftly and noiselessly from place to place, each little group in its own vehicle and each vehicle a perfectly constructed, swift-winged motor which will be one of our strongest agents for civilization, as well as a most delightful vacation agent, carrying rich and poor alike into a better understanding of nature and teaching them the pure and refreshing beauties of the country.

Index

CPSIA information can be obtained at www.ICGtesting.com
Printed in the USA
LVOW11s1114210716

497016LV00003B/4/P

9 780806 155951